Feminism
and Materialism

Feminism
and Materialism

Women and
Modes of Production

Edited by
Annette Kuhn
and
AnnMarie Wolpe

Routledge and Kegan Paul
London, Boston and Henley

First published in 1978
by Routledge & Kegan Paul Ltd
39 Store Street,
London WC1E 7DD,
Broadway House,
Newtown Road,
Henley-on-Thames,
Oxon RG9 1EN and
9 Park Street,
Boston, Mass. 02108, USA
Reprinted in 1979 and 1980
Set by Hope Services, Wantage
and printed in Great Britain by
Lowe & Brydone Printers Ltd
Thetford, Norfolk

British Library Cataloguing in Publication Data

Feminism and materialism.

1. Women — Social conditions
I. Kuhn, Annette   II. Wolpe, AnnMarie
301.41'2   HQ1154   78–40670

ISBN 0 7100 0072 3
ISBN 0 7100 0074 X   Pbk

Contents

Preface

The way in which this reader came to be produced and the rationale for its production are outlined by us in our introductory paper. As far as the main body of the book is concerned, readers will undoubtedly become aware that many of the contributors have felt the need to give a critical appraisal of the current state of work in their particular fields of interest before embarking on their own analyses. The prevalence of this strategy indicates the extent to which a move into new areas of work and forms of theorizing involves a necessary, and often a very difficult, break with the problematics which inform much of the existing work in the areas drawn on. The order in which the contributions are presented here has its logic in the two main themes which emerge constantly throughout the book — the family and the labour process. The recurrent concern with these issues is a demonstration of their centrality with regard to the position of women in society, and suggests that an understanding of the precise character of the position of women is necessarily based on an analysis of the operation of the structures of family and labour process; and more than that, as we indicate in our introductory paper, these structures are to be understood in their historical concreteness.

It will also be apparent that there are a number of concepts which reappear throughout the book — patriarchy, ideology, value, and so on, concepts which even if only in their repetition may be seen as giving some indication of their importance for the project of this book. This is not to suggest, however, that they have always been fully worked out or developed in the contexts in which they are mobilized: it is perhaps not yet the moment for that. They may, though, be taken as guidelines for the future work which obviously needs to be, and will be, conducted in the construction of a feminist theory; we have offered some suggestions as to the specific concerns of such future work in the brief introduction which precedes each of the papers. Nor are the various contributions uniform in their approach to the construction of such a body of theory: it might be argued, for instance, that some inscribe forms of determinism not present in others. Whatever the absences in or inadequacies of particular contributions, however, it is nevertheless hoped that the individual papers and the book as a whole will stimulate discussion and provide a focus both for ongoing work and for work which will be undertaken in the future.

We would like to acknowledge here the work done by the contributors to the book, who have worked together to a considerable extent in its production. Tribute must also be paid by both editors and contributors to the work of the secretaries who dealt with the manuscript: Daphne Clench and Shirley Webb in particular ensured, under conditions of their usual overwork, that the typescript was ready in time to meet our deadline. Christine Pearce gave indispensable last-minute support and assistance, and many other feminist friends, notably Mary McIntosh, offered the practical and intellectual support which women so often need in order to deal with their many and varied responsibilities: this, in many ways, is what the book is all about.

London
November 1977

Annette Kuhn
AnnMarie Wolpe

Notes on contributors

VERONICA BEECHEY is a lecturer in sociology at Warwick University. She has previously done a variety of work in education, including teaching retarded children, teaching on adult education and women's studies programmes in the USA, and shop steward education in Britain. She is actively involved in the women's movement.

LESLEY CALDWELL trained as a teacher and studied literature in her birthplace, Australia, before coming to Britain where she has done teaching of various kinds, and read for a degree in sociology at Manchester University. She is currently living in London and working on a thesis on 'The Family and Church in Italy' at the Institute of Education. She has two children.

EVA GAMARNIKOW teaches sociology and is a research student at the London School of Economics. She was born in Scotland of Polish parents who came to Britain at the end of World War II, and she grew up in Germany and England. She has been involved in the Women's Liberation Movement since 1970, in consciousness-raising, in campaigns, and in feminist theory study groups, and lives communally, sharing responsibility for child care.

RACHEL HARRISON took a degree in sociology after four

years as a nurse and several more bringing up a young family. She is now attached to the Centre for Contemporary Cultural Studies at Birmingham University, where she is working on a thesis on the conditions of existence of romance in three historical periods.

ANNETTE KUHN was born in London and educated at Twickenham County School and Sheffield University where she took degrees in sociology. She has taught sociology at Sheffield University and London University and currently lives in London and lectures, researches and writes on film. She is a member of the editorial collective of *Feminist Review*.

ROISIN McDONOUGH, who was born in Eire, is currently completing a doctoral thesis at the Centre for Contemporary Cultural Studies at Birmingham University.

MARY McINTOSH is a lecturer in sociology at the University of Essex, and has previously researched and written on homosexuality and professional crime. She is active in the Women's Liberation Campaign for Legal and Financial Independence and is a member of the editorial collective of *Feminist Review*.

PAUL SMITH was born in Hertford, and holds degrees in sociology from the University of Essex. He is currently involved in research on historical materialism and theories of ideology, also at the University of Essex.

JACKIE WEST is a lecturer in sociology at Bristol University and has taught women's studies both at undergraduate level and on extramural courses. She is involved in the women's caucus of the British Sociological Association and has been active in the Women's Movement, particularly in relation to campaigns around contraception and abortion. She has a small daughter.

ANNMARIE WOLPE, originally from South Africa, came to Britain with her family in 1963 and re-entered academic work when her youngest child was three. After undertaking research on women in engineering for a higher degree, she specialised in the sociology of education, and now teaches at Middlesex Polytechnic. She is a member of the editorial collective of *Feminist Review*.

KATE YOUNG worked in a number of areas prior to studying social anthropology, including editing, international bureaucracy (at the FAO), and documenting and cataloguing antique silver. She has spent some years living in Mexico and Italy, and is now living in London with her son and other friends. She is a Research Fellow at the Institute of Development Studies at the University of Sussex.

1 Feminism and materialism

Annette Kuhn
and
AnnMarie Wolpe

The nature of this book — the issues it addresses and the
direction from which they are addressed — has been shaped
from the very first by an assessment of the state of theoretical
work around the position of women. By the latter part of
1976, when we first discussed our general ideas for producing
a collection of essays dealing with the specificity of women's
position from a materialist perspective, a good deal of writing
from various 'feminist' points of view had been published.
Since only a few years earlier there had been virtually no
work in this area available at all, any published material
obviously filled what was by then a very great need within
the 'new' women's movement, and indeed was often grasped
with eagerness, sometimes regardless of its quality or coherence. Women, irrespective of nationality and class position,
were seen to comprise a homogeneous group bound together
by one characteristic held in common — their 'oppression' in
all aspects of life. Descriptions of this oppression covered
mental breakdowns, discrimination in jobs and education,
sexuality, dependence on men, sex-role stereotyping, and so
on. The list is long, and the need evidently existed to bring to
light and give recognition to the numerous ways in which
oppression was experienced by women themselves. In the
urgency to gain this recognition, little concerted effort was
made to develop a systematic analysis of the situations
described. When such work was begun, there was a tendency

to appropriate existing theory, first by pointing to its amnesia where women were concerned, and second, by attempting to insert the 'woman question' into existing work and hence to add to rather than transform it. This took place in a variety of areas — in the social sciences, in psychology, history, and art history in particular.

At the same time when feminists who were also marxists began to criticize the failure of marxist theory in coming to terms with the specificity of women's situation, attempts to construct theoretical work in this area tended, like similar projects elsewhere, to draw on existing concepts (in particular in this case the notions of value and productive and unproductive labour) and attempt to 'apply' them unproblematically in relation to their own situation. What, however, did distinguish work in these different areas at this point in time was not the nature of the work itself — progressive though it was in relation to what had, or more correctly had not, gone before — so much as the means by which it was produced: generally through group discussion and collective work, though usually with an awareness also of the needs of women working on their own. Hence although the nature of knowledge was not yet radically challenged by the 'additive' strategy, the ways in which work was produced constituted in themselves a transformation of traditional institutionalized modes of acquiring knowledge.

Partly as an outcome of, and partly in tandem with, this work, the last few years have seen the foundation and expansion of an area of academic and/or intellectual work called 'women's studies', the struggle for the establishment of which has a twofold and potentially contradictory rationale: women's studies was seen as a means by which women could produce knowledge about themselves, of their own history and condition, and disseminate that knowledge by means of a pedagogical practice. This very pedagogical impetus in the women's studies movement entailed a tendency towards its institutionalization as a discipline or field of study at various points within the education system — to date largely in further and higher education and adult education, and to a much lesser extent in schools. But appropriation may easily accompany such a process of legitimation, which at the same moment as accepting women's studies as a new 'subject' may either isolate it by 'ghettoization' or defuse its radical potential by incorporation. Here the contradiction, or perhaps more accurately the potential contradiction, turns on the character and provenance of women's studies and the implications for that character of its becoming a discursive practice of educational institutions. We would not want to suggest that because of this contradiction, women's studies should simply remain outside the formal education system: marginality is too high a price to pay for purity. What we do feel is that there has been a tendency of the contradiction, alongside its potential implications for the women's movement, to remain unremarked and hence impossible to deal with. Some of these implications revolve around the problem of 'theoreticism', which we discuss below. The point we would like to make here, however, is that we do see this book as an intervention in women's studies, the risks of which we are well aware. We also feel that the time is now past when almost anything written about women and informed by any kind of feminist perspective is to be taken automatically as an important contribution. What we aim to do in producing this book, therefore, is to confront in a systematic way a number of theoretical problems which arise in the various kinds of work being done in the name of 'women's studies' or 'feminist theory', particularly those problems which arise so acutely at the point when the posing of feminist issues constitutes an attack on existing theoretical frameworks, and can proceed only by actually transforming them. Although there is no total consensus among feminists on what the exact issues are, there is a widespread recognition of the need for development of a theoretical practice.

Indeed the need for theory formulated itself precisely out of the unifying eclecticism of descriptive and empirical work undertaken under the banner of women's studies. The original aim to produce knowledge out of little or nothing meant that much work of an exploratory nature — work which would by its nature be heterogeneous — needed to be done. There was a necessary and inevitable tendency to draw on a variety of theoretical positions, often without formulating or arguing out the implications of these positions. The problematic potential of such a situation did not, however, emerge as long as the fact of work of any kind whatsoever being done was to be regarded as progressive. But the expansion of work meant that the very problems raised by its eclectic and largely descriptive nature had to be addressed, and the need faced for a more precise and explicit articulation of theoretical groundings and a greater rigour in analysis. The risks of fragmentation and sectarianism attending such a development are evident, although the related danger of a retreat into 'theoreticism' — the construction of theory for its own sake — is perhaps less so. That is why, in arguing the need for a more rigorous and analytical approach to work on the position of women — in arguing, that is, for theoretical work — we have still to question constantly the purpose of such work. The need for theory cannot be taken for granted: theory needs to be justified for each specific situation within which and for which it is produced.

At a conference organized around the concept of 'patriarchy' which took place in London in May 1976, exactly at a moment when intellectual work within the women's movement faced a crisis of unity and direction, an urgent call was made for an explanation of the need for theoretical activity. It was — in our view rightly — felt necessary to justify theoretical work of the kind articulated in the papers presented at that conference as oriented towards 'the study of the forms of women's oppression both in the present and historically, the attempt to uncover the real basis for such oppression, and to explain why it takes the particular forms it does' (Himmelweit et al., 1976, p. 1). Nevertheless, some of that work did come under heavy criticism on the grounds of its inaccessibility and 'elitism': that is, it was felt that analyses were formulated in such a way as to exclude the majority of the participants from what was being said. It was also felt that any theoretically oriented enterprise by its very nature fails to take into account actions and events which ordinary women experience and understand as meaningful to themselves. Criticisms such as these rest on a set of demands and positions which, because they tend to be unvoiced in the criticisms as they are formulated, need to be drawn out and examined in the light of their implications for theoretical work within a feminist problematic, however defined.

It is perhaps too easy to meet criticism of theory with counter-accusations of anti-intellectualism. If anti-intellectualism is a relevant conceptualization to employ here, it can be seen as contingently, and not necessarily, related to the subjectivism underlying — albeit often unconsciously — the position adopted by critical tendencies. The injunction to produce 'analyses' which make sense of the everyday world is locatable within an epistemology articulated in the 'action theory' formulated by Max Weber as embracing

> all human behaviour when and in so far as the acting individual attaches a subjective meaning to it . . . . Action is social in so far as, by virtue of the subjective meaning attached to it by the acting individual (or individuals) it takes account of the behaviour of others and is thereby oriented in its course (Weber, 1947, p. 88).

In its demand for analysis — or perhaps more appropriately, description — of concrete situations, the 'subjectivist' position in effect argues for a concentration on specific areas of action which have meaning for the 'actors' immediately concerned: in this case, for women. The implication of the action frame of reference is that the world is reducible to and explicable in terms of subjective meanings produced and deployed by actors in concrete situations of face-to-face interaction.

From this position, criticism of theoretical work on the grounds that it does not immediately relate to 'reality' may then be seen as an assertion of the impossibility of describing, let alone of analysing, situations and instances which are not open to experiential observation. What must follow from the demand for making sense of the everyday world through meaningful experiences is not a rejection of *all* theory *per se*. Because such a demand is located within an epistemological base (largely unrecognized in this instance), the rejection is of specific theoretical positions, positions which may be described as 'structural' or 'holistic'. We should make it clear, however, that in arguing that certain demands to justify theory may actually constitute an effective rejection of particular types of theoretical work, we certainly would not wish to suggest that no justification is required for theoretical activity.

The problematic relationship between theory and 'practice' always poses itself quite acutely for the women's movement, precisely because it has been one of the projects of the movement to construct knowledge of the nature and causes of our oppression, with a view to changing that situation. The need for theoretical work arises quite simply from the very urgent and specific need for constructing an analytical and effectual understanding of women's situation. And an intervention in theory or knowledge may certainly be seen as itself constituting a change in the world. But none the less a distinction is to be made between theory and theoreticism. Theoreticism is not necessarily inherent in every theoretical enterprise, but tends to have its operation within a series of institutions and institutional discourses. Specifically in our society at present, the production and dissemination of knowledge is largely a specialized activity with its own institutions — a term which embodies not simply a concrete sociological conceptualization, but embraces also the very terms within which appropriate modes of inquiry, limits and boundaries of 'subjects', methods, ways of producing and making use of knowledge, are defined. This same institutional discourse incorporates also a mode of address which renders the theoretician as the authoritative source of knowledge. This is what we mean by theoreticism.

But it may, even with a full awareness of this pitfall, be the case that the way in which concepts are presented and argued results in apparent inaccessibility. However, the complexity of many of the issues to be grappled with does demand an engagement on the part of the reader as much as of the author, in the sense that both reader and author are involved in the production of theory. In pointing out the dangers of theoreticism we are calling attention also to the authoritarianism of theoreticist discourse which constitutes the reader as a passive recipient of the privileged knowledge of another. Theorizing is not a one-way activity. The very way in which the women's movement operates — the means by which women are acquiring and using knowledge about themselves — runs counter to theoreticist tendencies: for example, women's studies is by nature interdisciplinary, and hence subverts boundaries between subjects. Moreover, because of the means by which such knowledge is — or has been — produced, it may call into question the authoritarian character of traditional academic discourse. But, as we have already suggested, such a challenge is a possible and not a necessary accompaniment of the kind of work and ways of working done under the rubric of women's studies: the institutionalized character of its development can mean that work done within women's studies may become isolated from its origins and open to theorizing for its own sake. We very much hope that the work presented in this book is not read, or appropriated, in this way.

In arguing for theory in feminist intellectual work, we are arguing for a theoretical contribution of a particular kind, the nature of which is suggested by the second term in the title of this book: materialism. We are here adopting Engels' definition of the term:

> According to the materialist conception, the determining factor in history is, in the final instance, the production and reproduction of immediate life. This, again, is of a two-fold character: on the one side, the production of the means of existence, of food, clothing and shelter and the tools necessary for that production; on the other side, the production of human beings themselves, the propagation of the species (Engels, 1972, p. 71).

The materialist problematic is based on a conceptualization of human society as defined specifically by its productivity: primarily of the means of subsistence and of value by the transformation of nature through work. United with this is a conceptualization of history as the site of the transformation of the social relations of production and reproduction. As far as an analysis of the position of women is concerned, materialism would locate that position in terms of the relations of production and reproduction at various moments in history. In doing this, one of its central concerns would be with the determinate character of the sexual division of labour and the implications of this for power relations between men and women at different conjunctures. At the same time, however, the connection between this set of relations and the social relations specific to modes of production — that is, relations between classes — must also be thought.

It is at this point that the issue at the heart of the attempt to construct a marxist feminism is raised: although we regard its production as a priority, we have to recognize that marxist feminist theoretical work is as yet in its infancy. It is for this reason that we have drawn the theoretical boundaries of our work inclusively around the terrain of materialism, and have not focused attention exclusively on marxist feminist analyses; though we very much hope in doing this that some of the issues which are indicated in this book as of potential importance for a marxist feminist problematic will be taken up and developed further. The starting-point for a marxist — or a classic marxist — analysis, as opposed to a materialist one, would be an account of the laws of motion and transformation of modes of production, especially of the capitalist mode of production, and of the ways in which value is created and capital accumulated within this mode. The problem is that although in our view the subordination of women is to be thus analysed historically in terms of the relation of women to modes of production and reproduction, this particular issue is scarcely addressed within traditional marxist thought. In this sense the suppression and subordination of women as such is not seen as constituting a problem requiring analysis, beyond the assertion that the prior condition of women's 'emancipation' is that they be brought into the sphere of capitalist production. It is no coincidence that the attempt to construct analyses of the specificity of the subordination of women in capitalism in terms of orthodox approaches to the labour theory of value through an examination of domestic labour encountered such obstacles that attempts of this sort have by now been virtually abandoned: a situation which suggests that Veronica Beechey is right in her assessment that 'a correct analysis of the subordination of women cannot be provided by Marxists unless Marxism itself is transformed' (1977, p. 61): transformed, for instance, through an attempt to come to terms properly with the sexual division of labour. It is clear, as the papers in this book testify, that much marxist analysis, in subsuming women to the general categories of that problematic — class relations, labour process, the state, and so on, fails to confront the specificity of women's oppression. There is often an automatic assumption that there is no need to do so — analysis is applicable to all groups and fractions at any moment in history, and a transformation of capitalism according to marxist precepts would entail the emancipation of all members of society, whether male or female. Materialist analyses of women's condition, to the extent that they constitute an attempt to transform marxism, constitute also a move towards the construction of a marxist feminism.

Each of the original essays presented here in one way or another articulates the complex and problematic relationship between analyses operating within a materialist tradition and the issues and perspectives brought to the fore increasingly in recent years within and outside the women's movement: women's paid labour, housework, the place of women in relation to the family and the state, for example. The specific issues are addressed and the analyses put forward as work towards the construction of a theory: many of the questions raised are far from resolution. Whether or not, for example, the notion of 'proletarianization' is applicable to the class position of women white-collar workers, or whether it is possible to allocate a specific value to labour power and thus to conclude that in their paid labour women are remunerated at less than the cost of their own reproduction, are issues which are both debatable and debated. It is clear also that a materialist approach to the question of women's situation constantly comes up against the problem of the apparently transhistorical character of women's oppression, which immediately problematizes the relationship between such oppression and mode of production. Any attempt to deal with this fundamental issue necessitates a consideration of the relationship between patriarchy, however formulated, and history; or more particularly, mode of production. In this context two interrelated issues are raised — the family and the sexual division of labour — whose crucial importance to a theorization of the situation of women is constantly claimed but still remains to be analysed. In many respects, these questions constitute a central concern for all the contributors.

As editors of, as well as contributors to the book, we do not necessarily agree with each other, nor with all the contributors, in terms of specific analyses. What we hope to have done in producing this reader, however, is to have brought together a body of work which provides a coherent basis for an understanding of women's situation by means of outlining the foundation of a systematic approach to an analysis of that situation defined, as we see it, in terms of women's historically specific relationship to modes of production and reproduction.

References

Beechey, V. (1977), 'Female wage labour in capitalist production', in *Capital and Class*, no. 3, pp. 45–66.

Engels, F. (1972), *The Origin of the Family, Private Property and the State*, Lawrence & Wishart, London.

Himmelweit, S., McKenzie, M., and Tomlin, A. (1976), 'Why theory?' in *Papers on Patriarchy*, Women's Publishing Collective, Lewes.

Weber, M. (1947), *Theory of Social and Economic Organisation*, Oxford University Press, New York.

2 Patriarchy and relations of production

Roisin McDonough
and
Rachel Harrison

If only because patriarchy has from the very first been seized upon by the women's movement as a concept central to an understanding of the subordination of women both cross-culturally and transhistorically, it is crucial that it be seriously addressed in any theoretical practice which claims to be feminist. As Roisin McDonough and Rachel Harrison point out here, patriarchy has been understood in a variety of different ways, though there is an understandable tendency for it to be mobilized in universalistic terms as a concept through which women's oppression is thought as operating similarly across the boundaries of space and time. The project of this paper, and indeed in different ways of each of the contributions to this book in which patriarchy is specifically addressed, is to advance the notion that patriarchy may in fact be usefully thought in historical terms. In other words, although it is true that simply to address patriarchy as a concept is in some sense to take its validity for granted, the aim in taking it up here is to displace it, to move the terms of its discussion away from the terrain of universalism and to reappropriate it for materialism, for an approach to women's situation in its historical specificity. Hence the conclusion arrived at in this paper is that patriarchial relations take their particular form from dominant relations of production. For example, within the capitalist mode of production patriarchy has its operations through class relations, so that while the relations of human reproduction, which McDonough and Harrison see as the privileged site of patriarchial relations, 'are analytically central to an explanation of the subordination of all women, different contradictions inevitably arise for women inhabiting different class positions'. This implies that although patriarchal subjection exists, it is not necessarily and automatically the case that patriarchy is the main structure within which women are subjected, but rather that the precise character of the operation of patriarchal relations is shaped within the historical concreteness of a mode of production; even though at certain conjunctures patriarchal relations may operate in a relatively pristine form, as Eva Gamarnikow suggests below in her analysis of the nursing profession. It is, however, the task of theoretical work to establish the exact interrelation at specific moments of history between mode of production and structures of patriarchy.

Patriarchy has often been used as a central concept of analysis with which to understand the nature of women's oppression, both theoretically and politically. However, recent debates within the women's movement show that there is no consensus about the meaning or status of such a term. Whilst its usefulness as a concept is rarely contested, it is nevertheless the focus of much debate amongst radical feminists, separatists and socialist feminists alike, and the debate is often one which the very term patriarchy occludes as much as it illuminates. Yet there is agreement on one issue — there can be no understanding of the nature of contemporary capitalist society without placing the oppression of women at the centre of such an analysis. It is precisely this lack of centrality within marxism to date on the whole question of women's oppression — that is, the virtual dearth of any analysis concerned with the relationship between the social relations of production and the social relations of human reproduction — to which many feminists are addressing themselves. The questions posed by the attempt to understand the forms of women's oppression both in the present and historically, to uncover the material basis for such oppression and to explain why it takes the particular forms it does are the key theoretical and political tasks which the movement faces today.

One of the first major attempts to provide a thorough theoretical examination of the oppression of women using the concept of patriarchy was Kate Millett's *Sexual Politics* (1971). Patriarchy for Millett means not the rule of the father but the rule of men and, as such, is seen as a universal 'mode of power relationships' and domination: it is all-pervasive, for it penetrates class divisions, different societies and different historical epochs. It is *the* primary oppression simply because of its longevity, and specific variations within patriarchy are less significant than its general truth.

Whilst her analysis is able to draw upon and make comparisons between a vast range of transhistorical, empirical and cross-cultural evidence and thus give extremely important insights into the way in which patriarchy permeates our lives, its strength is ultimately its limitation. Millett's examination of patriarchy and the various domains of its operation remains discrete and abstract precisely because it is so general. She gives us no understanding of *interconnectedness* of the different mechanisms through which patriarchy works and how these have varied historically. In other words there is no analysis of the specificity of the operations of patriarchy throughout time and of its relation to other forms of domination at the economic and political levels. All is subsumed under the general rubric of patriarchy, which, however undeniable its universality may be, does not lead very far.

Sexual Politics does, however, represent one of the first serious theoretical attempts to come to grips with the specific nature of women's oppression and it signals the irreducibility of that oppression to any simple or even complex class analysis conceived through traditional marxist economic categories. But her attack on the inadequacies of traditional marxist analysis in its confrontation with the question of women's oppression, while correctly pointing out its deficiences and castigating it for its economic reductionism, can constitute no solution merely by means of inverting that lack. Thus one of the central weaknesses in Millett's position is revealed not when she states that most marxist analyses involve the presumption that the family and marriage are merely economic phenomena capable of transformation by economic or institutional methods alone, but when she attempts to redress this theoretical lacuna by asserting the primacy of sex over class. The problem (which still remains and to which Millett was one of the first to address herself systematically) is not solved by overturning the classic, crude, economistic position which stresses the simple determinacy of class conceived economically only to replace it with another primary determination — that of sexual oppression. Millett rejects not just a specific kind of marxism, but marxism *per se*, and in seeing patriarchy as equivalent to and at times more fundamental than the class system she moves away from a materialist analysis and into a sociological one.

Any adequate theoretical analysis of the position and oppression of women within capitalism cannot therefore be predicated theoretically on the mirror inversion and replacement of class determination with that of sex as Millett attempts to do. Nor is it a question of the addition of a 'missing ingredient' to an overall marxist theory, a missing ingredient which simply takes into account some seeming congenital deficiency within marxist theory in adequately coming to terms with the intransigent and the awesome (often referred to as 'the women's problem'). On this much Millett and many other feminists are correct. It seems that the task at hand is twofold: that is, it is necessary to question the nature and premises upon which marxism is itself based whilst at the same time asking feminist questions. This essay, in addressing itself to that project, attempts a displacement of the notion of patriarchy: first onto the terrain of psychoanalysis, specifically as explored by Juliet Mitchell (1975), whose project is to inscribe a theory of the unconscious within historical materialism by means of a re-reading of Freud; and then onto the more familiar domain of historical materialism in an attempt to re-locate patriarchy as an instance both of history and of class formation.

I

The appearance in this country of Juliet Mitchell's book *Psychoanalysis and Feminism* marks a significant departure within the theoretical development of the women's movement. The most striking feature of the book is its attempt to reappropriate that *bête noire* of the movement — Freud — and to cleanse him of all traces of anti-feminism. She wants to show how popular, debased versions of Freudianism mask the fundamental import of Freud's work for any understanding of women's oppression, and how psychoanalysis, in spite of its often quite reactionary use, is not a recommendation *for* a patriarchal society but an analysis *of* one. In embarking upon this project she runs counter to the whole mainstream of current feminist critiques of Freud and radical/existential/ phenomenological psychology, a task which is evidently unpopular within the canons of the prevailing orthodoxy. Yet the book is unique in another sense too, for while the synthesis of Marx and Freud has been attempted many times before (Mitchell's book is nothing new in that regard), it is distinct in two ways: first, in the *kind* of marxism that she uses in her synthesis, and second, in her uncritical acceptance of Freud in the effort to secure it.

In discussing the implications of Mitchell's work on patriarchy, we will begin with an exegesis and clarification of the underlying theoretical premises on which the book is founded. In the main this will draw out the major conceptual similarities between Mitchell's and Althusser's theoretical paradigms (in particular the Althusser of *Lenin and Philosophy*) and will show how these concepts are operationalised in her analysis. This will be followed by an account of her exposition of Freud's theory of psychoanalysis and patriarchy and of her attempt to 'historicise' his theory; that is, to situate historically Frued's concept of patriarchy within the development of capitalism. Third, we shall deal with both the problems of and the theoretical elisions made in the attempt to unite marxism and psychoanalysis.

In general terms, Mitchell holds a similar view to that of Althusser with regard to the nature of the social totality and how to think that totality. Against both the mechanistic interpretation of the base-superstructure metaphor and the essentialist or Hegelian view of the social whole, Althusser proposes a distinct concept of the social formation, fundamentally that the distinguishing feature of every social formation is to be found in the particular unity of the levels or instances which compose it—the economic base and the political and ideological superstructures. These levels are different not only because they refer to distinct objects or practices, but also because each of them differs in its capacity to determine the others. The unity which they form is based on a hierarchical relationship between the levels in which the economic 'determines in the last instance' the political and ideological levels, but is at the same time 'overdetermined' by them. Thus the political and ideological have a 'relative autonomy' with respect to the economic base; that is, they have a relative independence, the parameters of which are nevertheless fixed by their ultimate dependence on the determination by the economic 'in the last instance'. The concept of 'relative autonomy' is one of the key theoretical underpinnings of Mitchell's analysis of patriarchy. For her, patriarchy and patriarchal relations — the site of whose existence and formation is located within the unconscious — are relatively autonomous of the capitalist social formation which is the object of her analysis.

Mitchell, like Althusser, distinguishes between science and ideology, a distinction based upon a specific epistemological argument about the relationship between theory and reality. In his earlier works, Althusser argues that ideological discourse produces a defamation between theory and the 'real', in terms of both its production and what it claims to represent. For both Mitchell and Althusser, Freudian psychoanalysis is a science based on the discovery of a new scientific object — the unconscious:

> If psychoanalysis is a science because it is the science of a distinct object, it is also a science with the structure of all sciences: it has a *theory* and a *technique* (method) that makes possible the knowledge and transformation of its object in a specific practice (Althusser, 1971a, p. 184).

Perhaps the most important theoretical premise shared by Mitchell and Althusser is the conception of the structure and the functioning of ideology in general which, as Althusser argues in keeping with Freud's notion of the unconscious, are always the same. The mechanism of ideology in general, as of the unconscious, is an omnipresent, transhistorical entity. To that extent it is immutable in form throughout the course of history. Ideology, like the unconscious, is eternal, it has no history (Althusser, 1971b).

There are three main theses which Althusser uses to explain the nature of ideology in general. First, ideology is a 'representation' of the imaginary relationship of individuals to their real conditions of existence: this thesis implies a definite break with all conceptualisations of ideology as 'false consciousness' or as a distorted representation of reality. Ideology is not a representation of reality at all. What ideology represents is men's lived relations with reality: it is a relation of the second degree. Althusser insists that this lived relation is necessarily an imaginary one.[1] Ideology then is not a representation of real conditions of existence (that is, the existing relations of production and other relations that derive from them) but a representation of an imaginary relationship of individuals to these real conditions of existence.

Second, ideology has a material existence. This thesis implies that ideology is not an ethereal dross that exists only inside our heads, something which is to be counterposed to the real. On the contrary, ideology is a material force. It exists and is inscribed within a set of social relations, practices and rituals which have definite effects. Ideology is a level of the social formation which is articulated with the other levels. It is a structure of social relations which is both determined by other social relations and which has a determining effect upon them. Thus any analysis of ideology is an analysis of *social relations* themselves, not a reflection of social relations in the world of ideas.

Third, 'ideology interpellates individuals as subjects'. This thesis is based on the argument that the category of the subject is constitutive of all ideology in so far as the defining function of all ideology is to constitute individuals as subjects. This process of constitution is discussed by Althusser in terms of two notions. The first, 'interpellation', refers to the operation of ideology in that it constantly calls upon or 'hails' individuals as subjects – that is to say, the place of the individual within the concrete practices of ideology is always that of subject, individuals are always-already subjects within the practices that constitute them. Second, this process of constitution has a duplicate mirror structure, it is 'doubly specular'. The subject recognises itself as a subject only because it subjects itself to the central Absolute Subject[2] which provides the possibility of this recognition, and circumscribes the forms of subjection in which the subject is constituted. These forms of subjection are accepted by the subject in such a way that this recognition of being a subject appears to be an obvious and natural fact. But, as Althusser argues, they are the ideological recognition of an obviousness *imposed* by ideology. This implies that to be a subject (in the first place to recognise oneself as a free and unique being) is an effect of subjection to ideology.

Such a conception of ideology and the construction of subjects within and by ideology outlined by Althusser forms the theoretical basis upon which Mitchell argues that Freud's work, symptomatically read, can be reappropriated to provide a genuinely materialist theory of the constitution of subjectivity, and that such a reappropriation must trace as its point of departure Freud's two key concepts of the unconscious and psychic representation. *Psychoanalysis and Feminism* is an attempt to show how Freud's science of psychoanalysis provides the basis by which an understanding of mechanisms of women's oppression can be achieved, and also that this understanding is compatible with the basic tenets and premises with which historical materialism enables us to grasp the history and development of different modes of production. Psychoanalysis, like history, is a science, concerned with

> The material reality of ideas both within and of man's history . . . . The way we live as ideas the necessary laws of human society is not so much conscious as *unconscious* — the particular task of psychoanalysis is to decipher how we acquire our heritage of the ideas and laws of human society within the unconscious mind, or to put it another way, the unconscious mind *is* the way in which we acquire these laws (Mitchell, 1975, p. xvvi).

Freud's work, argues Mitchell, sets out to analyse the operations of ideology and the laws of the human order, both of which he saw as patriarchal: by patriarchy is meant the law of the father, and for Mitchell it is the operation of this law within the individual lives of men and women which Freud's work illuminates. Psychoanalysis gives us the concepts with which to understand the functioning and mechanisms of ideology and of the place and meaning of sexuality and gender differences within society. Where marxist theory explains the historical and economic development of society, psychoanalysis in conjunction with dialectical materialism is the way to understanding ideology and sexuality.

The importance of such a stance lies in its explicit rejection of theories about women's oppression which assume an easy malleability of human institutions. Mitchell stresses the need for a theory which provides a structural analysis of the ways in which ideology and the cultural construction of sexuality are rooted not only within our consciousness (in the ordinary use of the term) but crucially within our unconscious. Thus it is not merely a question of analysing and struggling against those structures or social institutions that exploit women, nor is it a question of being aware of 'sexist' attitudes towards women — though these do, of course, form a crucial part of the overall struggle — but rather that we need a different *kind* of analysis. Mitchell's main criticism of feminism lies in its denial of the existence of unconscious, its ultimate rejection of the domain of psychic reality and the realm of unconscious fantasy: in short she criticises it on the grounds of a social realism which leads it to deny any attribute of the mind other than rationality or consciousness. For feminism the reality principle is paramount. Penis envy, passivity, masochism and all the other 'invidious' concepts used by Freud to analyse the female personality, Mitchell forcefully argues, should not be extracted from a wider theory of psychoanalysis. It is within this context that these apparently value-laden terms become scientific concepts with which to analyse the perennial oppression of women, and properly understood they may play an important part in their liberation.

Mitchell's thesis is basically as follows: for Freud, entry into civilisation (that is, the acquisition of humanness) is entry into patriarchy. There is a homologous relationship between ontogeny (the development and genesis of the individual) and phylogeny (the history of the human race): one does not come before the other, they are the same event, the event of human society expressed on different levels:

> The myth that Freud rewrote as the oedipus complex epitomises man's entry into culture itself. It reflects the original exogamous incest taboo, the role of the father, the exchange of women and the consequent differences between the sexes. It is *not* about the nuclear family, but about the institution of culture within the kinship structure and the exchange relationship of exogamy. It is thus about what Freud regarded as the order of all human culture. It is specific to nothing but patriarchy which is itself, according to Freud, specific to all civilisation (Mitchell, 1975, p. 376).

In interpreting the validity of Freud's theory of the oedipus complex, Mitchell relies heavily on a particular reading of

Lévi-Strauss's anthropological studies of kinship patterns. Lévi-Strauss, she states, has shown that it is *not* the biological family of father, mother and child that is the distinguishing feature of human kinship structures. This biological base must be transformed if society is to be instituted. Marriage laws and the related incest taboo must be established in order to break out of the circular nature of the biological family and indeed these form the essential prerequisites for the inauguration of a cultural kinship system. Contrary to popular belief, there is nothing 'wrong' biologically with incest: it is rather that the command to exchange exogamously (that is, to marry outside one's own tribe) forbids the cul-de-sac of endogamy: in short, for humanity to establish itself, to enter culture, certain rules of kinship exchange must be enacted. That which is exchanged, according to Lévi-Strauss, is women and it is this legally defined and sanctioned exchange of women which is the primary factor in distinguishing mankind from other primates. Whatever the nature of society — patrilineal, matrilineal and so on — it is always men who exchange women. Hence women, it is argued, become the equivalent of a sign which is being communicated since it is communication and the act of exchange which binds human societies together.

The reading of Lévi-Strauss proffered by Mitchell accords with Freud's definition of culture as patriarchal, for culture is seen as predicated on the symbolic exchange of women by men. Thus she argues that Freud's myth of the oedipus complex represents the subjective acquisition of the social necessity of the incest taboo that Lévi-Strauss outlines: the oedipus complex is therefore not about the nuclear family, nor can it be limited to the capitalist mode of production. Freud was most insistent that the oedipal moment was a universal event signifying man's entry into culture, into all that defines him as human. However, this is not to say that the oedipus complex does not assume different forms of expression under different social and economic systems. In advanced capitalist society, its expression of the exchange relationships and taboos necessary for society takes place within the nuclear family. It is here that Mitchell locates the central contradiction of capitalism:

> In economically advanced societies, though the kinship-exchange system still operates in a residual way, other

forms of exchange — i.e. commodity exchange — dominate and class, not kinship structures, prevail. It would seem that it is against a background of the *remoteness* of a kinship system that the ideology of the biological family comes into its own. In other words, that the relationship between two parents and their children assumes a dominant role when the complexity of a class society forces the kinship system to recede (p. 378).

Historically we can locate this 'remoteness' with the shift from agricultural communities to industrial complexes. It is this shift which 'involved the final blow to the visible significance of kinship exchanges'. Under capitalism the vast majority of the population has nothing to sell but its labour power but it also has nothing to exchange save for this, and particularly in its early stages it has nothing to inherit or to give. For the first time in history it is no longer necessary for women to be objects of exchange, except amongst the bourgeoisie for the purposes of transmission of property. Thus Mitchell is arguing that the complexity and class nature of capitalist society makes archaic the kinship structures and incest taboo for the majority of people, and yet for some reason it preserves them. The specifically capitalist ideology of a supposedly 'natural' family unit appears to be in contradiction with the kinship structure as it is articulated in the oedipus complex, which in our society is expressed within the confines of the nuclear family. Capitalism has made the patriarchal law *redundant*. That is the basic contradiction. It is important to note here that there is no basic contradiction internal to patriarchy itself, but only as it relates to the social relations with which it is articulated, namely the nuclear family and the organisation of production. Under capitalism the mass of mankind, propertyless and working socially together *en masse*, would be unlikely to come into proximity with their kin, were it not for the preservation of the family; and if they did, Mitchell asserts, it would not matter. Mankind under capitalism has the potential to develop and realise its full sociality, its full humanness — there can be no return to 'nature' — the final and complete transition to culture will only be effected with the advent of socialism. Yet the oedipus complex, which denotes the individual's taking up of an asymmetrical sexed position in relation to the father, is

'unsuitably' contained and expressed in the socially and
ideologically reconstructed nuclear family. It is women in
their role as reproducers who stand at the crux of this contradiction.

> Men enter into the class-dominated structures of history
> while women (as women, whatever their actual work in
> production) remain defined by the kinship patterns of
> organisation. In our society the kinship system is harnessed
> into the family — where a woman is formed in such a way
> that it is there where she will stay. Differences of class,
> historical epoch, specific social situations alter the expres-
> sion of femininity; but in relation to the law of the father
> women's position is a comparable one (p. 406).

However, Mitchell's identification of patriarchy with the
inauguration of culture and her characterisation of patriarchy
as a transhistorical phenomenon leads her into the theoretical cul-de-sac of dualism. Her uncritical acceptance of Freud's
analysis of the laws and operations of patriarchy within the
unconscious as a temporal and universal structure vitiates her
claim to provide a historical materialist account of women's
oppression. She correctly refuses to discuss ontological questions of how it all began and instead stresses the dynamic
question of how sexual oppression continually recurs throughout history, but her notion of history is limited and at times
purely formal. History for her precisely equals patriarchy, the
universal culture of all previous productive systems. Each
specific mode of production expresses the universal patriarchal culture in differing ideological forms. Thus Marx at the
end is finally invited to augment Freud in the understanding
and overcoming of social and sexual oppression.

The parameters of her argument are defined by the attempt
to specify the relationship between kinship structures and
modes of production, with special emphasis on the ideology
of contemporary capitalism. Yet in analysing this nexus she
collapses its historical specificity because of her initial hypo-
statisation of the whole concept of patriarchy. Her starting
theoretical conceptualisation of the social totality as composed of 'relatively autonomous' levels is transmogrified into
an analysis of patriarchy which is no longer 'relatively autonomous' but *wholly* autonomous, and one which is not saved

for materialism by the injection of a historical syringe towards the end of the book:

> Though of course ideology and a given mode of production are interdependent, one cannot be reduced to the other, nor can the same laws be found to govern one as govern the other. To put the matter schematically, in analysing contemporary capitalist society we are (as elsewhere) dealing with two autonomous areas: the economic mode of capitalism and the ideological mode of patriarchy. The interdependence between them is found in the particular expression of patriarchal ideology — in this case the kinship system that defines patriarchy is forced into the straightjacket of the nuclear family. But if we analyse the economic and the ideological situation only at the point of their interpenetration, we shall never see the means to their transformation (p. 412).

It is precisely this failure to analyse in its historical specificity the point of penetration of these two related domains that results in prescriptions inscribing both a theoretical and a political dualism: her clarion call is for separate socialist (economic) and cultural (feminist) revolutions. The relationship between class and sex is not thought out dialectically but merely separated, each containing its own inner logic, each going its own separate way. The characteristic separation of sexual relationships and the family from the economy or the relations of production in the European marxist tradition is reproduced in her analysis. Not only is there an absence of consideration of the economic role of the family — domestic labour and its relation to the sexual division of labour — within capitalism, but the concept of ideology itself refers only to sexuality and the constitution of the sexed subject within patriarchal relations of domination and subordination. Masculinity and femininity imply class as well as sex designations and are contained by and constructed within the interface between specific class-familial ideologies and the naturalised reproduction of these relations in the operation of various sets of institutions and practices, each with its own set of internal contradictions. If the structure and functioning of the unconscious are eternal effects of the structure of society — that is if, as Mitchell argues, the construction of the unconscious is the effect of the universal laws by which human beings become social beings — then the problem for marxist feminists remains: how politically and theoretically to account for the way out of the impasse which reaffirms the 'natural' inferiority of the female sex. When Mitchell poses questions about the universality of the structures outlined by Freud (the oedipus complex, castration anxiety and so on) she asks whether or not they are appropriate to all forms of culture. In reply to herself she argues that although the basic structure is universal, its application may be varied and specific. Thus while the structure and functioning of the unconscious are immutable in form they may be filled with varying 'contents' dependent upon the mode of production and corresponding social relations to which it gives rise. It is here that the contradiction for Mitchell lies, a contradiction which signals the possibility of different kinds of social/sexual relations. The oedipus complex and the constitution of sexed subjects in capitalism which take place within the nuclear family are established in the context of redundancy: the prescriptions against incest and exogamy that the patriarchal law expressed in the oedipus complex have become irrelevant.

Mitchell's attempt to specify a set of general, abstract, formal propositions about the nature of the unconscious and ideology is theoretically incompatible with a concrete understanding of the forms and conditions and effectivity under which ideology operates and of their relation to other structures within the wider social totality. This disjuncture between immutable forms and historically variant specific contents — the distinction made between the abstract and the concrete — which underpins her analysis is untenable because both these things are conceptualised at different levels of abstraction and there is therefore no homology between the concepts and that to which they allude. A similar point has been made by Hirst concerning Althusser's theory of ideology which, as we already noted, forms the theoretical paradigm on which Mitchell's analysis is based:

> Althusser makes use of the abstract/concrete distinction
> to rectify the generality of his analysis. A general func-
> tional mechanism is modified in its effects by the 'concrete'.
> This abstract/concrete distinction is an impossible one . . . .
> Althusser seeks to counteract the theoretical effects of this

mechanism (functionalism) by reference to its inhibition
by 'concrete' conditions (Hirst, 1976, p. 386).

The result, then, of such an attempt is a formalism which
relates separate structures in an extrinsic fashion rather than
dialectically integrating them. This tension in Mitchell's work
stems from a failure to resolve theoretically the conceptual
'difficulties' contained in Althusser's essay on the ideological
state apparatuses, which arise from the distinction made
between ideolog*ies* — which are always class (and sex?)
specific — and ideology in general, which is common to all
social formations. What we are arguing is that the unconscious
can be analysed only in its historical specificity, within the
concrete kinship structures and class ideologies in which it is
located. Such an analysis should demonstrate the ways in
which historical variation in these latter structures has materially affected the 'necessary' universal precondition for
the acquisition of humanness — the oedipus complex.

II

Given that the way forward for an analysis of patriarchy
necessitates an engagement with historical materialism, there
remain immense problems surrounding the application and
extension of that method to the subordination of women.
These are due mainly to the 'fact that the feminist problematic, the fact and implication of women's subordination to
men, and of women's struggle against that subordination'
(Mackintosh, 1977, p. 119) is not the central problematic
of marxism. One of the major problems encountered in
trying to understand the material and historical bases of
patriarchy is that of conceptual ambiguity and absences in
analysis. A clarification of terms is therefore a necessary part
of a discussion of the concept of patriarchy in a materialist
analysis. In addition, it will be argued that the orthodox
marxist definition of patriarchy as a form of organisation of
labour in the household is inadequate without, at the same
time, locating how the sexual division of 'the social relations
under which women work in the home, social relations generated by the reproductive role of women' is structured in
such a way that relations between the sexes are relations of
domination and subordination. Hence further development

of the concept of patriarchy must lie in the interrelation between the relations of production on the one hand and what Maureen Mackintosh has termed the 'relations of human reproduction' on the other. To attempt a theoretical understanding of the family and of human reproduction in relation to the subordination of women is not to return to the kind of biological determinism that the women's movement has rightly rejected: rather, it is an attempt to show how patriarchal oppression of women in the family is crucially connected with the need to control their fertility and sexuality. In the pre-capitalist producing family and in the working-class family in capitalism, patriarchy is also connected with the need to control the wife's labour.

Although her emphasis is on patriarchy as a labour relation, Sheila Rowbotham calls attention to the double-sided nature of patriarchal relations:

> The oppression of women differs too from class and race because it has not come out of capitalism and imperialism. The sexual division of labour and the possession of women by men predates capitalism. Patriarchal authority is based on male control over the woman's productive capacity, and over her person (1973, p. 117).

An analysis of transhistorical oppression must lay emphasis on the social relations of human reproduction, the control over the woman's 'person'.

> One has to admit to the relation of human reproduction some autonomy of content. The characteristic relation of human reproduction is patriarchy, that is, the control of women, especially of their sexuality and fertility, by men. The first necessity is to separate the fact of this control from the question of the form in which it is exercised: e.g. through a patrilineal and patrilocal system or in some other way; through ideology; through various forms of economic subordination. This then specifies clearly the theoretical problem: what are the forms taken by patriarchy in this society, and how are they interrelated with the social relations of production? How, in other words, do changing modes of production change the forms of patriarchy without destroying its existence? (Mackintosh, 1977, p. 122).

It is important to note in this context the ways in which the concept of 'reproduction' has shifted in content between its early formulation in *The German Ideology* and its later formulation in *Capital*. In *The German Ideology*, Marx suggests three aspects of social activity which are 'the first premise of all human existence and therefore of all history'. The first is the means to satisfy needs, the second is the production of new needs, and

> The third circumstance which, from the very outset, enters into historical development, is that men who daily remake their own life, begin to make other men, to propagate their own kind; the relation between men and women, parents and children, the family. The family, which to begin with is the only social relation, becomes later, when increased needs create new social relations and the increasing population new needs, a subordinate one . . . . These three aspects of social activity are not of course to be taken as three different stages, but as three 'moments', which have existed simultaneously since the dawn of history and the first men, and which still exert themselves in history today (Marx, 1970a, pp. 49–50).

The problem is, however, that once the family social relation has become a subordinate one it becomes analytically peripheral for Marx. In particular, the last of the three 'moments', propagation of their own kind, becomes designated as 'natural', and so outside of history:

> The production of life, both of one's own labour and of fresh labour in procreation, now appears as a double relation: on the one hand as a natural, on the other as a social relation . . . the nature of society must be studied in relation to the history of production and exchange (p. 50).

This naturalisation of the reproduction of fresh labour also occurs in *Capital*:

> The maintenance and reproduction of the working-class is, and must ever be, a necessary condition to the reproduction of capital. But the capitalist may safely leave its fulfilment to the labourer's instincts of self-preservation and of propagation (Marx, 1970b, p. 572).

In *Capital* it is stressed that the reproduction of the social relations of production (class relations determined by ownership and non-ownership of means of production) takes place primarily at the site of production: 'Capitalist production . . . also produces and reproduces the capitalist relation: on the one hand the capitalist on the other the wage labourer' (p. 578). Brigit O'Loughlin argues that for Marx production and reproduction are a unitary process, with production taking analytic precedence, so that 'if production is capitalist in form, so also is reproduction' (1977, p. 6). She refers to Marx's critique of Malthus, in which it is argued that 'the biological reproduction of people is a contingent outcome of the ways in which the production and reproduction of the means of subsistence are socially organised' (ibid.). In *Capital*, the question of value of labour power, the costs of its reproduction in terms of the commodities consumed, is the central focus of analysis. In other words what is at issue is the contribution of the productive worker, the wage labourer, to the reproduction of labour power, rather than the social relations of human reproduction themselves.

Although as marxists it is essential for us to give analytic primacy to the sphere of production, as feminists it is equally essential to hold on to a concept such as the relation of human reproduction in order to understand the specific nature of women's oppression. This means that we must distinguish clearly between the two kinds of reproduction associated respectively with the sphere of production (the reproduction of the conditions of production, the means of production, commodities and so on) and the reproduction of the relations of production; and in the sphere of the family (the reproduction of the labourer and the non-labourer) O'Loughlin in fact criticises Engels' treatment of production of the means of subsistence and human reproduction as two distinct and co-ordinate aspects of the process of production, and accuses him of giving them equal analytic weight. It would seem, however, that in making such a distinction Engels was drawing on the earlier formulation of *The German Ideology*, in which the propagation of fresh labour was seen as one 'moment' of social activity, before social relations came to refer only to the organisation of labour. When Marx spoke of patriarchy he was invariably referring to a specific relation of domestic production, in which the head of the household owned or controlled the means of production and organised the labour of its members. Similarly, when he referred to the 'slavery latent in the family' the reference is to the organisation of labour resources and not of procreative resources. 'This latent slavery in the family, though still very crude, is the first property . . . the power of disposing of the labour power of others. Division of labour and private property are, moreover, identical expressions' (1970a, p. 52). The sexual division of labour is not an important component in this analysis. In connection with guild production, Marx argues that:

> Capital in . . . towns was naturally derived capital, consisting of a house, the tools of the craft, and the natural, hereditary customers; and not being realizable, on account of the backwardness of commerce and the lack of circulation, it descended from father to son (p. 71).

There is no explanation given for the system of male inheritance of productive property in connection with either land, guild or factory production: like the sexual division of labour, the sexual division of property is regarded as natural, and therefore not a problem.[3] Marx does, however, mention the changing relations in the family once its means of production have been expropriated by the capitalist. *The Communist Manifesto* states that 'modern industry has converted the little workshop of the patriarchal master into the great factory of the industrial capitalist (Marx and Engels, 1967, p. 87). 'The proletarian is without property; his relation to his wife and children has no longer anything in common with the bourgeois family relations' (p. 92). From this point, Marx makes a distinction between the bourgeois family and the proletarian family, calling for the abolition of the bourgeois family based 'on capital or private gain' and the abolition of all right of inheritance.

There is little analytic concern, therefore, in Marx's work for the specific subordination of women. Although he speaks of the slavery latent in the family, this refers equally to women and to children. In stating that 'in the relations of slavery and serfdom . . . one part of society is treated by the other as itself merely an inorganic and natural condition of

its own reproduction' (1973, p. 489), Marx is as usual referring to labour even though the definition might evidently be
particularly applicable to women as procreators and labourers.
It is not recognised that women are subject to specific contradictions in connection with their double role, nor that this
might pose political problems in relation to the unity of the
working class. When he calls for working men of all countries
to unite it is probably exactly *men* that he means. And when
in *Grundrisse* the relation of the worker-proprietor to his
means of subsistence (in the pre-capitalist mode of production) is analysed, the worker-proprietor is undoubtedly seen
as male: and it was the male labourer who was 'prised from
the land — from the raw material, the instruments and means
of subsistence to become a "free labourer" for capital' (1973,
p. 498). Women, generally speaking, were not of course
proprietors except in default of brothers or temporarily as
widows until their sons attained majority. Women were also,
generally speaking, excluded from apprenticeships. Even
when Marx is referring to transformations in the organisation
of labour which crucially affected women, for example
('manufacture seizes hold initially not of the so-called urban
trades, but of the secondary occupations, spinning and
weaving, the two which least require guild level skills, technical training . . .' (p. 511)), there is no mention of the ways
in which the sexual division of labour and family relations
were thereby changed.[4]

In order to understand women's subordination, wives must
be seen to stand in a particular relation to the male head of
the household. Because of their additional procreative function, they cannot be unproblematically put together with
children as dependent labour. At one point, Marx does mention a modification in the relation of slavery in the family,
the power of disposing of the labour power of others:
'Previously, the worker sold his own labour power, which he
disposed of nominally as a free agent. Now he sells his wife
and child. He has become a slave dealer' (1970b, p. 396). The
question arises — now that capitalism, which is in theory
progressive for the woman providing as it does the means of
achieving an independent income — as to why adult women
are none the less regarded as dependents whose labour power
is not their own to sell. The answer lies in a recognition of

the fact that a wife cannot be regarded as 'free labour', because she is bonded to her husband for the purpose of pro-creation and the reproduction of the bearers of labour power. A wife's relation to capital is always a mediated one because of her primary responsibility to service the family: her relation to production is always mediated through her relation to her husband, precisely through the relation of human reproduction. As Sally Alexander writes:

> Women's vulnerability as wage-workers stemmed from their childbearing capacity, upon which 'natural' founda-tion the sexual-division of labour within the family was based. The pre-industrial family had a patriarchal structure . . . . The father was head of the household . . . and his authority was sanctioned . . . by law . . . . In spite of the wife's contribution to production, her responsibility for the well being of her husband and children always came before her work in social production, and in a patriarchal culture, this was seen to follow naturally from her role in biological reproduction (1976, p. 77).

However, Marx remained consistent in his formulation of relations between the sexes following uproblematically from changes in their respective relations to production. In *Capital*, for example, it is argued that

> However terrible and disgusting the dissolution, under the capitalist system, of the old familial ties may appear, nevertheless modern industry, by assigning as it does an important part in the process of production, outside the domestic sphere, to women, to young persons, and to children of both sexes, creates a new economic foundation for a higher form of the family and of relations between the sexes (1970b, p. 490).

Because Marx allows no autonomy of content to the social relations of human reproduction, women are seen to inhabit only capitalist relations, rather than both capitalist and patri-archal relations: it follows then that there is no sense of con-tradiction in this analysis of women's position. And so while the concepts of *Capital* are essential to an analysis of women's wage labour, and those of *Grundrisse* can be used, when suit-ably modified, to look at structures of dependence of women on men, Marx provides no conceptual tools for theorising the subordination of women in terms of the social relations of human reproduction. It is for these reasons that marxist feminists are obliged to return to Engels, in spite of the many inadequacies of his theorisation.

Engels follows quite closely Marx's use of the concepts of patriarchy in that he sees the patriarchal family as a historically specific institution based on the organisation of labour in household units of production. But the fact that he actually regards women's oppression as an analytic problem *per se* leads him to superimpose on the analysis of family forms a critique of monogamy. Hence Engels is attempting to relate a number of different concepts all of which are sexually specific in content: the sexual division of labour, forms of ownership of productivity property, and corresponding forms of marriage. Engels associates hunting and gathering societies with 'group marriage', and animal breeding and plant cultivating societies with 'pairing marriage'. He speculates that an original 'natural' sexual division of labour in the pairing marriage was accompanied by the ownership of domestic utensils by the female and of extra-domestic implements by the male. This was not asymmetrically structured — there was no domination of the female by the male. This pattern of owning personal effects changed rapidly once domesticated animals and cultivated land became part of the system of production. As Karen Sacks notes, Engels does not attribute the development of private property to a greedy male nature. 'The qualitatively different nature of these "effects" — that they could reproduce themselves and their fruits — led to the destruction of the communal political and economic order that had created them' (1974, p. 210). Once a surplus which could be appropriated as wealth became a regular feature of the male sphere, men gained a new economic power over women, and 'with this political revolution came a new form of the family, the patriarchal family tied to agriculture, which incorporates bondsmen into its structure as a transitional form before the appearance of the monogamous family' (Delmar, 1976, p. 274). For Engels the monogamous family means the individual family of procreation rather than the household family unit of production, the patriarchal family. This has to be distinguished from the monogamous form of marriage that is imposed upon women once there is a surplus in the form of productive property to be passed on to heirs. Engels writes in *Origin of the Family, Private Property and the State*: 'In order to guarantee the fidelity of the wife, that is, the paternity of the children, the woman is placed in the man's absolute power . . . . With the patriarchal family we enter the field of written history' (Marx and Engels, 1970, p. 489). (Engels equates history with the permanent production of a surplus, class appropriation, exploitation, civilisation, the beginnings of Roman and Greek society.) This analysis permits a relationship to be posed between class appropriation and women's subordination: 'The first class antagonism which appears in history coincides with the development of the antagonism between men and women in monogamous marriage, and the first class oppression with that of the female by the male' (p. 495).

Juliet Mitchell reads (without warrant, perhaps) this account of history to substantiate her thesis that patriarchy is the universal culture; that is, that patriarchy is coincident with the institution of civilisation or history:

> However, there is an aspect of Engels' thesis that is usually overlooked by revolutionary optimists, and it is an aspect that allies it far more closely with Freud's apparently opposite hypothesis than anyone cares to contemplate. Monogamous marriage, inheritance and the first class oppression are — for Engels — also coincident with civilization. Patriarchy and written history are twins. The group marriage that precedes it takes place under conditions of savagery, the pairing family of barbarism. The freedom of women is pre-historic, pre-civilization (Mitchell, 1975, p. 365).

There is a pertinent argument in *Origin of the Family, Private Property and the State* which relates to the privatisation of female labour in the home. In the patriarchal family and even more in the 'monogamian' family, 'the administration of the family lost its public character . . . . It became a private service . . . based on the open or disguised domestic enslavement of the woman' (Marx and Engels, 1970, p. 501). Here we have a clear indication that Engels recognised that although the patriarchal family decreased in its importance as an organisation of male labour, the control of the wife's labour in the family continued. Although Engels associates women's oppression with the sexual division of labour into private domestic labour for the woman and social public labour for the man, with the male ownership of productive property, and with monogamous relations of human reproduction, he does not distinguish sufficiently between the different procreative functions of women of different classes. In other words, although there is an indication of how class divisions at the level of production distinguished between owners and slaves, the way in which this functional differentiation was reflected at the level of procreation within the first differentiation of function *for women* is not in fact shown. Women were divided into those who procreated heirs (future owners of the means of production) and those who procreated future slave labourers. Thus the natural and material function of women to procreate for social use is transformed into two economic functions necessary to perpetuate the social relations of capitalist production. From the moment of the asymmetrical appropriation of the surplus product, women came to perform two separate functions appropriate to the class position of their husbands. It follows from this that the form of the family in class societies must be seen as arising not directly from the mode of production but as mediated by its accompanying relations of production.

The social relations of human reproduction, then, are class specific relations. They comprise the form of control of the wife's labour in the family and also the form of control of the wife's sexual fidelity. Just as the labour process is always situated within a particular mode of production and its social relations, so is the procreative process. Historically, too, the procreative process has — like the labour process — been shaped by a relation of control, specifically in this instance by a relation of patriarchy. At marriage, the wife gives into the control of her husband both her labour power and her capacity to procreate in exchange for subsistence for a definite period, for life. Whether or not her capacity to labour is actually realised depends upon her husband's class position. Both the feudal lord and his lady suffered loss of nobility, meaning the right to live off the surplus, by performing manual labour: on the other hand, the wife of the self-sustaining peasant family laboured incessantly. So, too, in capitalism, the wives of the appropriating bourgeoisie (bourgeois women) are excused the need to labour, and their economic dependence provides the condition for their sexual fidelity. When the male heads of household production became propertyless through the gradual appropriation and concentration of the means of production in the hands of capital, the basis of their authority over their wife's productive labour was lost, also to capital, and the consequent entry of women into the labour force allowed for the possibility of the wife's independence from her husband with respect to the exchange of her labour power in a 'free' market, as indeed Marx and Engels had predicted. But what had not been envisaged was the 'inefficient' reproduction of the labour force which ensued. Capital's greed for cheap labour meant that the employment of women was favoured over that of men. In *The Condition of the Working Class in England* Engels points to the reversal of labour relations in the family which followed from the 'emancipation' of proletarian women in wage labour and the unemployment of the husband:

> We must admit that so total a reversal of the position of the sexes can have come to pass only because the sexes have been placed in a false position from the beginning. If the reign of wife over the husband as inevitably brought about by the factory system, is inhuman, the pristine rule of the husband over the wife must have been inhuman too (Engels, 1969, p. 174).

The sexual division of labour is evidently not seen as in any way 'natural', but rather the result of the particular economic conditions of early capitalist industrialisation.

In order that the 'problem' of the dissolution of the family (meaning the dissolution of patriarchal family relations) should be 'solved', women's dependence was historically re-secured in the first half of the nineteenth century by the intervention of legislation. This was done not directly in the family, but indirectly by restricting the conditions under which female labour power could be sold. In other words it was state intervention whose effect was to limit the progressive tendencies of capitalism that replaced women in the home, rather than the logic of capitalism. Sally Alexander argues:

> The intervention of capitalism into the sexual division of
> labour within the patriarchal family confirmed the econ-
> omic subordination of women . . . by confirming produc-
> tion for use to the home . . . and production for exchange
> to the workshop . . . capitalism ensured the economic
> dependence of women upon their husbands and fathers for
> a substantial part of their lives (1976, p. 77).

However, she correctly insists that 'it is the consistency of
this articulation of the capitalist mode of production through
a patriarchal family structure — even at the most volatile
moments of industrial upheaval — which must form a central
object of feminist historical research' (p. 111). The mechanisms by which patriarchy is secured vary according to the
class position of women and the different procreative functions they perform. Just as it is impossible to generalise about
'the family' in a class society, so it is impossible to generalise
about mechanisms of subordination. Brigit O'Loughlin has
argued that production must be analytically posited before
reproduction and it follows from this that the social relations
of production must be posited before the social relations of
human reproduction. Though women are placed simultaneously in two separate but linked structures, those of class
and patriarchy, it is their class position which limits the conditions of the forms of patriarchy they will be objectively
subjected to.
    A wife inhabits her husband's class position, but not the
equivalent relation to the means of production. Whichever
class she inhabits, the crucial mechanism of her subordination
enabling the male control of her 'person' is that of differential
male and female access to the means of production (for the
owning class) and the wage (for the non-owning class): on the
one hand the sexual division of productive property, and on
the other the sexual division of labour. These patriarchal
structures of economic dependence in marriage (which are
specific to women but different for each class) function
ultimately in the interests of the male capitalist, of his need
for legitimate heirs and for fresh labour power. So it is that
women's subordination serves the same system, but in different ways. Thus to speak of situating the social relations of
human reproduction in the context of the relations of production means to understand the perpetuation of these structures

in both the bourgeois and the proletarian family as being primarily determined by the need to control woman's procreative capacity and her sexuality, in connection with heirs on the one hand, and the efficient reproduction of the next generation of labour power on the other. While the relations of human reproduction are analytically central to an explanation of the subordination of all women, different contradictions inevitably arise for women inhabiting different class positions. As we have seen, the contradiction for the working-class woman was between the possibility of material and social independence from men and the family (with her entry into social production), and her legal and economic dependence as wife.[5] This contradiction clearly did not exist for the bourgeois woman, since in the nineteenth century especially there was no possibility of an independent existence for her: the contradiction for the bourgeois woman was that she was only an honorary member of the bourgeoisie without its defining characteristic, the ownership of the means of production.

Engels noted the contradictions arising from sexual control especially in the bourgeois family. For example, he indicates that while monogamy with respect to the bourgeois woman was functional for the bourgeois male because it guaranteed legitimate heirs, it had different outcomes from men — whose refusal to give up sexual freedom resulted in prostitution — and for women — whose sexual rebellion took the form of adultery. We would agree with Delmar, then, that Engels must be given credit for asking crucial questions about the twofold but linked character of production and reproduction:

> If the origin of the family constituted an achievement it
> was this, that it asserted women's oppression as a problem
> of history, rather than of biology, a problem which is the
> concern of historical materialism to analyse and revolution-
> ary politics to solve (Delmar, 1976, p. 287).

However, as Veronica Beechey argues, 'Engels fails to recognise what feminists have consistently argued, that the patriarchal family remains within industrial capitalist society, and its persistence is of fundamental economic and ideological importance to the capitalist mode of production' (1977, p. 47). It is necessary, therefore, to be wary of the one-sidedness of the argument put forward by Zaretsky that 'the rise of modern industry centralised private property and thus eliminated the economic basis for the patriarchal family' (1976, p. 107). We can agree that the patriarchal family as a productive unit in which the head of the household organised male, female, and child labour has been eliminated. But it must be stressed that because the labour of the working-class wife remains an aspect of the family organisation of labour, then even within the orthodox marxist definition of the term an element of patriarchy can be said to persist. There is still a sense in which 'the family under capitalism is a producing unit: production of use of values by the wife who is maintained in a subordinate social, economic and legal position, with an overwhelming emphasis on production for children's needs' (Mackintosh, 1977, p. 124). If we understand patriarchy also to include the concept of male control of female fertility and sexuality, then it can certainly be said that patriarchy in this sense persists across all classes of women. Whether it is maintained directly by the husband as in the bourgeois family or reinforced by welfare provision as in the proletarian family, the institution in which such control is exercised is still the patriarchal family. In other words, the family remains what Engels termed an 'economic unit', one in which the wife is dependent on the husband.

We have seen that Marx used the notion of the patriarchal family to refer, without exception, to the social relation of domestic production in pre-capitalist modes of production. Engels followed this argument by referring to patriarchal relations as those concerned with the sexual division of labour primarily in the household, but also as it spilled over into industrial labour relations. The employer, he writes, is not only sovereign over the labour of his female employees, but also over their 'persons and charms . . . . His mill is also his harem' (Engels, 1969, p. 177). Engels attempted to theorise the relation between the sexual subordination of women in monogamous marriage and the economic subordination of women in respect of the sexual division of labour both within the home and between private and public spheres. Both aspects of women's subordination, the control of her fertility and sexuality and also the sexual division of labour (and property), must form the basis of a theoretical analysis of patriarchy. Engels' critique of monogamy, the lifelong depen-

dence of the woman on the man for the purpose of the legitimate inheritance of the means of production, applied in
particular to the bourgeois family and to the self-subsisting
family in the pre-capitalist mode of production. While
virginity and monogamy are still arguably relevant to the
bourgeois social relations of human reproduction, it is less
clear according to Engels' analysis why monogamy persists
in the non-bourgeois family where logically, at least, it is
redundant. The inadequacy of economic explanations of
working-class women's continued sexual subordination in the
family suggests that patriarchy as an ideology which defines
women's place with regard to the family, must be an important feature of the complex of mechanisms that underlie the
perpetuation of patriarchal relations. Any adequate analysis
of relations in the family must take into account the specific
political and ideological oppression of women, as it relates
both to their sexual subordination in the family and to their
economic subordination in wage labour.

It must be stressed, however, that in spite of women's
transhistorical sexual subordination in the family with respect
to their procreative function, this function can only be understood in the context of the particular historical conjuncture.
Historical analysis necessarily entails an examination of the
social relations of production and the corresponding social
relations of human reproduction. It also requires an examination of the shifting weights of the various components that
secure women's subordination in any specific instance. One
of the problems with the definition of patriarchy as the law
of the father is its attendant confinement to a symbolic
instance. Historically and concretely, however, the patriarchal
nature of laws defining women's exclusion from rights to
ownership, to labour, to control of their own fertility and
sexuality, and so on has been an arena of constant challenge
by women.

We have attempted here to show how an analysis of patriarchy in its symbolic aspect and also an orthodox marxist
analysis are both one-sided, and we have argued that an
adequate marxist feminist analysis must attempt to relate
the form of organisation of the sexual division of labour in
the home and in production to the historically specific form
of organisation of procreation and sexuality. The implications

of holding on to a dual notion of patriarchy as, first, the control of women's fertility and sexuality in monogamous marriage and, second, the economic subordination of women through the sexual division of labour (and property) means that women's procreative function, or rather its relations, are not subsumed under the sexual division of labour: hence patriarchy should be understood as more than the sexual division of labour. Like the exchange of women, the sexual division of labour requires explanation, it is not itself a cause. Patriarchy, then, remains a key object for marxist feminist analysis.

Notes

1 Althusser's concept of the Imaginary is indebted to Lacan's development and modification of Freud's account of the construction of sexuality in the individual. For Lacan the Imaginary is the relationship of self to self in the formation of the child's identity, an identity which is not real but imagined. The child has been 'given' itself in the privileged moment of recognition of 'otherness' constituted by the 'mirror phase' (see Annette Kuhn's contribution to this volume). The self is constructed upon the recognition of absence or the discovery of *difference* in the alienated reciprocity of the self-other dialectic between the mother and the child.

2 Althusser (1971b) introduces the concept of the Absolute Subject in relation to Christian ideology, where God is the Absolute Subject *par excellence* (p. 167) who needs His subjects as much as His subjects need Him.

3 Pierre Bourdieu, in 'Marriage strategies as strategies of social reproduction' in R. Forster and P. Ranum, *Family and Society* (Johns Hopkins University Press, Baltimore, 1976), makes a careful analysis of the way in which the family as a property-owning unit 'manages' the transmission of the patrimony in the male line.

4 Alice Clark in *Women in the Seventeenth Century* (Frank Cass, London, 1968) examines in detail changes in domestic production, the exclusion of women from apprenticeships, the sexual division of labour and the subordination of women.

5 The 'concrete contradiction' is noted by Hilary Wainwright, Margaret Coulson and Branka Magaš in 'Some critical notes on Wally Seccombe's "The housewife and her labour under capitalism"', *Women and Socialism Conference, Paper 3*, published by Birmingham Women's Liberation Group, 1974.

References

Alexander, S. (1976), 'Women's work in nineteenth-century London' in

J. Mitchell and A. Oakley, *The Rights and Wrongs of Women*, Penguin, Harmondsworth.

Althusser, L. (1971a), 'Freud and Lacan' in *Lenin and Philosophy and Other Essays*, New Left Books, London.

Althusser, L. (1971b), 'Ideology and ideological state apparatuses' in *Lenin and Philosophy and Other Essays*, New Left Books, London.

Beechey, V. (1977), 'Female wage labour in capitalist production' *Capital and Class*, no. 3, pp. 45—66.

Delmar, R. (1976), 'Looking again at Engels's "Origin of the Family, Private Property and the State" ' in J. Mitchell and A. Oakley, *The Rights and Wrongs of Women*, Penguin, Hardmondsworth.

Engels, F. (1969), *The Condition of the Working Class in England*, Panther, London.

Hirst, P. Q. (1976), 'Althusser's theory of ideology', *Economy and Society*, vol. 5, pp. 385—412.

Mackintosh, M. (1977), 'Reproduction and patriarchy', *Capital and Class*, no. 2, pp. 119—27.

Marx, K. (1973), *Grundrisse: Foundations of the Critique of Political Economy*, Penguin, Harmondsworth.

Marx, K. (1970a), *The German Ideology*, Lawrence & Wishart, London.

Marx, K. (1970b), *Capital* vol. I, Lawrence & Wishart, London.

Marx, K., and Engels, F. (1969), *The Communist Manifesto*, Penguin, Harmondsworth.

Marx, K., and Engels, F. (1968), *Selected Works*, Lawrence & Wishart, London.

Millett, K. (1971), *Sexual Politics*, Hart-Davis, London.

Mitchell, J. (1975), *Psychoanalysis and Feminism*, Penguin, Harmondsworth.

O'Loughlin, B. (1977), 'Production and reproduction: Meillassoux's "Femmes, geniers et capitaux" ', *Critique of Anthropology*, vol. 2, pp. 3—32.

Rowbotham, S. (1973), *Women's Consciousness, Man's World*, Penguin, Harmondsworth.

Sacks, K. (1974), 'Engels Revisited' in M. Rosaldo and L. Lamphere, *Woman, Culture and Society*, Stanford University Press.

Zaretsky, E. (1976), *Capitalism, the Family and Personal Life*, Pluto Press, London.

3 Structures of patriarchy and capital in the family

Annette Kuhn

The article that follows may be read as a continuation and elaboration
of the discussion begun in the previous contribution, whose authors, in
arguing that a materialist understanding of patriarchy would grasp it
as the structure informing the determinate social/historical organization
of procreation and sexuality, suggest that the family is the principal site
of the operation of patriarchal relations. Annette Kuhn takes up this
point in a criticism of the determinism which has informed a great deal
of theoretical work on the family and the position of women within it.
Although this issue is also addressed here by Veronica Beechey in her
critique of sociological approaches to women's work in relation to their
position in the family, the focus of Kuhn's argument is the way in which
the family is constantly resorted to as an 'explanation' of women's subordination, without in fact any genuine analysis of its autonomous
operation in this respect. Existing work, whether sociological or marxist,
tends to be functionalist in its assumption of certain sets of determinations, which suggest that the form of the family is determined by the
social system or mode of production, and/or that women's consciousness is determined by the form of the family and ultimately therefore
by the character of the social totality. Hence no degree of autonomy is
allowed in such analyses for either the family form or the positioning
of subjects within that form. The argument advanced here, that the
family is definable exactly as property relations and psychic relations
(both of which are historically specific) between men and women, and
that patriarchy is a structure which unites both sets of relations, assigns
an autonomous — or relatively autonomous — effectivity to the family

as a historically specific form of social organization. The notion of subject positioning drawn upon in the discussion of psychic relations comes from an area of work which constitutes itself as a materialist theory of subjectivity whose relevance for an understanding of the placing of women within patriarchal relations is paramount. The question of the subject in patriarchal psychic relations was introduced by Juliet Mitchell in *Psychoanalysis and Feminism* (1975), which is in fact criticized in the previous article on grounds of the universalism implied in its adoption of a Lévi-Straussian problematic. Other work in this area has been informed by the insights of structural linguistics, and the psychoanalytical work of Jacques Lacan in particular has been seen as the source of an understanding of the construction of the sexed subject. A conceptualization of subjectivity in relation to women within patriarchy is seen by its proponents as necessary because the position of women cannot be described or explained solely in terms of mode of production (Coward *et al.,* 1976). This is precisely what is implied in the suggestion in several of the papers in this volume that patriarchy may be conceived as a structure relatively autonomous of mode of production. The distinction, however, between the psychoanalytical problematic and the kind of appropriation of patriarchy for materialism which is part of the project of the papers presented here is more fundamental, and centres on the question of subject relations and their historical specificity. In arguing for a conceptualization of the subject as the site of the representation in ideology of relations of production and reproduction, the psychoanalytical problematic evidently presupposes a relative autonomy for ideology with regard to other instances of the social formation. Perhaps the main difficulty here, though, is that despite the fact that at present the psychoanalytic problematic can chart the formation of the sexed subject in ideology through the operation of patriarchal family relations, it is difficult to see how the structures it mobilizes can be seen in a more precise historical specificity through, for example, a conceptualization of class or mode of production. To say this, however, may be to make a premature demand, and it is perhaps for future work to examine in their conjunctural specificity the operations of ideology through structures of capital as well as of patriarchy.

The family occupies a strange position in analyses of various kinds which attempt to locate the effectivity of that formation within a social totality, historically, or with regard to the

structural subordination of women.[1] In some ways it constitutes an area of very obvious terror. It is constantly referred
to, or deferred to, as the crucial site of the subordination of
women, and its absence or dissolution, it is implied, would
pose a threat to property relations both patriarchal and capitalist and even to the psychic relations through which, it is
argued, social relations are mapped onto relations of subjectivity. In this sense, the family is very often invoked as a
final, catch-all explanation of the various characteristics of
women's position in different societies and at different times,
constantly referred to but still to be analysed without recourse
to various forms of functionalism. The same can be said —
with perhaps even more force — of ideology, and this is probably no coincidence: materialist analyses in both areas are
notoriously underdeveloped and it is perhaps true to say that
this lack has only just begun to be attended to, largely with
the impetus of the kind of criticisms offered and theoretical
work begun within the women's movement. But to the
extent that the kind of work required has been attempted, it
has tended hitherto to be either sociological or sociologistic.
In making this distinction, I am referring separately to an
ongoing tradition in sociology, namely a preoccupation with
the 'functions' of the family and the 'fit' between the family
and the wider social structure (Morgan, 1975), and to various
problematics, not simply avowedly sociological ones, in
which the family is seen as a repository of a social totality,
or as having its effectivity in the maintenance of such a
totality.

The concern with maintenance, whether the totality to be
maintained be seen as one in harmony — as in sociological
functionalism — or as one in contradiction — as in materialist
'functionalism' — tends in the first case to the effacement of
history altogether and a consequent tendency to universalise
a historically specific social formation, or in the second to
the displacement of the effectivity of history away from
the family and onto other formations, such as class. This displacement is by no means to be dismissed as crude economic
determinism, but its significance here is that the family is in
fact emptied of all social significance in such a way that it
becomes merely the vehicle of the reproduction of existing
relations of production. In both cases of functionalism — the

sociological and the materialist — the family is thought as the non-contradictory site of socially necessary activities such as 'pattern maintenance' (ideological reproduction) and 'tension management' (psychological renewal of labour power). The terms 'pattern maintenance' and 'tension management' are taken from the sociologist Talcott Parsons's functionalist analysis of the nuclear family, and the bracketed terms are of the sort frequently mobilised in marxist analyses of the family. What I am suggesting by juxtaposing the language of such different traditions is that in spite of differences in terminology, both approaches share a similar orientation (Middleton, 1974) because the question they both attempt to answer — how is it possible for the family to exist? — is a functionalist one. And both see the family as the transmitter or repository of social forces the site of whose real operation lies outside itself. If this is indeed the case, then it is no wonder that the family can be referred to only as crucial (and so on) for the continuation or reproduction of a social order, for many of the existing analyses which attempt to specify its effectivity relegate it, paradoxically, to the status of what may be termed an empty signifier.

What I want to do in this paper is to begin to shift the terms of the debate around the family, but of necessity by means of drawing upon existing analyses whose aim is to locate forms of the family with regard to history and social formation — materialist analyses, that is — because it is such analyses which through the centrality within them of history, however thought, contain the potential for a reformulation of the question. I would argue, however, that materialist analyses relapse so readily into sociologism because they tend to take for granted the place of the subject in history and fail to grant it an autonomous field of operation; the 'agent' (to use a term widely deployed in recent materialist functionalist analyses) is thought precisely as a vehicle through which the forces of history are acted out. A criticism of such a determinate conceptualisation of the subject does not, however, constitute a demand for voluntarism, which effectively denies any autonomous operation for history, but does simply suggest that things are perhaps more complex than either of these two positions suggest when they both from their opposite points of view implicitly or explicitly pose a model of the subject as coherent, without contradiction and, in one sense or another, outside history. By looking at classic work — in particular that of Engels — which offers a materialist analysis of the family, I shall emphasise the important place occupied by property relations in inscribing family, household and production relations, and I shall attempt to open up the question of the problematic status of history in relation to the very crucial notion of patriarchy. This focus permits a consideration of attempts to construct a theory of the subject as the site of psychic structures of patriarchy; and in particular of the production of the male/female subject. Such theorising may be read as drawing on, and as written in terms of, the materialist notion of the family as historically inscribing property relations. By these means I aim to displace or alter the terms of the way the family is thought by suggesting that patriarchy unites property and psychic relations and that it is this unity which is effected in the operation of the family.

I

It is perhaps not surprising that many of the attempts which have been made within a materialist problematic to locate the significance of the family in relation to mode of production or social formation have tended towards sociologism: for much of the classic work in this area is notable largely for the schematic character of its analyses with regard to the family. The project of *Capital*, for example, is to dissect the laws of motion of the capitalist mode of production, which means that analysis tends to focus on the production of exchange value under conditions within which capital is accumulated through the expropriation of surplus value — that is, under conditions of capitalist production. Within this problematic, the means by which labour power, the source of surplus value, is reproduced, are of obvious importance. Marx argues in the first volume of *Capital* that:

> The value of labour power is determined . . . by the labour time necessary for the production, and consequently also the reproduction . . . of this special article . . . . Given the individual, the production of labour power consists in his reproduction of himself or his maintenance . . . . The value

of labour power is the value of the means of subsistence
necessary for the maintenance of the labourer (Marx, 1954,
p. 167).

However, the institution of those means tends to fall outside
the scope of analysis and is in some sense seen as arbitrary or
even natural:

> The maintenance and reproduction of the working class is,
> and must ever be, a condition to the reproduction of
> capital. But the capitalist may safely leave its fulfilment to
> the labourers' instincts of self-preservation and of propaga-
> tion (p. 537).

Thus the necessity to capital of the reproduction of labour
power is acknowledged, while the proletarian family, the site
of that reproduction, is not: possibly because of the implication that within the proletarian family in its pure form under
capitalism no exchange values, but use values only, are directly
produced — and hence the family is seen as beyond the scope
of the analysis of the operation of capital accumulation.
Marx's references to the reproduction of labour power and
his simultaneous failure to consider the full implications of
its institutionalisation have been the source of some contention as to the relationship between the relations of domestic
labour, that socially necessary labour which takes place in the
household, outside the conditions of capitalist production,
the reproduction of labour power, and the expropriation of
surplus value which takes place outside the household; all of
which questions revolve around the issue of the sexual division
of labour and its instantiation and mobilisation within particular modes of production. I shall deal with these questions in
more detail below, and simply point here to the fact that it
is possible either to hold to the immediate implications of the
analysis put forward in *Capital* by arguing that the free labour
of the housewife benefits capital without creating value, or to
argue that domestic labour benefits capital because it creates
value for which the housewife is unpaid (approaches which
have been labelled respectively 'orthodox' and 'unorthodox'
(CCCS Women's Studies Group, 1976, p. 102) with regard to
classic marxist positions).

It is perhaps of relevance to note, alongside this relative
lack of attention devoted to the proletarian family, the import

of the fact that one of the historical features of the development of capitalism *per se* is the tendency for more and more
sectors of the population to be drawn into the realm of
capital accumulation, capitalist production itself — that is, to
become proletarianised: a tendency particularly evident in
Britain during the period of industrialisation up to the time
of writing of *Capital*, and one which implied the increasing
proletarianisation of women and children, as well as of men.
Gardiner, Himmelweit and Mackintosh, however, argue that
in his analysis of the value of labour power, Marx assumed a
proletarian family unit in which wife and children did not
work (1975, p. 3), a situation in evident contradiction with
the noted tendency of capital to draw such groups into the
working population. This contradiction, unspoken by Marx
and clearly an outcome of the very exclusion of family/
household relations of production from the terms of the
analysis put forward in *Capital*, permits the escape from
attention of something vitally important — that the proletarianisation of women posed a very real threat to the continuation of family relationships within the industrial working
class and hence to the benefit accruing to capital of the family
based labour of the housewife, which secures the reproduction
of labour power at relatively low cost. This risk, always
ultimately posed for capitalism, of course has been and continues to be recuperated at various conjunctures through the
overdetermining operation of such factors as the intervention
of the state in the conditions of employment of women, in
poor laws and social security, which are discussed by Mary
McIntosh in her contribution to this volume. Recuperation
has also and relatedly operated through structures of *patriarchy* which have a specific effectivity in relation to structures of capital but which maintain a relative autonomy with
regard to these structures.

Although there is little systematic attempt on the part of
Marx in *Capital* and elsewhere to provide an analysis of the
relationship between the forces of capital and the proletarian
and bourgeois family forms under capitalism (indeed the
project of analysing the laws of motion of the capitalist
economy would exclude such a preoccupation), the family
is in fact addressed as a central issue by Engels in his *Origin
of the Family, Private Property and the State*, but the question

is displaced here in such a way that the historical instantiation of family forms is seen precisely in terms of patriarchal (as opposed to, say, feudal or capitalist) relations. The relationship between patriarchy and mode of production is problematic in that each inscribes a different notion of history, and the two structures can in no way be seen as homologous, nor can either be understood as determining, or determined by, the other. As is implied elsewhere in this volume (see Chapter 2, contributed by McDonough and Harrison), patriarchy is most appropriately seen as having a relative autonomy with regard to mode of production. It is clear that Engels follows Lewis Morgan, on whose anthropological researches much of the evidence on kinship in *Origin of the Family* is based, in deploying an evolutionary model of history of very much the kind set out by other nineteenth-century thinkers and social theorists. Each of Engels' three stages of history – savagery, barbarism and civilisation – corresponds to a particular family form: respectively group marriage, pairing marriage and monogamy. Since, according to Engels, the overthrow of mother right, 'the world-historic defeat of the female sex', predates written history, the conditions for patriarchal social/ familial relations came into existence well before the rise of capitalism. Indeed the importance of one form of patriarchal family in 'civilisation' – the *familia*, 'a new social organism whose head ruled over wife and children and a number of slaves' (Engels, 1972, p. 121) – is particularly emphasised, and it is clear that it is a form precisely characteristic of slave societies. Feudal societies, too, are characterised in terms of the break-up of the kinship structures of the *gens*, or clan, in favour of those of the monogamous family. It is clear, therefore, that although Engels' analysis of the social relations of family forms does inscribe history as a crucial component, the model is founded in an epistemology different from that articulated in an analysis which treats of the dynamic of transitions between different modes of production *within* 'civilisation'. What this means in effect is that although Engels' notion of the social relations of patriarchy is a historical one, nevertheless it cannot be mapped unproblematically onto the social relations characteristic of a mode of production. The two histories are, so to speak, out of step. This clearly has implications for the development of an analysis of patriarchal structures in the family in capitalism as a specific mode of production and indeed at conjunctures within that mode, since the concept of private property put forward by Engels cannot be conceived in terms of the specific relations of private property under capitalism: a point to be borne in mind in examining the question of the rise of the monogamous family and the attendant growth of private property. The monogamous family, like private property, predicate capitalism and 'is based on the supremacy of the man, the express purpose being to produce children of undisputed paternity' (p. 125). Its conditions of existence, then, are provided by the economic necessity of property relations as written into patriliny: since inheritance of property is from father to son, the paternity of children must not be in question. And hence the fidelity of the wife is to be ensured and social fatherhood brought into identity with biological fatherhood. The prehistoric origin of the appropriation by males of property is described in terms of a social overdetermination of a 'natural' sexual division of labour: domestic labour performed by women continued to produce use values exclusively, while work done by men became a potential source of exchange value (Sacks, 1974). As far as the capitalist mode of production is concerned, Engels sees the property relations of monogamous marriage as having a historical effectivity only in the bourgeois family, the inheritance of property only being an important issue in that class. The 'higher' form of the family envisaged by Engels lay in the potentiality of the proletarian family in which, since with the lack of private property the question of inheritance was not relevant, the choice of marriage partner could be free from such considerations. Since Engels' argument is based on the premiss that male supremacy is a phenomenon of private property, then for him the abolition of the latter would accordingly entail the disappearance of the former. The implication of this analysis of family relations is that patriarchy as an abstract structure pervades the social/familial relations of all social formations in which private property exists, but, to take the analysis further, that the precise form in which patriarchal relations are expressed varies according to the particular character of property relations, or of class relations, within any social formation.

Although Engels' description of forms of the family under capitalism is rather unsatisfactory — on the bourgeois family he is very sketchy and on the proletarian family he is actually wrong in a number of respects — this reading of *Origin of the Family* does constitute a possible means of filling a gap in the classical marxist approach to the political economy of capital and signals a potentially productive way forward from socio-logical and sociologistic explanations of the social and histor-ical effectiveness of the family.

If patriarchy is seen as a relatively autonomous structure written into family relations — the privileged site of social relations between men and women — whose operation is broadly historical in the evolutionary sense adopted by Engels but overdetermined by specific features of the con-juncture, then the terms of its operation in history with regard to the position of women can also be thought. Patri-archy, as McDonough and Harrison argue in Chapter 2, is a concept which has been appropriated in a variety of ways by the women's movement, and it is quite readily seized on as a universal structure through which the oppression of women can be understood without reference to history. This is to a certain extent true of those analyses which draw on the con-cept of patriarchy to put forward some notion of a collective female unconscious, which then becomes the repository of an archaic femininity, in a way rather analogous to that by which myths of archaic matriarchies and societies of Amazons are sometimes put forward as the kind of forgotten, or repressed, history which resides in the Jungian notion of archetypes. It can, however, be argued that the unconscious is not in any necessary sense transhistorical, that it does not in fact exist outside history. What is perhaps nevertheless problematic about a statement of this kind is that it is not immediately evident precisely in what way the relationship between history and the unconscious can be posed. Although Juliet Mitchell (1975) is surely correct in arguing that such a relationship does exist, she is unable to cope with the question of the immediate relationship between the unconscious and the social formation, because she is unspecific about the character of the historicity for which she argues. By this I mean that she conflates the two kinds of history which I have distin-guished: the history of patriarchy and the history of modes of production. She is right to argue for a historical inscription of the unconscious as expressing patriarchal relations in the broad social sense of the law of the father as head of the household and controller of the labour power of members of the family or household; but to move immediately from this to assert a more precise relation to mode of production and social formation involves the elision of two problematics — easy enough to do in the sense that they both place themselves under the banner of both history and materialism. The point I am making here is that patriarchy tends to be understood either as a structure informing social relations, relations of production and private property in the sense argued by Engels; or as an alternative position it is seen as a structure informing psychic relations, subject positioning and symbolic structures. What I want to suggest is that these two positions are not necessarily alternatives, that psychic relations can be seen as the site and expression of the symbolic operation of social and property relations, and that such a way of posing this relationship involves a rethinking of the nature of family relations and a reformulation of the question of ideology. It is important that the juxtaposition of family and ideology be made here, in the sense that the family is — as I have suggested above — commonly seen as merely the place of the operation of ideology, the reproduction of relations of production whose real effectivity lie elsewhere, outside the family. Such a notion is immediately displaced by the redefinition of ideology in terms of the creation of subjects for a set of representations of social relations. The suggestion that patriarchy is a structure which unites property relations and psychic relations entails a number of problems, however, not the least of which is the ever recurrent question of the place in this scheme of history as operating through the mode of production.

I shall outline below some of the arguments which, drawing on readings of psychoanalytic work done by Freud, offer a theory of the positioning of the subject and the constitution of the unconscious whose project is to historicise both. It is perhaps sufficient simply to indicate at this point that such work, to the extent that it mobilises the notion of partriarchy, does so precisely in the sense in which Engels relates the monogamous family, private property and patriarchal oppression to a stage of history which predates capitalism and may well survive it: that is, that the work I shall be referring to can argue an inscription of the unconscious in history, but not in a social formation. A certain number of difficulties are raised with the question of more precisely conjunctural approaches the aim of which is to analyse the relation between, say, the capitalist mode of production or moments within that mode and the social relations of the patriarchal family or household; and the mode of operation of psychic relations at this level is somewhat problematic. The problems which are immediately raised here include the question of property relations in particular modes of production — in capitalism expressed as relations of class. The definition of patriarchy as a relatively autonomous structure whose operation is over-determined conjuncturally by precisely such structures as class may be enlightening as far as the connection between patriarchy and property relations is concerned, but how can the connection between patriarchy and *psychic* relations be thought? The question of the construction of the sexed subject has been addressed productively in the psychoanalytic problematic, but the question of the two modes of history must inevitably lead to the question of the construction also of the class subject. Before attempting to suggest how this might be dealt with, it is important, given the argument that patriarchy unites property and psychic relations, to first examine the question of patriarchy, property relations and the family in greater detail.

In the family, property relations are historically expressed in social relations between men and women, in particular between husbands and wives. Or more correctly, perhaps, the family is definable exactly as property relations between men and women, and the social relations of the family are those property relations in action. Since the materialist problematic concerns itself with the production and reproduction of immediate life, then the implications of any division of labour must be crucial to that problematic. A great deal of anthropological evidence has been put forward on the question of the sexual division of labour, its main import being that such a division appears to be common to all kinds of societies, but that the actual concept of the sexual division of labour as an abstraction is of little analytical use because of the wide variety, social and historical, of concrete expressions of that division. Furthermore, the sexual division of labour in itself bears no necessary implications for power relations between the sexes. Karen Sacks (1974), taking up in part one of the strands of Engels' argument, suggests that relations between men and women in non-capitalist societies are open to transformation as soon as household production ceases to be confined to use values, and a relation of patriarchal control obtains when the sexual division of labour operates so that the means of subsistence is in male hands. In societies in which production takes place exclusively in the household, a base for unequal power relations between men and women in the household exists under conditions which are defined by the production of exchange values and the operation of a sexual division of labour such that women's productive labour is confined to use values while men produce for exchange and acquire property. With the development of forms of social organisation in which production for exchange takes increasing precedence over production of simple use values, the social impact of such a sexual division of labour is intensified, with the result that 'women now worked for their husbands and families instead of for society' (Sacks, 1974, p. 211). At this point, women's labour becomes subject to appropriation by men even in societies characterised by household-based production. To the extent that such a development can draw upon and exploit existing sexual divisions of labour, these relations of production become intensified with the growth of production for exchange outside the household. In capitalism a separation is set up between relations of production and labour processes in two spheres, household and industry, and the relation of exchange is displaced from household commodity production to the sale of labour power in exchange for a wage.

This brief outline of the terms of the effectivity of the sexual division of labour for relations between men and women in the family contains a number of points which require further elaboration. The first relates to the sexual division of labour itself. Although on the one hand Engels argues that it is a natural and entirely unproblematic division — 'the division of labour is determined by entirely different causes than those which determine the status of women'

(Engels, cited by Delmar, 1976, p. 285) — on the other his main argument about the subordination of women rests on a position as to the growth of private property, which he sees as primarily the outcome of a sexual division of labour in terms of which the productive potential of men's labour was realised through their tools, the means of production, which became the first private property and was owned by men. If this is the case, then the sexual division of labour cannot be seen as a natural one, certainly as far as its effectivity is concerned; it has its historical expression in social relations. This has important implications for the relationship between men's labour and women's labour in the household; to the extent that women's labour becomes increasingly confined to the production of use values for consumption in the family, women's work is increasingly done in the service of family members. This becomes institutionalised in the social relations of marriage to the extent that husbands are in a position of owning or controlling the labour power of their wives, a situation which may be legitimated in the written or unwritten terms of marriage contracts. With the transition to capitalism, these social relations are carried further. The distinction between the production of use values and of exchange values is concretised in two separate sets of relations of production, those of the family and those of the factory. The sexual division of labour takes on specifically capitalist social relations in being overdetermined by the separation of work and home. Indeed the very formulation 'work and home' only becomes possible in capitalism, signifying as it does a qualitatively new kind of distinction between the production of use values (by domestic labour) and the production of exchange values (through wage labour). The latter comes to be exclusively defined as work, partly because of the exchange value of the commodities produced, but crucially and specifically in capitalism because that work is performed in exchange for a wage. Labour in the household — domestic labour — remains the province of women, of wives, although at the same time women of the proletarian class are drawn also into commodity production. The terms of their entry into the capitalist economy are, however, given by their pre-existing relation to domestic labour in such a way that they take on some of the characteristics of an industrial reserve army, as

Veronica Beechey argues in Chapter 7 of this book.

Male property *per se* ceases to constitute the basis for male supremacy in class societies (Sacks, 1974, p. 219), at least as far as the proletariat is concerned; but this does not mean that male supremacy ceases to exist in the proletarian family. The marriage contract is based partly on bourgeois property relations, and the implications of such relations as to the legal rights of the husband over the person and property of the wife come to be applied also to marriages within the working class. Moreover, the implications for the expression of property relations in relations between the sexes come to be displaced onto the wage, which is seen as the legitimate property of the 'breadwinner' (that is, the husband) in return for a part of which the wife is obliged to render up her labour power, or part of it. Thus the marriage contract gives the husband the right of access to his wife's labour in reproducing his labour power and by bearing and rearing his (*his*) children, even where questions of property, inheritance, and so on are not involved. Although the marriage contract can therefore be seen in some ways as a contract of employment, it differs from contracts between employers and employees in two crucial respects: first, in that the wife is not free to change her 'employer' — the marriage relationship tends to be seen as a permanent one ('till death us do part'), to be dissolved only by the extreme measure of divorce, which is still illegal in certain societies. Second, in the marriage relationship the wife does not exchange her labour power for a wage. The domestic labour she performs is unpaid.

The relations of domestic labour are thus crucially different from the relations of capitalist production, and they place the wife in a position of subordination *vis-à-vis* the husband, who through the marriage contract becomes in effect the controller of her labour power. At the same time, the relationship between wage labour and domestic labour is effaced in the fact that one precisely is wage labour while the other is not. Because the wage appears to be a payment solely for labour performed outside the home, it conceals the fact that labour power, the source of surplus value, is a commodity whose value must be the cost of its production and reproduction. Since the production and reproduction of labour power take place substantially within the family through the labour of the housewife, then it is clear that her labour is in one way or another crucial to the generation of surplus value:

> On the one hand, then, since the value of labour power assumes a domestic unit and must include means of subsistence for wife and children, its value is higher than if society were made up of individual productive units. On the other hand, the labour that she necessarily has to perform is unacknowledged, completely absent from the wage (CCCS Women's Studies Group, 1976, p. 111).

Although then, domestic labour is both socially useful labour and beneficial to capital, it is performed within an arena of social relations in which these economic relations are displaced onto and take the appearance of personal relations between two individuals. The wage, because it is apparently given as a return for work performed outside the home, is seen as the property of the wage-earner, and that part of it which is passed on to the housewife then appears as a gift.

In considering the marriage contract and the wage form I have been able to point to only a few of the characteristics of the relations between men and women in the family under capitalism. What I want to argue is that property relations which pre-exist capitalism take on an expression particular to that mode of production by being inscribed in the characteristic feature of the wage form and by being expressed within the legal definitions of the marriage relationship in all classes. What I hope also to have suggested is the way in which a sexual division of labour has a specific effectivity in capitalism, as mapping itself onto the spatial separation of the site of production of use values (home and family) and that of the immediate production of exchange values (workplace). In arguing this, I do not in any way wish to underestimate the significance of the fact that most women for most of their lives are not wholly engaged in domestic labour: indeed, it must be one of the contradictions of capitalism that the continuation of male supremacy and the family form is under potential threat from the development of female wage labour. But as long as marriage exists as in part a labour contract, then the labour for which that contract provides — domestic labour — will remain 'at the heart of both class and sex oppression. It is the role to which all other roles within a capitalist mode of production will refer' (CCCS Women's Studies Group, 1976, p. 112): women occupy a particular relation to the capitalist mode of production, characterised by their concentration in semi-skilled and low-paid work, their tendency to move into and out of the labour market, their marginality in regard to state social security provisions, and so on, and that relation is at all moments associated with their *de facto* position or potential position within the family and with regard to domestic relations of production. The patriarchal relations implied in a social/sexual division of labour and in the appropriation of women's labour by men within the family are 'worked on' by the forces of capital and re-emerge at each conjuncture as particular forms of social relations.

II

In putting forward the argument that the concept of patriarchy unites property relations and psychic relations, I have already pointed to the problematic status of the history in theoretical work which aims to locate the production of subjects for ideology in patriarchal relations, in that the history appealed to in such work draws on the sort of evolutionary model adopted by Engels in *The Origin of the Family*. Within this problematic, the unconscious is thought as the repository of the structural relations of patriarchy, and the subject — 'the individual in its social relations' — produced in the interaction of psychic representations and physical relations. It is argued in this reading of psychoanalysis[2] that the crucial moment of subjectivity is constituted in the entry into the Symbolic order of language, and that this entry is predicated in two dominant moments: the mirror phase and the castration complex. The beginning of subjectivity — posed by Lacan as the constitution of the 'I' (Lacan, 1968) — is explained in terms of the metaphor of the mirror in which the infant sees its own reflection for the first time: this is a moment of simultaneous unity and separation, in that the body is experienced as whole and yet as outside the previous operation of the drives:

> The mirror-phase is seen by Lacan to be the moment at which the infant's first movement towards a unified sense

of itself is set in motion. Prior to this, the infant is dominated by the constant flux of instinctual energy across its body . . . . The identification of the image in the mirror is the first moment in which the infant comes to form an image of itself (Coward and Ellis, 1977, p. 110),

an image experienced as exterior, a model for the world of objects and separation of subject and object. In the mirror phase the subject adopts a relation to the ego characterised by narcissism, in the Imaginary wholeness of the ego-ideal. The impetus of the Imaginary relations which characterise the mirror phase is then a reconstitution of subject and object into a unity. The mirror phase is crucial in the production of the subject in ideology, since the operation of ideology is to reconstruct the coherent subject problematised by the very splitting which defines this specular relation. The movement of ideology in this definition becomes the institution of a lost ideal, a closure, a lived representation of the Imaginary unity and coherence of the world. The mirror phase in its operation as the production of the 'I', of subjectivity, is an important moment in the entry of the subject into language — 'once we can imagine ourselves as whole selves, an image that is also an alienated one of self as other, we have the possibility of symbolising' (Coward *et al.*, 1976, p. 11). This notion of otherness is implicit in language, which inscribes a source of address, a speaker, and an object of address, a recipient, in the register of discourse; which is distinguishable from any other register precisely on grounds of subjectivity: 'it is by identifying himself as a unique person pronouncing *I* that each speaker sets himself up in turn as the "subject" ' (Benveniste, 1971, p. 220). It is in this sense that the Symbolic order of discourse presupposes subjectivity and the self-other split.

If in the Lacanian problematic the mirror phase is the structural and developmental moment which institutes the possibility of discourse and ideology, then it is the castration complex, in completing the process inaugurated by the mirror phase, which is the privileged moment of the construction of the sexed subject, the social male or the social female. As a precondition of gender identification, children of both sexes have to give up their mother as a love object, the little boy having to choose a woman other than his mother, at the same time resolving the threat of castration, implied in the intervention of the father at this stage, through masculine identification and through repression of desire for the mother. This, according to Freud, is the origin of the superego, the internalised source of morality derived from the authority of the father. Since the female subject is formed in a different set of relationships with the love object and the 'third term' – the father – she undergoes a different entry into the Symbolic, the metaphor for that difference consisting in the notion of the phallus as the privileged signifier. (The use of the term 'phallus' emphasises the symbolic function taken here by the penis.) Because the relationship of women to the phallus as signifier is one of a lack, then she enters the Symbolic negatively. This particular argument is based in a dictum of Saussure, the founder of structural linguistics, that language is made up of differences (that is, that meaning is produced in language out of relations of difference between the components of a speech act), extended to the notion of the phallus as signifier fixing difference according to possessing or not possessing it:

> The phallus functions as the term representing plenitude (having the phallus) when the differences previously established receive their cultural form. For this reason the female entry (into the Symbolic) is an articulation of lack, and therefore a negative entry (Coward *et al.*, 1976, p. 15).

A most important point for the present argument with regard to the construction of the sexed subject is that entry into the Symbolic takes place through the intervention of the 'third term', and it is at this point that the import of the family form in the construction of the subject becomes more clear. The third term in the (bourgeois) 'family romance' is the father, whose intervention in the mother–child relationship constitutes a demand that sexual identification be made. The moment of the castration complex is, as has been noted, the moment of the instantiation of the superego, the internalisation of paternal authority; so that in some sense the entry into the Symbolic is also the inauguration in psychic terms of the rule of the father. It is arguable, therefore, that the family form in its historical specificity is crucial in providing the conditions for certain kinds of entry into the Symbolic, and hence that the precise character of social relations within the family is also crucial here. Freud, and also Lacan, in arguing for a particular mode of resolution of the castration complex, assume a patriarchal family. The implication of this is that the production of subjects in ideology does have its effectivity as a historical process. The problem remains, however, that the notion of the patriarchal family involved here is such a broadly historical one that it is difficult to propose any immediate relation between subjectivity, family relations and social formation. Specifically, as far as the capitalist mode of production is concerned, psychoanalysis does not yet address the formation of the class subject within either the bourgeois or the proletarian family. However, to state this is not to suggest a necessary transhistoricism in the psychoanalytic problematic. Lacan argues that 'changes within the economic, political and ideological break down the fixed positionality in which ideological discourse sustained itself' (Coward and Ellis, 1977, p. 155), and given that concrete family relations in capitalism are in a sense its property and productive relations mapped onto patriarchal property relations, the precise character of, for example, paternal authority will take various forms which must in some as yet unspecified way provide different conditions for the entry into the Symbolic and the construction of the sexed subject.

In many descriptions and analyses of the family, it is seen as that social formation within which people are assigned a place in society and 'internalise' the nature and conditions of that place: in sociological terms, the family is the site of both the primary socialisation of children and the continuing socialisation of adults. Sociological explanations of this process range from the extreme determinism of the Durkheimian problematic — pre-existing rules and roles are internalised, represented in consciousness in an unmediated fashion — to the extreme voluntarism of symbolic interactionist and phenomenological perspectives — actors negotiate roles, construct a life-world for themselves, in concrete situations of face-to-face interaction. In many marxist approaches to the family, the neutrality of the concept of socialisation is displaced, often unproblematically, onto more or less elaborated notions of ideology, so that the family becomes the scene of the operation of ideological processes whereby the reproduction of existing relations of production takes place. The notion of socialisation then becomes a deproblematised and deterministic notion of manipulation: in either analysis, the sociological or the marxist, the maintenance of the existing order is secured. The main difference between the sociological position and the mechanical marxist one is that the model of the social totality operating, at least implicitly, in the latter is one characterised by contradiction rather than by the harmony of the functionalist totality, the 'social system': this means that ideology can be seen not as a neutral or pervasive but as a partial worldview, that of the dominant class. And hence emerges the concept of 'bourgeois ideology', seen as a more or less coherent value system the terms of which are imposed on the dominated class through various apparatuses such as school, or family, operating in the interests of the dominant class in capitalism. In his discussion of the state apparatuses which contribute to the reproduction of capitalist relations of production, Althusser argues in terms of 'a reproduction of submission to the ruling ideology for the workers, and a reproduction of the ability to manipulate the ruling ideology correctly for the agents of exploitation and repression' (Althusser, 1971, p. 128).

Certain notions of culture, such as that mobilised in versions of the sociology of education, draw on this problematic of a dominant class with its own worldview, and also argue the existence of a countervailing culture of the dominated class which finds expression in certain (recuperable) displacements such as truancy, vandalism, and certain forms of language use (Young, 1971; Keddie, 1973). Other things being equal, however, it is the culture of the ruling class, seen as the dominant culture, which has at its disposal the most effective vehicles of transmission of dominant ideology. This line of argument is put forward by Bourdieu and Passeron, for example, who see the dominant culture as 'contributing to the reproduction of the structure of power relations within a social formation', and 'the one which most fully, though always indirectly, corresponds to the objective interests . . . of the dominant groups of classes' (1977, pp. 6 and 7). Ideology is understood here as the direct and unproblematic expression of class interests, and its character determined by those interests. Ideology, thought in these terms, 'functions'

(Hirst, 1976) to reproduce the class relations of production, and becomes simply a vehicle for the transmission of representations of those relations, and the family one among a number of sites for that transmission. And presumably, to the extent that patriarchy is a structure of dominance, ideology can likewise be seen as a means by which representations of *sexual* relations of production are transmitted, and the family can be seen as the arena of such transmission in much the same sense as the notion of 'sex role socialisation' is mobilised. This approach is unsatisfactory, and for two principal reasons. First, it deprives the family of all autonomous effectivity as a social formation and reduces it to an empty space filled by the operation of ideology, merely the scene of the re-enactment of social/sexual relations reflected in representations of those relations. Ideology can, on the other hand, be thought as a level or instance of the social formation which maintains a relative autonomy with regard to other levels, the economic and the political in particular. The notions of theoretical practice as developed by Althusser and of hegemony as developed by Gramsci both imply an attribution of relative autonomy to the ideological level. What this means is that ideology is not necessarily a direct expression of ruling-class interests at all moments in history and that at certain conjunctures it may even move into contradiction with those interests. Second, the notion of 'dominant ideology' de-problematises the subject in ideology, which is seen simply as a vessel to be filled with a pre-existing set of representations, defined by an essential unity, a coherence either mystified through the imposition of a 'false consciousness' or given in terms of the subject's being the repository and vehicle of non-contradictory representations of social/sexual relations.

The notion of the subject in ideology was referred to above in the context of the argument that the mirror phase is a crucial structural and developmental moment in the construction of the subject. Within this problematic, ideology is seen as a set of lived relations constructing subjects in relation to the social formation through representations: 'Ideology consists of a practice of representation and a subject constructed for that representation' (Coward and Ellis, 1977, p. 71), and hence in the moment of its operation inscribes both a subject positioning and a set of relations.[3] The non-unified character of the subject posed by psychoanalysis is argued in relation to the implications of the splitting involved in the specular relation of the mirror phase, so that the operation of ideology is seen as a lived relation of the Imaginary ego-ideal, the unified self, and hence as involving an attempted closure or recuperation of the subject–object split, an Imaginary coherence. The work of ideology is to construct a coherent subject: 'the individual thus lives his subject-ion to social structures as a consistent subject-ivity, an imaginary wholeness' (Coward and Ellis, 1977, p. 76). The structural relations of the castration complex — the relations of the Symbolic order of language — at every moment pose a threat to this Imaginary coherence, precisely because language is predicated in otherness, the address inscribed in discourse bearing a notion of separation. The point to be emphasised here is that the psychoanalytic problematic offers a conceptualisation of the subject in ideology which is not coherent; not simply an 'agent' of ideological practices, but potentially the site of contradiction or 'perpetual retotalisation'. As soon as ideology is thought in this way, and the effectivity of the subject in ideology argued, then the family itself is seen in a different light: instead of being understood as the site of the unmediated imposition of representations of social/sexual relations, it becomes the place of the construction of subjects in ideology. And because the precise historical character of social relations within the family must be crucial in this operation, then the family in its historical specificity must possess its own effectivity in this process.

III

I began this paper by pointing to the deference with which the family is routinely treated in analyses which seek to locate the conditions for the subordination of women in patriarchal and capitalist structures. Deference is an indicator of fear, and repeated references to the importance of the family in the operation of these structures can indeed be seen as something like terror, particularly given the fact that the family has come to serve as a final and last-ditch 'explanation' for the reproduction of labour power and relations of production, while at the same time its actual *operation* remains largely unanalysed, and apparently unanalysable. It seems to be possible only to pose the family as a repository of a social totality – whether such a totality be in harmony or in contradiction – an empty signifier, a terrain on which the forces of history are acted out, played out, exhausted. What I hope to have pointed to here, apart from the simple existence of this situation, is the possibility of examining a number of issues whose bearing on the question of the family with regard to women and structures of patriarchy and capital is immediately evident, and of raising other issues whose relevance to that question is at first sight perhaps not quite so apparent; with the aim of offering some suggestions as to how the terror might be come to terms with, how analysis of the family might begin. The central term here is 'patriarchy', and I would argue that the use of this term both to describe concrete relations of property and power between men and women as expressed in particular family forms and to locate the terms of the positioning of the subject, specifically the sexed subject, and the constitution of the unconscious, is no coincidence: that the notion of patriarchy does indeed unite property relations and psychic relations. Patriarchy – the rule of the father – is a structure written into particular expressions of the sexual division of labour whereby property, the means of production of exchange values, is appropriated by men, and whereby this property relation informs household and family relations in such a way that men may appropriate the labour and the actual persons of women. Patriarchal structures have their operation within history, but not within modes of production: they are overdetermined in particular modes of production by more immediate characteristics of the social formation: in capitalism, for example, the family is the site of the operation of the structures of patriarchy and capital as they have specific conjunctural effectivity. In fact, the family may be defined exactly as property relations between husbands and wives and those property relations in action. The family so defined provides the terms for psychic relations, for the production of sexed and class subjects for representations of relations of patriarchy and capital, that is, for the constitution of subjects in ideology. In these terms, the family becomes more than simply one ideological state apparatus

among many, but the privileged place of the operation of
ideology.

Notes

1 Thanks are due to Michèle Barrett and Mary McIntosh for their comments on a draft version of this paper, which is dedicated to
   Brodnax, Buster and Oliver.
2 This is available as a body of work which is in many respects difficult
   to deal with: I cannot attempt here to give any complete or detailed
   acount of it, but it might be helpful to the reader to locate the work
   as an effort to construct a materialist psychoanalysis, the general
   terms of which are very accessibly outlined in Althusser's essay
   'Freud and Lacan' in his *Lenin and Philosophy and Other Essays*
   (1971). Perhaps the most widely known exponent of this work,
   in Britain at least, is Jacques Lacan, most of whose writings were
   until recently not available in English: his *Écrits* are, however, now
   published in translation by Tavistock (1977). Useful explanations of
   the psychoanalytic terms adopted in the present paper may be found
   in J. Laplanche and J.-B. Pontalis, *The Language of Psychoanalysis*,
   Hogarth Press, London, 1973; and an account of Lacanian psychoanalysis in relation to the development of semiotics is put forward in
   Coward and Ellis (1977), especially Chapter 6.
3 In describing ideology in terms of a set of lived relations, Althusser
   (1971) is evidently attempting to express this relation of overdetermination, although it can be argued that even in the second part of
   this article when he discusses 'ideology' rather than 'ideologies' he is
   still thinking the subject as without contradiction.

References

Althusser, L. (1971), 'Ideology and ideological state apparatuses' in
   Lenin and Philosophy and Other Essays, New Left Books, London.
Benveniste, E. (1971), *Problems in General Linguistics*, University of
   Miami Press.
Bourdieu, P., and Passeron, J.-C. (1977), *Reproduction in Education,
   Society and Culture*, Sage Publications, London.
Centre for Contemporary Cultural Studies Women's Studies Group
   (1976), 'Relations of production: relations of reproduction', *Cultural
   Studies*, no. 9, pp. 95–118.
Coward, R., and Ellis, J. (1977), *Language and Materialism*, Routledge
   & Kegan Paul, London.
Coward, R., Lipshitz, S., and Cowie, E. (1976), 'Psychoanalysis and
   patriarchal structures' in *Papers on Patriarchy*, Women's Publishing
   Collective, Lewes.
Delmar, R. (1976), 'Looking again at Engels's "Origin of the Family,
   Private Property and the State" ' in J. Mitchell and A. Oakley, *The
   Rights and Wrongs of Women*, Penguin, Harmondsworth.

Engels, F. (1972), *The Origin of the Family, Private Property and the State*, Lawrence & Wishart, London.

Gardiner, J., Himmelweit, S., and Mackintosh, M. (1975), 'Women's domestic labour', *Bulletin of the Conference of Socialist Economists*, vol. 4, part 2, pp. 1—11.

Hirst, P. Q. (1976), 'Althusser's theory of ideology', *Economy and Society*, vol. 5, pp. 385—412.

Keddie, N. (1973), *Tinker, Tailor: the Myth of Cultural Deprivation*, Penguin, Harmondsworth.

Lacan, J. (1968), 'The mirror-phase as formative of the function of the "I"', *New Left Review*, no. 51, pp. 71—7.

Marx, K. (1974), *Capital*, vol. I, Lawrence & Wishart, London.

Middleton, C. (1974), 'Sexual inequality and stratification theory' in F. Parkin, *The Social Analysis of Class Structure*, Tavistock, London.

Mitchell, J. (1975), *Psychoanalysis and Feminism*, Penguin, Harmondsworth.

Morgan, D. H. J. (1975), *Social Theory and the Family*, Routledge & Kegan Paul, London.

Sacks, K. (1974), 'Engels revisited' in M. Rosaldo and L. Lamphere, *Woman, Culture and Society*, Stanford University Press.

Young, M. F. D. (1971), *Knowledge and Control*, Collier-Macmillan, London.

4 Church, state, and family: the women's movement in Italy

Lesley Caldwell

This is the only contribution to the book whose specific and explicit topic is a feminist political practice, in that it is an analysis of the condition of a conjuncture at which the women's movement occupies a position of central significance. Activity on the part of the Italian women's movement in the 1970s has turned on two issues, divorce and abortion, neither of which are in themselves revolutionary. But the very effectiveness with which these issues have been taken up is an indicator of the extent to which they are phenomena of a series of fundamental contradictions in Italian society. In her analysis, Lesley Caldwell draws on a model of the social totality as composed of relatively autonomous levels and instances which at certain moments may move into contradiction; and the precise character of the contradictions within Italian society is seen as residing in the nature of the development of Italian capitalism, or more precisely in its uneven development, which is evident not only in enormous regional variations in forms of social organization, but crucially in this particular case in the underdevelopment of the capitalist state apparatus in relation to power exerted by the Church. The relationship between Church and state, which is in many respects pre-capitalist in character, combined with the particular nature of the hegemony of Catholicism, has meant that certain representations of the 'role' of women and the 'functions' of the family written into the Church's account of itself have enormous resonances beyond their point of origin. The model of the family as patriarchal — the site of the legitimate authority (coming from God) of the father/husband has informed and continues to inform legal structures in such a way that the 'rule of the father' had until very recently a literal and very forceful meaning in Italian law. The enormous difficulty encountered by campaigns to legalize divorce and abortion is only one symptom of such a situation. However, to challenge the basis of the law in such matters, as is happening in Italy, is immediately to challenge the hegemony of the Church and the character of its relationship with the state. But since the formal target of opposition is the state, whose position is weak, mobilization around the specific issues of divorce and abortion has led to a more fundamental questioning of the position of women and the implication of the family in this, and may even become instrumental in setting the terms of the crisis in which Italian society finds itself. The analysis put forward here, as well as documenting a particular situation, should serve to suggest that feminist practice relates at every moment to the specificity of its social-historical context, and that the features of such contexts, in determining the character of appropriate practice at any moment, are the legitimate and necessary object of theoretical and analytical work.

The importance of feminist issues in Italy in the 1970s has generalised the nature and broadened the extent of political struggle.[1] But it has also created difficulties for feminists both in the presentation of these issues and in the kinds of activity that are seen as relevant for a feminist political practice, above all in the area of confrontation between class struggle and struggles around sexual oppression. The divorce bill of 1970 and the repercussions following its acceptance provided the first opportunity for the widespread diffusion of discussion of specifically feminist issues and for the mobilisation of sectors of Italian society for whom politics had previously been an irrelevance; and this trend has been continued with the debate on abortion. In this paper I will look at the ways in which divorce came to assume such importance in the Italian context; and in doing this I shall present a brief account of the social and historical circumstances which were the preconditions for this particular issue attaining such political priority. This involves, first, situating the Catholic Church at an institutional level and indicating the extent of its influence on state laws; and, second, looking at the divorce bill and the role played by the left, especially the Italian Communist Party (PCI)[2] and the feminist movement, in the campaign. Central to this discussion is an account of the relations of these groupings to the Church and of the Church's place in Italian society, relating its position to that of the Italian liberal-democratic state with regard particularly to conceptualisations of sexuality, women and the family.

I would suggest that the crucial position occupied by the Church in Italy is the primary factor in explaining the political relevance of issues such as divorce and abortion, and that this also provides one key to the militancy of the Italian feminist movement: the Catholic Church, in other words, must be seen as a central protagonist in the postwar political situation. The Church traditionally occupies an important place in Italy, a place which has indeed been given a considerable degree of legitimation in the twentieth century through the Concordat (part of the Lateran Pacts which finally established the Church's position in Italy and marked the resumption of diplomatic relations between Church and state) which Mussolini signed with Pius XI in 1929. As the official state religion, Catholicism has been influential in maintaining the place of the family as both a focus of Italian life and the only area in which women have been permitted any scope for development in a sphere acknowledged to be their own. With the inclusion in 1947 of the Concordat as article seven of the new constitution, the Church confirmed the strong position that it had already gained during the Fascist régime; and Vatican involvement in a specifically anti-communist campaign around the first elections in the new republic in 1948 signalled the direction of its interest. With and through the Christian Democratic Party (DC) it has influenced and continues to influence the priorities of Italian governmental policy, and has enjoyed a measure of success which, in spite of a decrease in real Vatican power, nevertheless still attests to the fact that the Catholic Church is a factor which should be neither underestimated nor overlooked in any analysis of the Italian social formation.

The attempts to introduce a divorce law and the political manœuvrings that followed its eventual approval in 1970 provided the initiative for a political campaign which served to focus the discontent felt by many sectors of the Italian population with regard to the power of the Church and the extent of Vatican influence in political decisions, especially as exercised through the clerical wing of the Christian Democrats. Nominally the party of organised Catholicism, DC is internally divided on the extent to which it sees itself as bound by the demands of the Vatican, and yet it has continued to press for the inscription of Catholic conceptualisations of the family in the laws of the Italian state. The Church's teaching on the family legitimises what can be seen as an authentically bourgeois conception of the family by means of an insistence on a particular social order as the natural order. Thus a specific male–female division of roles within the family is upheld, and positions and roles in general are allotted in terms of the family's declared functions. The Christian texts — or rather a selection of certain pertinent ones[3] — provide authoritative reference for this set of views. The Church's attitude to the family, in particular its insistence on the primacy of reproduction and the rejection of sexuality, has helped to create and justify a repressive set of formulations which permit strong sanctions against women who do not conform to them, and even the construction of laws which distinguish the importance of crimes according to whether they are committed by men or by women. Thus it is that the subservience of women to their fathers and husbands is actually written into Italian law.

The feminist challenge to the Church was focused initially by the political campaign around the referendum for the abrogation of the divorce law. Because of the Concordat and the Catholic position on the indissolubility of marriage, and because the organised political parties were unwilling to challenge the Church and risk losing votes, there had been no divorce in Italy. However, in 1965 a bill was presented by Loris Fortuna, and it was basically this bill which was finally approved in 1970. After the bill became law, the decision on the part of the right wing of DC to begin the collection of signatures for a referendum for its abrogation initiated a countrywide discussion which continued until the referendum took place in May 1974. Discussion, although originally on divorce *per se*, inevitably moved towards a critical analysis of the implications of the referendum itself, of the power of the Church, and in some areas (though, for reasons I shall attempt to assess, not in all) an examination of the whole idea of the family and its importance.

The Church's doctrine on the family insists on its eternal quality and sacramental significance. Any notion of the family as an historically specific institution is rejected: it is seen rather as 'divinely instituted' and indissoluble, its primary end being 'the procreation and education of offspring'. Within the family and within marriage there is said to be a natural ordering on which the welfare of home and family depends. *Casti connubii*, the papal encyclical of 1930, reiterated the importance of the gender-based hierarchy of authority within the family and the tasks assigned to the partners on the basis of it. It argued against the movement of women towards emancipation on the grounds that this would be unnatural and constitute a perversion of family life, and would even result in 'crime' because 'it would free the wife from the domestic cares of children and family, enabling her to the neglect of these, to follow her own bent, and engage in business and even in public affairs' (p. 37). In the past thirty years the qualities associated with the Christian family have adjusted to the changing needs of a changing society so that the papal pronouncements of the 1960s place a much greater emphasis than previously on reciprocal love and shared companionship and play down the insistence on a hierarchical ranking stressed in earlier documents. This might be seen as a reflection on the changing attitudes of the times, but in fact the concept of the family and Christian marriage embodied in *Casti connubii* still substantially represents official Church policy. It must, however, be added that this particular view of the family has been emphasised in the Church's position on the family, matrimony and women only since the latter half of the nineteenth century: that is, that it is itself historically specific.

While it must be recognised, and this has some importance at the political level, that there are many divisions within the Church, it is the official Church which has pursued a policy which denigrates women and in effect refuses them the right to the control of their own lives. It has done this and it continues to do it not only through its attitude to contraception and abortion, although this has considerable implications for the way in which these issues can even be raised in some parts of Italy (Cantarow, 1976), but also through the more general frame of reference of which this attitude forms part – the

Church's view on sexuality as a whole. In 1975, the Sacred Congregation for Doctrine issued a publication — *Dichiarazione circa alcune questioni di etica sessuale* — which provided the opportunity for a restatement of the Church's position on sex. It confirmed that premarital and extramarital sex and any form of homosexuality or masturbation were forbidden, the only legitimate sphere of the expression of sexuality being sex between married couples. This position is said to be derived from divine law by the Church in its position as sole interpreter of that law. Thus any notion of sexuality as conditioned by social relations or mode of production and any argument for the expression of sexuality as a right are automatically rejected. Sex is seen as permissible only when it is tied to the possibility of reproduction. This has considerable importance in attempting to arrive at an understanding of the specificity of the situation of women in a country whose Catholicism represents a continuing strand in its traditions.

Italy is distinguished by extremes of economic development, and both the kinds of social relations and the forms of religion found there display notable regional variations. Even given these differences, however, Catholicism still represents the predominant ideological force, not only for women living in the less industrialised areas or in small towns in the south, in the mountains or in the islands, but for all women, whether they have rejected the Church or not. The depth of this influence points up the Church's entrenched position which is further attested by its involvement in wider networks of social and welfare services. In many cases these Church-based institutions provide prior or equal socialising structures to those of the state, and indeed supplement the very inadequate state-provided facilities, at the same time, of course, rendering less urgent the need for serious attention to this inadequacy. These services include schools, universities, clinics, hospitals, homes for the sick, the handicapped and orphans, sports clubs and cultural and social organisations. It is obvious that these networks place the Church in a position that is central to and highly influential in the everyday lives of many sectors of the Italian people. This retention by a non-state institution of a whole series of responsibilities which have been associated with the growth of the capitalist state in other European countries, in a sense highlights the weakness of the Italian state in its failure to assume responsibility for cultural and servicing functions which in other capitalist societies were gradually lost by religious institutions in the course of the establishment of the bourgeoisie. Althusser (1971) points to the role of the Church under feudalism as that of the dominant ideological state apparatus, one whose hegemonic control had to be destroyed in the establishment of capitalism as the dominant mode of production and the concomitant attainment by the bourgeoisie of state power.

Although the Church did in fact suffer a certain loss in power at the time of the unification of Italy in 1861, setbacks were very much offset by the continuing strength of its position as a cultural institution and the extent to which the support it enjoyed among the masses permitted it to develop other networks of an economic and social character. From its beginning, the position of the state was relatively weak, with regard both to the power and influence wielded by the Church and to its own lack of real strength as a territorial unit, for little effort was made to reconcile the differing cultures, languages, and rates of development of capitalist relations of production in Italy. The unity of 'unification' did not signal any real attempt to see Italy and its development as a whole, whereas the Church enjoyed a much more effective unity of purpose and organisation. The extent of the Church's continuing power is evidenced in the spread of its secondary networks; and awareness of the extent of its incursion into the sphere of people's ordinary lives — particularly the lives of women — provides the context for feminist identification of the Church and its authority as oppressive and for the development of organised resistance to it. In that Catholicism denies the right of women to control their own fertility, in that it rejects the possibility of 'unpaid-for' pleasure, in that its own organisation is an active perpetuation of a belief in the inferiority of women and their unsuitability for certain tasks, it is seen by the feminist movement as one of the prime targets for an attack on the patriarchal basis of social organisation. This position immediately raises a need to address the concrete ways in which the Italian state (in its government, in its administration and in its laws), the Catholic Church and the most reactionary strata of the bourgeoisie are interrelated, both politically and economically, and to identify the areas in which their interests are similar and the areas in which they diverge.

The Concordat remains the legal agreement through which the Catholic Church's position of dominance is assured. Through it the Church became the official state religion and obtained a guarantee of religious instruction in all state schools; through it Christian marriage became the form of marriage sanctioned by the Italian state and — most important in emphasising the link between Church and state — religious marriage ceremonies were given civil status (about 98 per cent of Italian marriages take place in church (Clark and Irving, 1972)). In return the Vatican recognised the Italian state, committed itself to strict political neutrality, and gave the government access to knowledge of ecclesiastical appointments before they were announced. The Church thus gained a set of privileges which it did not hesitate to put to use and, in the postwar period of liberation and reconstruction, actually strengthen. For example, under the Fascists, Catholic organisations were the only ones permitted to operate, so that when the régime fell Catholics had developed strong links and organisational bases which put them in a position to become the most strongly organised political grouping, apart from the Communists (Clark and Irving, 1972). The inclusion of the Concordat in the postwar constitution was a victory for the Church in maintaining the position it had won under the Fascists.

By making the concept of the Christian family a part of the new democratic state, the constitution legitimated the traditional roles of husband and wife and their duties towards each other and their children. While according to article three of the constitution all citizens are equal before the law, regardless of sex, article twenty-nine makes some qualifications to this. It states:

> The republic recognises the rights of the family as a natural society based on marriage. Marriage is organised on the moral and juridical equality of the spouses within the limits set by the law in guaranteeing the unity of the family.

The ambiguity of this working nods in the direction of article three (all citizens are equal before the law regardless of sex, race, language, religion, political opinion, social or personal condition), but basically reaffirms the principle of a sexual hierarchy within the family. The vague formulation 'the unity of the family' actually sanctions the Catholic idea of the family and the unequal position of the wife. The considerable dissent around the assumptions underlying this wording on the part of the members of the assembly responsible for the drawing-up of the constitution is indicated by the intervention of the Hon. Calamandrei:

> moral [equality] certainly, but it can't be assured by legal means, this moral equality. The law that is in force at present — and as far as I know, none wants to change it — is not based on the juridical equality of the spouses because the head of the family is the husband. It's he who gives his name to his family and to the children. It is the wife who is obliged to follow him [Article 144 Civil Code] and not vice versa. And this juridical inequality of the two adults in a family follows from the unity of that family in this society. To function successfully it needs to be directed by a single person. The system could be changed so that the wife was the head of the family . . . it would be another system. But you have to choose. A middle way that gives both spouses absolute legal equality doesn't exist. And for now, I don't think there's any intention of changing the traditional choice made by our laws. So this section just doesn't correspond to the truth (quoted in Alfieri and Ambrosini, 1975, p. 48).

On the level of general citizen's rights, the Italian constitution was prepared to claim the equality of all its citizens, but on the specific question of the family, a patriarchal formulation derived from the Catholic tradition is still insisted upon.[4]

Furthermore the subordination of women is written into Italian law, both civil and penal. The inferiority of women and their necessary subordination to their husbands actually constitutes a basis of the Civil Code of 1940: it states that a wife must be protected and maintained, that she is to assume the surname of the husband, that she has an obligation to go wherever *he* decides they are to live and that she has no right to work outside the home without his approval. It also upholds the rights of the father over those of the mother in relation to children and states that in the event of the death of the husband, a wife can still be held responsible to his family. And until 1968 it allowed a wife's adultery, but not that of a husband, as legal grounds for separation (Alfieri and Ambrosini, 1974, p. 51). The importance of the family and its honour also informs the laws written into the 1930 Penal Code, and the family is seen as the property above all of its male members. Women are identified as requiring special care and as occupying a status similar to that of minors. Until 1965 only fathers could institute criminal proceedings in cases of crimes against members of a family. In situations in which the honour of the family is interpreted as the honour of its male members, the law upheld this abstraction rather than the rights of women who may actually have been violated: this arose primarily in cases of sexual assault, for instance where an illegitimate baby was killed against the will of the mother in the interests of protecting the 'honour of the family'. The law also encouraged marriage between a rape victim and her oppressor by disallowing prosecution if a marriage could be arranged. Thus the standpoint of the law was that of the family (meaning the father) which desired to avoid the sanctions which sometimes ensued against a 'sullied' daughter; it clearly did not give its weight to support or defend the victim. The centrality of this notion of family honour permitted reductions in sentences imposed on husbands, fathers or brothers who killed their wives, daughters or sisters if it could be established that such women were involved in 'illegitimate' sexual relations – that is, sexual relations with a person not their husband. The reverse procedure, however, did not apply: women in a corresponding position were still liable to a charge of homicide rather than of manslaughter. Until 1968, adultery was an offence subject to penal law, though sanctions differed for men and women: the adultery of a wife was punishable by up to a year in prison, but a husband was liable to punishment only if he brought a concubine to live in the house.

While it seems clear that these laws represent an extreme example of the perpetuation of practices firmly embedded in pre-capitalist relations, the move for their repeal began only in the 1960s, and eight years elapsed between the initial government proposal for the reform of family law embodied in the Civil Code and its final approval in 1975, because conservative elements in the Italian parliament were concerned to hold it up for as long as possible. The almost general consensus — the neo-fascist MSI being the sole exception — on the need for the abrogation of these laws constituted a demand for the re-evaluation of the overt sexual inequality inscribed in the whole corpus of Italian law. The kind of changes which had occurred in the lives of the majority of Italians, implemented above all by the policies that had brought about the economic miracle of the 1950s, underlined the necessity for a reappraisal of those areas of political and social life which came to seem increasingly inappropriate as Italy consolidated its position as an advanced capitalist country. Italy does not totally conform with the characteristics of a highly industrialised country because of the persistent underdevelopment within its own boundaries of certain geographical areas, notably the south and the islands. This has given it an extremely skewed regional distribution of economic activity, goods and services. In spite of this, the conditions of existence of its population, affected by large-scale migration within the country and abroad, the overcrowding of cities and the resulting lack of amenities and the growth of mass production of consumer goods, are indeed the social conditions of advanced capitalism. The persistence alongside capitalist social relations of a set of legal practices based in pre-capitalist structures and increasingly at odds with the methods of organisation associated with capitalism was recognised not only by militants and pressure groups, but also by liberal elements within the ruling class. A commitment to the reform of the Legal Code, especially in so far as it related to women, formed part of the platform of the 1964 centre-left government, but such a commitment did not in fact constitute an attack upon the patriarchal structures from which those practices derive.

Of course, given that they remain the laws of a social formation divided by class and sex, the lack of guarantees of women's equality provided by them is no surprise, nor could it be maintained that changing the laws in itself entails very radical changes in the basis of social organisation. What the updating of laws such as these perhaps actually does is to provide a model — albeit an inadequate and cautious one — which while it conforms to the situation of some sections of the population, represents a range of possibilities not previously allowed of for others; and it is argued on these grounds that within the extended provisions of a set of laws which are to an extent appropriate to the lived experience of the majority of people, new practices can be fought for and new rights won. What seems very striking about these legal structures is that they represent a situation of backwardness in many ways unsuited to the practices of a capitalist social formation and they also indicate a failure to reform legal structures in line with changes in the lives of people, the functions of the family and the demands made upon it in the new situation of the postwar period. These changes reflect others which have been brought about in an extremely short time through the postwar reconstruction and extension of capitalism. Italy had been a semi-industralised country with low productivity in both agriculture and industry, with a large proportion of its workforce being concentrated in textiles and on the land. The injection of American capital and the decision to gear production to foreign markets, and the availability of a large pool of labour together with repressive government attitudes to strikes and workers' struggles, led Italy to develop one of the highest growth rates in the world and a GNP which increased at a rate of 5.3 per cent per annum during the 1950s (Proctor and Proctor, 1976). The fact that this speedy development was grafted onto a country already distinguished by a split between north and south and between country and city meant that unevenness of productive activity (in terms of industrial sector and geographical area) was perpetuated, and industry also developed in two separate sectors: an efficient export oriented sector and an inefficient one geared to home consumption. It also meant that the land in the south became less utilised as the north developed and migration continued. The extremely high levels of internal migration (between 1952 and 1962, 16 million people changed residence: internal migration involved 1.5 to 2 million persons a year, and about 2 million emigrated abroad in that decade (Halliday, 1968)) pushed the problems associated with rapid urbanisation to the fore; and the gaps in state services in vital areas exacerbated these difficulties. These gaps may be seen in part as a reflection of the inability of the state to provide services, but given the links that had been developed between the administration and Church organisations in the Fascist period, and continued with the added advantage of a Christian Democratic Party in government, meant that the advisability of weakening Church structures and decreasing public expenditure on them (or the desire to do so) must also feature as a possible explanation (Rodotà and Rodotà, 1977).

Quite apart from, though obviously not unrelated to, the intertwined networks of the Christian Democratic Party and the Church's own organisations and the powerful mutual help that these permitted, the sheer *economic* strength of the Vatican is enormous. It has been demonstrated (*The Economist*, 1965) that the Vatican's economic interests are to a large extent linked with the development of Rome, and also of Italy. In Rome, the Vatican is one of the biggest landlords and its connections with the administration have enabled it to avoid disclosure of its involvement in building speculation scandals. Its realisable assets are estimated conservatively at £2,000 million, making the Pope the largest shareholder in the world. These figures suggest that the Vatican holds an investment portfolio only exceeded by large US mutual life insurance companies. It has large interests in land and real estate throughout the world, plus the world's most valuable art collection. The Vatican administrators have total freedom, being answerable neither to parliament nor to shareholders. It does not pay tax and it operates across frontiers. The article claims that requests from the Vatican for special concessions are treated sympathetically because they have 'an historic and moral foundation'. The economic and organisational strength of the Church in Italy, the extent of interrelation between its networks and those of the Christian Democrats — and therefore its implication in political struggles — have meant that while it has continued to press for the retention of laws which are increasingly at variance with the needs and the image of a modern country and with the lives of the masses, it experienced little organised resistance until the 1970s.

The Church stands firm in its belief in the rightness of its cause and in the need to guard itself against forces that may seek to destroy it. This, quite apart from the implications of its economic situation, has linked it to political groupings of a virulently anti-communist type. Thus, it has close links with the right wing of DC and with groups to its right such as MSI, the neo-fascists. But after the death of Pius XII the papacy intervened less in internal Italian politics and there was increased tolerance to communism and socialism both in Italy and abroad. The social problems generated by the end of the economic miracle of the 1950s, and the continuing ineffici- ency of governments implicitly supported by the Vatican, rendered much more difficult the use of religion as a unifying issue overriding more fundamental contradictions. The Second Vatican Council had opened up debate within the Church and there was growing dissent among Catholics about the Vatican's political links. The internal crisis of the Church began in earnest around the divorce bill.

The absence of rights to divorce was the direct result of the wholesale adoption of the Catholic conceptualisation of the family in the constitution. Fear of Vatican censure, alienation of Catholic voters and consequent loss of parlia- mentary seats had led to a tacit decision on the part of all parties not to press this issue. The bill proposed in 1965 by Loris Fortuna, a socialist deputy, allowed for divorce on a number of grounds: prison sentences of more than fifteen years; incest; crimes of sexual violence; incitement to prosti- tution of wife or children; criminal insanity; failure to con- sumate a marriage; a divorce or another marriage abroad on the part of one of the spouses; and separation of spouses for five years (Alfieri and Ambrosini, 1975). Within parliament and within the government itself this minimal bill posed such problems for the centre-left government that it was effectively delayed until the 1968 elections, at which time all the lay parties endorsed their support for it. The bill was approved in the Chamber of Deputies in November 1969 and despite further government delays and Vatican pressure, became law in December 1970. It was revealed that since the law's first proposal in 1965 the Vatican had sent the government three diplomatic notes, which were not shown to DC's coalition partners, aimed at encouraging the government to suspend the debate and reopen a discussion of the revision of the Concordat (Clark *et al.*, 1974). This would mean that any dis- cussion of the bill on divorce would have to await lengthy dis- cussion of all the terms of the Concordat and especially the constitutionality of the issue at all since the wording of article seven did not make it clear whether the introduction of divorce was possible or not.

With the approval of the bill, the Holy Rota (the Vatican court) immediately lowered the cost of its own annulments, the only legal means of obtaining separations before the passage of the divorce law. The most conservative Catholic elements initiated a procedure for the implementation of a referendum to 'abrogate' the law. According to article seventy-five of the constitution such a referendum must be held if half a million signatures are collected. None of the political parties wanted a referendum, fearing that it would set an unwanted precedent; nor did they want the kind of political campaigning that would presumably ensue, which would undoubtedly open up the question of relations between Church and state, and hence raise possible difficulties for future DC governments and their supporters. And so a whole series of delaying tactics were introduced. These included an attempt to introduce a new bill which would alter the orginal sufficiently to render it invalid. This failed because it involved making divorce harder to obtain, and the lay parties — with the significant exception of the Communist Party — would not agree. Eventually parliament was dissolved and new elections were called. The constitution decrees that the procedure for a referendum must be postponed for one year after a general election is held; and since this was the first time a general election had been held before the end of a government's full term of office it seems clear that, while there were other reason for holding a general election, the referendum played a large part in the choice of an early date. This resulted in the delay of the referendum from the spring of 1972 to the spring of 1974 (since referenda can be held only within a specified time, namely on a Sunday between 15 April and 15 June, which meant that spring 1973 was too soon after the elections which had been held in September 1972). The extreme sensitivity in the issue of the role of the Vatican and its relations with political structures meant that all the political parties, with the exception of the Radical Party and the extra-parliamentary groupings, attempted to pitch the campaign at a very general level — the Fascist menace, law and order, and so on. However, the women's movement, with the Radicals and the far left, employing slightly different perspectives and emphases, developed a campaign which aimed at a more comprehensive analysis.

While the question of divorce has been generally seen in bourgeois law as relating to the right of the individual, the dissolution of marriages has never provided any serious challenge to the family or to the relationship between husband and wife. What divorce primarily enabled was remarriage for persons already separated, as well as giving legal standing to the many cases of *de facto* separations and new unions that had come about with the large-scale migration of the 1950s. It is only within the problematic of the Concordat and the consequent insertion into the constitution of a certain view of the family that divorce could come to be the origin of such controversy as came to surround the question. The conjuncture within which a specifically Catholic formulation could be written into the constitution was characterised also by 'the increased clericalisation of the state' (Rodotà and Rodotà, 1977) – hence the immediate practical difficulties raised by the conflicts over the presentation of Fortuna's bill. The legal framework and the ways in which it had been utilised over the postwar period meant that any challenge to the indissolubility of marriage and any attempt to allow the inscription of such a challenge in the provisions of Italian law evidently necessitated entry into a whole discussion around the relation between state and Church institutions and around the ties between the government and the Vatican. This, given the continuing inability of the government to effect any necessary reforms or to manage the economy, in turn threw open to question the very nature of the Italian state. In this way divorce, itself not a revolutionary issue nor – it could be argued – even a personally salient one for the majority of Italians, provided a means of mobilising the masses of people and for beginning a continuing debate on the family, on women's position within it, and on the specific articulation of these instances within and with a capitalist social formation. The divorce referendum campaign itself facilitated the widespread dissemination of the debate around abortion which took place after the referendum, although organised demand for abortion had begun before the actual voting took place. The abortion issue and before it the divorce issue have both developed a mass base, with the result that the wider issues of feminism, introduced through these campaigns, have become a basis of continuing widespread discussion and action.

The strong emphasis on the centrality of the family in Italian society is associated with a set of attitudes towards motherhood in which its vital importance is overtly stressed. But this has not been paralled by any great concern to provide material assistance for either childbirth or aftercare. The list of issues raised by UDI[5] at its convention on women and maternity in 1971 demonstrates the precise nature of the material conditions of motherhood in Italy. There is a general lack of hospital facilities for deliveries, which results in a situation in which 50 per cent of Italian women give birth at home, and in some regions of the south the percentage is as high as 80 per cent. An estimated 1.5 to 2 million illegal abortions are performed every year, and Italy has the highest infant mortality ratio of Western countries (32.2 per thousand). There is a serious shortage of aftercare facilities for mothers and babies; and unmarried mothers are heavily discriminated against and receive minimal welfare assistance. Until recently the Church actively discouraged adoption and there were large numbers of children in institutions. There is an extreme scarcity of nursery places (in Milan one to every 52,800 residents, and in Naples one to every 236,000 residents), and a high incidence of abortions, stillbirths, sterility and deformed babies among women workers. Child labour is prevalent. There are distinctions in kind and method of administration of social security for legitimate and illegitimate children; and maternity acts as a severe handicap to work outside the home, and vice versa.

The examination of the roots of women's oppression brought about through this development of discussion on the family highlighted the 'woman question', and the earlier positions of the political parties with regard to that question were seen as an important issue. The PCI had been involved in drawing up the constitution, had actively assisted in the inclusion of the Concordat, and by so doing had effectively agreed to the state's position as guarantor of the Christian tradition of the family and of the relations within it. At the same time, however, until the mid-1960s it had been the only political party to emphasise the importance of the 'woman question' and the need for the extension of laws in the area broadly designated as women's rights. With the growth of the feminist movement and the elaboration of feminist theory (in a way that would have been impossible in the Italy of the 1940s fresh from the rule of Mussolini and the degrading account of the place of women embodied in Fascism), the inadequacies of PCI politces on women became apparent. These policies, particularly as they had been pursued in the 1950s by UDI, had already been the subject of much self-criticism within the Communist Party on the grounds of their lack of specificity.

The way in which the question of women has been inserted into overall PCI theory in the postwar period is posited on the necessity, following Engels, of bringing women into capitalist production. This is seen as contributing to their emancipation and also as necessary for the advance of the whole country. Immediately after the Fascist era there was a new evaluation by Togliatti, secretary of the PCI, of the balance of forces, which addressed the necessity for the workers' party to ally itself with a range of other sectors, primarily women, Catholics and the middle classes, to undertake the democratic socialist revolution. The revolution was not seen as something that began with the seizure of state power, but a process that could begin and be broadened through the full implementation of the renewal initiated by the defeat of the Fascists, the role of the Resistance in this defeat, and the subsequent establishment of a democratic state. Women are given a central place for the role they can play in assisting the development of this new society, but their particular oppression is seen only in relation to the uneven developments of economic relations and the backwardness of certain regions. This means that their situation is articulated within an overall analysis of the unequal presence of capitalist relations of production which in their turn lead to outmoded forms and antiquated customs which affect women especially. Togliatti argued:

> The true cause of the backwardness of Italian women is to be found in the backwardness of economic relations and in the backwardness of civil relations that are in evidence in our country. This is true first of all for the countryside,

where the remnants of feudalism are still in evidence even
in those places where before they are tending to disappear.
They were reinforced, above all, after the Renaissance and
are still active in almost all the regions of central and
southern Italy. The backwardness of women results from
the fact that backward social and civil relations are transferred from country to city and to almost all the strata of
the male and female population. They enter into the family
and create there a particular atmosphere of inequality and
oppression, giving rise to a family that in some areas of
Italy is still of a strictly feudal kind (Tisi, 1976, p. 46).

Given the institutional changes in Italy brought about by the
setting up of the democratic (bourgeois) state, the problems
of the emancipation of women achieves a considerable degree
of importance. Again in Togliatti's words:

Today we have reached such a point of economic development and such an awakening of the popular conscience
and such are the exigencies that are put to us, that the
emancipation of women must be one of the central problems of the renewal of the Italian state and society. If we
want to effectively lead to its conclusion a democratic
revolution in Italy, one that transforms our political
institutions, our economic life and our customs, we must
solve the problem of women's emancipation and we must
solve it in all its aspects i.e. economic, political, social,
moral in the widest sense of the word. If we don't succeed
in this task we shan't be able to give to Italian democracy
the new popular, progressive stamp that we meant to give
it (Frabotta, 1975, p. 237).

The relevance of women's emancipation was seen to lie in its
importance for the generalised struggle in which the workers'
party must consolidate, with other groupings, the advance
towards a more democratic Italy. Women, along with the
south and the peasants, represented three vast areas to be
conquered. Women, in struggling for their rights, contribute
to the good of the whole of the country (Tisi, 1976, p. 68).
These programmes are inserted into an overall strategy which
aims at gaining a series of reforms for the conditions of
women at work and for health, insurance and child care, but
at the same time denies the necessity for an analysis of the

particularity of their oppression. As a result there is little effort to develop an adequate theory of the family, little or no discussion of the implications of the role of the family in Catholic tradition and little challenge to the Church's position on birth control.

In all its relations with the Church, the PCI appears to have been reluctant to confront either the economic role of the Vatican and the significance of Vatican interference in politics, or – an even more significant omission – the ideological hegemony of the Church and its role in organising conservative reaction. This conciliatory approach continued despite provocations such as the Church's attempted organisation of the elections of 1948 as an anti-communist offensive, and the threat of excommunication in 1949 to Catholics who professed themselves communists. If, as is often suggested, the strategy of the PCI has been aimed at detaching the masses from the rulers of the Christian Democrats, the party has been constrained in its relations with organised Catholicism to opt for a policy arguably more expedient than the strategy for electoral success outlined in the *Italian Road to Socialism*. The stress on the dangers of a vulgar anticlericalism that have formed a large part of PCI criticism of the Radical Party and the members of LID (Lega Italiana per il divorzio)[6] is argued on the grounds of the extent of the Catholic tradition in Italy and its importance for the large masses of working people: however, the Church's interest in pursuing an agreement with DC appears to have caused the Communists to adopt a position *vis-à-vis* the Church which evades certain of the most serious problems. This is true above all for the question of women, apparently a central part of communist strategy, but one in which an investigation of the role of the Church in perpetuating the secondary status of women is nevertheless absent. In Togliatti's words:

> I don't believe that the religious faith of Italian women is the cause of their backwardness, just as I don't believe that this faith need be an obstacle in the struggle of women for their emancipation and for democracy (Tisi, 1976, p. 69).

The refusal to develop the connection between the question of Catholicism and the problem of women represents one of the most serious lacks in the development of Communist Party theory in the postwar period. Neither has the absence been addressed by the party programme's stress on the justice of an appeal to *all* women: in fact it has been exaggerated, first by attempts to 'improve' the divorce bill, and then by the reluctance to fight the campaign around the referendum on the central issues.

This reluctance to take up these issues — the family and related questions — was not, however, confined to the PCI: much of the left initially denied their importance, seeing divorce as an abstract legal right which could have little relevance for the working class and which indeed represented a battle of priorities within the different groupings of the bourgeoisie on a theme proposed by the right. Specific reasons for the adoption of this position varied, but apart from an unwillingness on the part of the PCI to predispose the Christian Democrats to break off moves towards an agreement that the Communists might take some share in government, the failure to confront the question of women and Catholicism was also a sign of the party's theoretical unpreparedness, as it was of the whole of the left. The Communists fought the campaign round the slogan 'per una famiglia rinnovata e democratica' (for a renewed and democratic family), stressing the general danger from the right and appealing to the maturity of all Italians. Along with all the lay parties, they pointed out that the divorce law had not, as was argued by the right, constituted a sustained attack on the family. The law had been in effect for four years and there had been a relatively small number of divorces, many of which regularised already existing situations. One of the reasons for this approach to the campaign was the fear of alienating women voters; this in itself actually underlines the incomplete understanding of the situation, which can only be exacerbated if the specific question of divorce is not inserted into discussion of the whole situation of women, of their economic and emotional dependence on their husbands and families, and of why, in this situation, it is quite reasonable for women to see divorce as a potential threat. To engage in debate at this level is to pose the issue in an entirely different way: '[the referendum] represents a moment of reappropriation direct, not delegated, on the part of the masses, of the politics of their own bodies and their own lives' (Gramaglia,

1974, p. 57). The right, on the other hand, unhesitatingly exploited the theme of the family. The campaign fought by DC centred on the family and its place and importance in society, and pointed to the threat to the family that divorce represented and to the challenge to the whole organisation of the country that a threat to the family meant. The MSI slogan was: 'Now they even want to destroy the family.'

But on this occasion the appeal to the personal could not be separated from the events of the previous period and DC's implication in them. Significantly, the Vatican entered the campaign with an appeal to women: it publicised its position in all the women's magazines, arguing that divorce acted as an encouragement to male licence and provided a quick, hasty solution when things went wrong; and it stressed the availability of annulments through its own court for situations of real gravity. The post-conciliar Catholic world was divided over the referendum and the political support of the DC-MSI campaign. The steps towards the radicalisation of Catholic organisations which had followed after Vatican II were reinforced by the general radicalisation of workers' movements which accompanied a number of strikes and sit-ins and the winning of considerable wage increases during 1968 and 1969. In the 1970 regional elections ACLI, the Christian Workers' Organisation, had officially refused to support the Catholic party: its document on divorce, condemned by its own leadership, represented an attempt by a Catholic organisation to confront a class analysis of the family (Castellina, 1974). The Catholic union CISL refused to adopt a position, leaving the referendum to a free vote. A variety of liberal to socialist elements within the Church itself, among them ACLI, Christians for Socialism, and Catholic Action, argued for the liberty of the individual conscience, the irrelevance of civil law for Church law, the importance of the decision for the future of democracy and the inadmissibility of Church intervention in state matters.

Equally important, there was an attempt to subject the concept of the 'mondo cattolico' (the Catholic world) to a more rigorous analysis aimed at delineating the social divisons reflected in that world and the inadequacy of an analysis which saw the force of religion as an unifying principle in the face of other divisions within the social formation. This centred on the need to separate the 'Catholic world' — or rather the masses of Catholic people — from institutional support of the Christian Democrats by showing the implications of a vote for DC in other, more evidently political, areas, and signalled a marked determination among large numbers of Catholics to confront the issue of Church and state in the postwar period. The results of the referendum reflected this lack of unity. Catholics have continued to be divided on the debate surrounding women and the anti-feminist practice of the Church. In June 1977, for example, Catholic Action ran a conference on 'The Church and the Position of Women' at which the professor of history at Padua denounced the scandal of a Church where 'women have to be quiet and pray'. He traced the influence of the philosophies of Augustine and Aquinas and of male power and authority, and maintained 'Christianity has betrayed the Christian values and has tied itself to the capitalist bourgeoisie' (quoted in *La Repubblica*, 26 July 1977). The position of the Church on this issue continues to be challenged from within and outside its own ranks.

The feminist movement by contrast placed divorce — and more recently abortion — within its overall analysis of women's oppression. It sought to clarify the contradictions relating to the accepted importance of voting against abrogation in the referendum in a situation in which the relevance for the majority of Italian women of parliamentary laws is itself open to question: that is, it pinpointed both the importance and the limits of divorce. With this perspective the feminists hoped to use the campaign to raise all the concerns — the family, sexuality, marriage, child care, work — that would enable the limitations of a single issue campaign to be overcome. In a specific political and economic conjuncture the divorce referendum became a vital issue. Given the limited personal significance that divorce had for perhaps the majority of women, given the fact that divorce not only does not threaten the structure of the family, but may actually strengthen it, and given the way in which divorce underlines woman's economic dependence, any concern for the position of women meant that the campaign certainly had to be fought, but not as if it were the only or the ultimate campaign. The slogan of the feminists of Milan — 'This is only the first of our Noes' — demonstrated the spirit of the campaign.

It is obvious, then, that the defeat of the Christian Democrats had wider ranging implications than a simple decision on the divorce law: the debates that began around the referendum have continued and form part of an ongoing discussion about the central institutions of the Italian formation — the Church and the family. In effect the boundaries of the area designated previously as political have been expanded. This has meant the mobilisation of large sectors of the population never before reached. Many groups set up for educational purposes by feminists in the women's movement and feminists in left groupings at the time of the divorce campaign have continued to meet and to develop critiques of the organisa- of those areas that directly impinge on the family and the home, such as schools, housing and nurseries.

The referendum represented a defeat both for the strength of Catholic control within Italy and for the power of the links between the Church and conservative groupings. The outcome gave impetus to the continuation of campaigns to bring discussions of feminist issues into many facets of Italian life, not least parliament, and the struggle to gain the legal right to abortion has developed from the discussions that began with divorce. Abortion has united feminist groupings which have fought to demand abortion rights from the state through parliament, but which have also insisted on the necessity of seeing abortion in the context of motherhood and of women's conditions of existence. This refusal to confine the debate to the area of the law or to the institutional level has resulted in widespread discussions of health and welfare facilities and more generally of the relationship of maternity to other aspects of women's existence. Feminism has received vast amounts of publicity since 1974: it is debated on television, on the radio, in the newspapers and in the weekly magazines. It is a mobilising issue in the schools and in the unions. The presence of a specific struggle — over abortion — has obviously assisted in this process, but discussion has never been confined to a single unrelated demand. Italian feminism has argued for the necessity to address the multiple contradictions that comprise the Italian formation and the impossibility of subsuming the relationship between the sexes entirely under an analysis of capital.

The existence of a strong workers' movement and a long

tradition of political struggle meant that the feminist movement developed out of, and as a response to, an existing situation in which the language of politics and the awareness of class contradictions comprised a taken-for-granted part of experience. Struggles against Fascism, the development of a partisan movement, the lack of a strong social democratic force and the presence of a growing Communist Party have resulted in the development of a high level of political consciousness in Italy, which was heightened by the events of the 1950s and the increased militancy and strength of the unions which developed in the 1960s. The existence of a women's organisation within the Communist Party, and the party's concern — albeit in an unspecific and undeveloped way — for the position of women and its interest in the raising of issues concerned with women's rights, provided important influences in the development of the feminist movement. The economic and political situation of the 1960s had exacerbated the difficulties faced by Italian women. Growing prosperity had led more women to seek employment outside the home; but Italy still had an extremely low rate of female participation in the workforce, and in fact throughout the 1960s there was a continual expulsion of women from the labour force (May, 1977). Nor could provision be made for the re-entry of women to paid employment after their children were at school, as has been the tendency in other Western societies. At the same time, however, the development of enhanced expectations had been fostered by mass production and the more widespread availability of consumer goods. Inflation and heightened demand for consumer goods led to the necessity for a second wage. The tendency towards increased decentralisation of productive activity characteristic of many sectors of Italian industry created the conditions for the widespread existence of home work — non-unionised, very minimally paid and performed preponderantly by women workers (May, 1977). At the same time the inability of the government to remedy deficiencies in the provision of social services has meant that the family, and primarily the mother, has been called upon to provide these necessities (Balbo, 1976). The demands raised by UDI at their convention in 1971 highlight the extent of the state's failure to provide: while the strength of the Catholic tradition has assisted in the perpetuation of a view of women as sources of potential evil and disaster, and has continued rigidly to delimit roles for men and women and responsibilities for the occupiers of these roles. The Church's stress on the importance of mother-hood and the distinctions made between mothers (and wives) and all other women have led to a contradictory over-indulgence of the activities of mothers and an attendant dis-missal of the seriousness of women in any other context.

The debate which began with divorce and the family, and was extended by abortion and the implications of maternity, was further widened by a series of cases of sexual violence and murder throughout 1975 and 1976. The publicity which attended these events further challenged bourgeois (and Catholic) categories of sexual acceptability and provided grounds for an attack on the Italian traditions of male dom-inance and the subordination of and contempt for women implied in these traditions. The recognition of these tenden-cies within the Italian social formation has informed the ways in which the feminist movement has addressed the problems of its own relationship to class struggle and the extent to which it is prepared to work with political groupings, both parliamentary and extra-parliamentary. The mass base of the movement's support and the unity with other organisations which were notable features of the campaign for divorce and abortion have ensured that the feminist point of view has not been lost by being situated only within the confines of the movement itself. At the same time a decided commitment to the methods of group discussion and of consciousness raising has ensured that the limited aims of fighting for legal rights do not result in failure to address the more general issues raised by such campaigns.

Since 1975, even the PCI has begun to consider the implica-tions of the growth of the feminist movement. On the question of abortion, UDI rejected the official position of PCI and linked itself with the feminists and their demands. The groups of the extra-parliamentary left whose own impetus arose from the same conjuncture as feminism (1968 to 1969) have been pushed to debate with the assumptions and posi-tions of feminism and with the inadequacy of their own analyses: this has been initiated by women within these groupings who have argued for their own autonomy over against the male-dominated practices of the group. The impact of these criticisms has resulted in considerable realignment of the extra-parliamentary left groupings and a continuing internal debate on the methods employed in all struggles.

The increased importance of women and the necessity to take account of their interests was attested by the play made for their vote by all the political parties in the 1975 and 1976 elections and by the recent DC proposal for the passage of a bill along the lines of the British Sex Discrimination Act. The recognition of the necessity to address the specificity of the position of women has been forced into the party programmes even of the Christian Democrats, but much of this play for votes is of little practical use for the situation of most Italian women. However, the challenges to the Church and to the workers' movement that have been posed in the context of the struggle for the legal right to divorce and abortion have initiated profound changes within the Italian social formation and ones which are vital to the development of class forces in the present conjuncture.

Notes

1 The paper contains some quotations from Italian sources which I have translated into English without also including the passage in Italian.

2 Italian political groupings are known by their initials, and where relevant I have followed this convention. There follows a list of the abbreviations used in the text:

DC — Democrazia Cristiana, the Christian Democrats: the majority party for the whole of the postwar period.

PCI — Partito Comunista Italiano, the Italian Communist Party: the second largest party.

PRI — Partito Radicale, the Radical Party: a small party active in the area of civil rights.

PSI — Partito Socialista Italiano: the main coalition partner in the years of the centre-left governments.

MSI-ND — Movimento Socialista Italiano-Nazionalisti di Destra: the neo-fascists.

3 See the section on 'La Famiglia Cristiana' in Fossati (1977).

4 'Every family is a society. Every well-ordered society needs a head. All the power of that person comes from God. And so the family has a head whose authority comes from God. This authority is over his wife, given to him as companion, and over his children' Pius XII, 'The authority of the family: an address to newlyweds', 10 September 1941; quoted in Fossati (1977).

5 UDI — Unione Donne Italiane, the Union of Italian Women: a group

founded in 1944 which grew from an organisation of women who had participated in the Resistance, it is largely made up of communist (PCI) and socialist (PSI) women, but there have been representations from all parties except DC and MSI. See Frabotta (1975).

6 An organisation set up during the 1960s for the purpose of conducting an educational campaign on the divorce issue: this campaign had taken an overtly anticlerical line.

References

Alfieri, P., and Ambrosini, G. (1975), *La condizione economica, sociale e giuridica della donna in Italia*, Paravia, Turin.

Althusser, L. (1971), 'Ideology and ideological state apparatuses' in *Lenin and Philosophy*, New Left Books, London.

Balbo, L. (1976), *Stato di famiglia*, Etas Libri, Milan.

Cantarow, E. (1976), 'Abortion and feminism in Italy: women against Church and state', *Radical America*, vol. 10, no. 6, pp. 8–28.

Castellina, L. (1974), *Famiglia e società capitalistica*, Alfani, Rome.

Casti connubii (1930), English translation published by Catholic Truth Society, London, 1965.

Clark, M., Hine, D., and Irving, R. (1974), 'Divorce – Italian style', *Parliamentary Affairs*, summer 1974, pp. 333–58.

Clark, M., and Irving, R. (1972), 'The Italian political crisis and the general elections of May 1972', *Parliamentary Affairs*, summer 1972, pp. 198–223.

Economist, The (1965), 'The Vatican's riches', 27 March, pp. 1403–5.

Fossati, R. (1977), *E Dio creò la donna*, Mazzotta, Milan.

Frabotta, B. (1975), *Femminismo e lotta di classe in Italia 1970–1973*, Savelli, Rome.

Gramaglia, M. (1974), 'Referendum e liberazione della donna' in Castellina (1974).

Halliday, J. (1968), 'Structural reform in Italy: theory and practice', *New Left Review*, no. 50, pp. 73–92.

May, M. P. (1977), 'Il mercato del lavoro femminile in Italia', *Inchiesta*, anno VII, numero 25, gennaio-febbraio 1977, pp. 56–73.

Proctor, J., and Proctor, R. (1976), 'Capitalist development, class struggle and crisis in Italy, 1945–1975', *Monthly Review*, vol. 27, no.8, pp. 21–38.

Rodotà, C., and Rodotà, S. (1977), *L'articolo sette e il dibattito sul concordato*, Savelli, Rome.

Tisi, A. (1976), *I comunisti e la questione femminile*, Riuniti, Rome.

5 Sexual division of labour: the case of nursing

Eva Gamarnikow

Eva Gamarnikow's work on the nursing profession in its early years m
be productively read through the definition of patriarchy which has
already been advanced in the first two contributions to this book: that
is, that patriarchy is a structure of dominance which operates across
different modes of production, but which takes its precise character
from the features of class and property relations of the dominant mode.
One of the implications of this is that it is difficult to think patriarchy
in the abstract, as it were outside history: and this being the case, it is
important that theoretical work which mobilizes this concept should
examine it in terms of its precise conjunctural effectivity. If the rise
of the nursing profession is considered in relation to the growth of
capitalism, it then appears as no coincidence that nursing emerged as
an independent occupation in Britain in the mid-nineteenth century, by
which time large sectors of the population had been drawn into capitalist production. In this situation, the position of women was affected
differentially according to their class — although the situation is made
rather complex by the introduction at this period of 'protective' legislation. It is perhaps true as a generalization, however, that proletarian
women were drawn into wage labour, while most women of the land-
owning and bourgeois classes were ensured a livelihood only if they
married; and this was perhaps also true, in a different way, of women of
petit bourgeois origin. The range of paid work open to non-proletarian
women was at this time extremely limited — virtually the only 'respectable' occupation being that of governess — and it is interesting in this
context that nursing saw itself from the first as an occupation precisely

for women, and for women of all classes. It grew up in a situation
whose limits were drawn by capitalist social relations, but at the same
time it adopted and 'worked over' features of the structure of patriarchy
in an entirely specific manner. The argument here is that in the particular case of nursing, the structure of the profession and everyday work
relations in it inscribe patriarchy in a particularly pristine way; such
that, for example, the relationship between doctor and nurse as manifest
in their relative powers *vis-à-vis* the patient is essentially a patriarchal
relationship. It may well be the case that the central place of specifically
patriarchal relations in this particular instance is to be seen in terms of
the relatively inclusive class character of the profession and the easily
appropriable 'womanly', caring characteristics of the 'good nurse'. In
other occupations entered by women, the relative balance of structures
of patriarchy and structures of capital would no doubt be different,
though the precise character of such differences must be the subject
of further investigation.

This paper is concerned with the structural determinants of
the sexual division of labour, with particular reference to the
occupational structure of nineteenth- and early twentieth-
century nursing. The period I shall be looking at stretches
from 1860, the year in which Florence Nightingale opened
the Nightingale Fund School of Nursing at St Thomas's
Hospital (a traditional landmark in the history of modern
nursing), to 1923 when the profession elected its first General
Nursing Council. I shall argue that the patriarchal character
of the sexual division of labour manifests itself in the nursing
profession in a number of interrelated ways. First, in the total
operation of health care, nursing occupies a role in subordination to medicine, in that it is the medical profession which
possesses the sole right of decision as to who is to be defined
as a patient. This subordination structures the nurse–doctor–
patient relationship, which comes to take on the ideological
resonances of power relations between men, women and
children within the patriarchal family – the doctor being the
incumbent of the 'rule of the father'. The female dominance
of the nursing profession and the male dominance of medicine
are of obvious relevance to the situation, the implications of
which none the less obtain in the 'anomalous' instances of
woman doctors and, particularly, male nurses – although in

such cases the tensions and contradictions in the situation are perhaps more likely to surface in the doctor–nurse relationship. Moreover, in the period under consideration, the moral traits of the 'good nurse' were evidently seen within the profession itself as identical with the characteristics desirable in a 'good woman'. Finally, I shall argue that the character of nursing as a profession for 'good women', together with the patriarchal and familial character of authority relations within the health care professions, meant that many aspects of the nurse's work became identifiable with domestic labour; but that because of the claim of nursing to some professional status, certain tasks commonly defined as within the province of domestic labour – cleaning and 'hygiene' in particular – come to occupy a central, but at the same time a problematic, position.

I

The sexual division of labour is a complex analytical concept. In spite of its theoretical importance for feminism it has often remained unanalysed – as, for example, in the domestic labour debate (Gardiner *et al.*, 1975). This situation is probably attributable to an implicit biologism; and indeed certain theorists consciously employ references to biology as an explanation (Marx, 1970; Engels, 1970; Gilman, 1966, de Beauvoir, 1970; Firestone, 1971). Such biologistic explanations treat the sexual division of labour as a natural division, springing from or ultimately rooted in reproductive functions. This 'naturalism' is seen to underpin women's labour in both the family and the wage sector, because both are characterised by sex specific task and job allocation. The ideology of naturalism, therefore, represents labour processes, or parts of labour processes, as specifically 'feminine' or 'masculine'. This is achieved either by direct reference to biology (motherhood, for example), or by drawing analogies between such apparently biologically determined activities as motherhood and particular types of work – such as, say, nursing which is frequently defined as 'maternal' caring for the sick. Biological determinism, or naturalism, underpins technological determinism, which locates divisions in the labour process in terms of technological imperatives rather than relations of production.

In the particular case of health care as a labour process a distinction is made in this frame of reference between caring and curing tasks. and functions which are allocated to nurses and doctors respectively because they seem to coincide with 'natural' biological functions (Thorner, 1955; Schulman, 1958; Maclean, 1974).

However, marxist analyses of the labour process have shown that technical divisions are determined by capitalist relations of production in the process of production of surplus value (Braverman, 1974; Marglin, 1976; Palloix, 1976), and technological determinism is seen as an ideological operation — a representation of exploitation. Similarly, materialist feminist analyses of naturalism demonstrate the way in which power relations between men and women are effectively obscured within this problematic (Delphy, 1977b; Mathieu, 1977). A theory which claims to be materialist must locate the sexual division of labour in the relations between men and women as social rather than biological categories. This approach constitutes an attempt to move away from, or perhaps rather to develop, the classic marxist theoretical concern with tracing necessary links between capitalism and women's oppression, generally by rendering the subordination of women solely as an aspect of capitalist class structure. It situates the problem within an analysis of patriarchy.

Patriarchy can be defined as an autonomous system of social relations between men and women in which men are dominant. Patriarchy designates male–female relations as social relations which among other things organise biological reproduction, rather than being themselves determined by biology. Patriarchy as an analytical category thus inscribes the sexual division of labour as a social division and not a natural one. According to Delphy (1977a), the patriarchal exploitation of women by men is located in the family. In marriage women exchange their labour power (that is, they provide unpaid services) for their upkeep. The value of this upkeep is, however, less than the value of the goods and services which the woman-wife produces. At the same time, because the marriage contract gives the man-husband control over the woman-wife's labour power, the goods and services she produces are use values rather than exchange values — they cannot be sold on the market, but belong to the man-husband.

Thus, it is argued that the marriage contract is a labour contract by which men appropriate women's labour power, and marital male–female relations, characterised by the husband's ownership and control of his wife's labour power, constitute the relations of domestic production and hence structure the domestic mode of production.

The domestic mode is different from the capitalist mode of production in that the latter depends on the free sale of labour power while the former depends on the transfer of ownership and control over the woman-wife's labour power to the man-husband. In the capitalist mode of production the wage relation is impersonal and the wage rate is determined by an abstract socially necessary subsistence level. In the domestic mode of production there is no socially determined subsistence level for all domestic labourers-wives: the wife's upkeep/consumption is a function of her husband's class position and income. Her own labour power has no exchange value. Under capitalism women-wives are doubly dependent on men-husbands, as owners of their labour power and as wage earners. The wife has no direct access to raw materials and means of production, but has to buy these in the market, and her primary link with the sphere of circulation is through her husband's wage.

This form of patriarchal exploitation is common to all married women because it is only they who are expected to perform free domestic services for men. Thus patriarchal marital relations are, according to this argument, class relations. Whereas, however, the marriage–labour relation between men and women functions to the extent that it affects the majority of the adult population, the sexual division of labour encompasses all men and women. It is an ideological representation of work distribution in society and extends patriarchal relations into areas where patriarchal exploitation does not exist, that is, into the non-familial labour process. The sexual division of labour treats all women as potential wives-mothers — that is, as dependent on men — precisely because they are biological females. The ideologically implicated nature of this mode of work and task allocation lies in its emphasis on sex differences rather than on, say, human similarities (Pedinielli-Plaza, 1977); and the priority granted to biological differences rather than human similarities provides a focus and a legitimation for hierarchical differentiation between men and women. The sexual division of labour as ideology is articulated at the point of differentiation and hierarchisation in the patriarchal labour process.

Thus the sexual division of labour identifies *all* women as a separate category of worker and integrates into patriarchy women who are not married and therefore not subject to direct patriarchal exploitation within the family. As a mode of work organisation, the sexual division of labour divides all discrete work processes into male and female tasks and jobs. As a patriarchal structure, it subordinates — either directly (secretarial work) or indirectly (low-paid women's work in industry) — tasks defined as female to those defined as male. The 'maleness' or 'femaleness' of a task is thus not inherent in the operation itself but in the ideological identification and distribution of tasks. The sexual division of labour then situates individuals in jobs and designates jobs as sex specific. This is an ideological operation specific to patriarchy. It is not an *ex post facto* description of occupational sex ratios. Thus it is possible for some women to enter 'male' jobs and vice versa without these jobs losing their ideological designation as sex specific: rather, this becomes an individualised act, frequently resulting in contradictory and difficult work relations — female executives and male nurses being cases in point.

II

Traditionally, nursing history has implicitly employed a sociological model of professionalisation (Johnson, 1972) to analyse and interpret events (Abel-Smith, 1975). In discussing this period, the account tends to focus on the creation of the occupation by Florence Nightingale and the political struggle for and against registration. What this approach fails to recognise, however, is that the conflict between the anti- and the pro-registrationists was not concerned with occupational hierarchy in health care and its effects on nursing so much as with definitions of nursing within an unquestioned hierarchical mode of work and authority distribution between nursing and medicine. The two factions disagreed about the desirable class origins and educational background of applicants, and about the length and type of training required for entry. But all this was prefaced by and inferred from identical models of the nurse–doctor relation, the central interprofessional relationship which subordinated nursing to medicine.

In their evidence to the 1904—5 Select Committee on the Registration of Nurses, for example, Dr Fenwick (the husband of Ethel Bedford Fenwick, who founded the Royal British Nurses' Association — the first nursing organisation in Britain — in 1887, and the International Council of Nurses — the first international nursing organisation — in 1899, and himself a leading pro-registrationist), and Sydney Holland, chairman of the London Hospital and an important anti-registrationist, provided strikingly similar descriptions of the nurse–doctor relation. Thus Fenwick told the committee:

> If a nurse does not possess technical knowledge, she is unable to do two things which are most essential for her patient: she is unable in the first place to carry out the duties entrusted to her by the doctor for the patient efficiently; and in the second place she is quite unable to report to the doctor efficiently what particular symptoms the patient has shown between his visits (House of Commons Select Committee, 1904, p. 3).

A week later Holland stated:

> If registration were to pass it could lead nurses to consider themselves as belonging to what is called a 'Profession'. The tendency would be to think of themselves much more the Colleagues of doctors instead of simply carriers out of the orders of the doctors; in fact they would be some pseudo-scientific person (p. 29).

For the purposes of this paper, the consensus about the structural location of nursing within the occupational organisation of health care is more relevant than the traditionally emphasised disputes. Thus, irrespective of the ferocity of these internal struggles and disputes, nursing will be treated as an occupation united by a common recognition of the existence and nature of the boundaries between itself and medicine.

The pivotal interprofessional relationship within health

care is that between the nurse and doctor. However, the division of labour between these two occupations is not primarily a technical one. The dividing line between their tasks is flexible, both historically and across the range of institutions in any given period. Rather, the division of labour must be located in the division of health care into two spheres of competence, based on unequal interprofessional relations. That this division was resolved into a sexual division of labour can be understood in terms of the fact that it was women who entered nursing. Professional power relations were overdetermined by the patriarchal relations implied in the sexual division of labour: hence the subordination of nursing — whose tasks were defined and practices limited — to medicine. The justification for this division of labour in health care drew upon existing representations around 'naturalism' within patriarchal ideology.

Nineteenth-century nursing reforms had two aims. The first was to establish a single stratified occupation with responsibility for patient care and the organisation and management of nursing; and the other was to introduce this occupation into existing health care institutions or to reform nursing arrangements to accord with the Nightingale blueprint. The growth of reformed nursing, therefore, also brought with it the organisationally autonomous nursing hierarchy, located in a separate department:

> Vest the whole responsibility for nursing internal management, for discipline and training (if there is to be a Training School) of nurses in one female head of the nursing staff
> .... The Matron (Superintendent) should be responsible to the governor of the infirmary alone for the efficient discharge of her duties; and the Nurses should be responsible to the Matron alone for the discharge of their duties (Nightingale, 1874, pp. 5 and 9).

Moreover, this autonomous nursing hierarchy was responsible for the training and professional socialisation of future nurses. The occupational hierarchy was constituted as a training hierarchy:

What makes a good Training School for Nurses?
1. A year's practical and technical training in hospital wards, under *trained* head-nurses (so-called 'sisters' of

London hospitals), who themselves have been *trained* to *train* . . . .

4. The authority and discipline over all the women of a trained lady-superintendent, who is also matron of the hospital . . . .

5. An organisation not only to give this training systematically, to test it by current tests and exams, but also to give the probationers, by proper help in the wards, time to do their work as pupils as well as assistant-nurses (Nightingale, 1882, p. 2).

Nursing control over training and its organisational form strengthened the position of the matron as the head of the hospital nursing department: 'The superintendent of the training school is the matron of the hospital, and head of all the women in the hospital' (Nightingale, 1882, p. 4). Responsibility for directing the probationer's apprenticeship widened the sister's role in the ward: 'The ward-sister must train the probationers in all the duties of a nurse' (Nightingale, 1882, p. 5).

This organisational autonomy of nursing, strengthened by the overlap between occupational career and training structures, provoked fear in some quarters of the medical profession. By this time (1860–80, the initial period of reform), the dominant tasks which initiated health care diagnosis had come under the control of medicine. This had been the outcome of a long struggle by the profession for state recognition of their monopoly, culminating in the 1858 Medical Registration Act (Parry and Parry, 1976). Organisational and training autonomy, however, made nursing a source of potential independent quasi-medical practitioners. Thus a good deal of medical opposition to registration (and this included women doctors like Elizabeth Garrett Anderson) was based on the fear that state–sanctioned organisational independence could lead to the development of occupational independence for nursing:

There is this great danger in having a register of nurses that it would lead to the establishment of an imperfectly educated order of medical practitioners. That has been the experience all through. When the Society of Apothecaries was established in the reign of King James I, it was laid down that, under no circumstances were they to attend people in disease. They were merely to dispense the pre-scriptions of physicians. They first came to attend patients in this way: when they went round in times of epidemics they made a small extra charge for delivering medicine, say at a house where there was the plague. In that way they came to be asked about illness, and so they gradually came into practice, and at the present time that has been re-formed by their receiving a thoroughly sound medical edu-cation, but it was impossible to prevent them entering into practice. Exactly the same thing happened to surgeons, and the very same thing would happen with regard to nurses (House of Commons Select Committee, 1904, p. 45).

Whatever the medical fears, the organisational autonomy of nursing hid its actual position of occupational dependence and subordination: nursing organisation in effect supervised and taught a form of nursing care which established and main-tained the hierarchical divisions between nursing and medicine, being based on the structure of the nurse–doctor relation which subordinated nursing to medicine in all matters defined as 'medical' by medicine itself. The divisions mapped out spheres of competence which made nursing practice depen-ent on medical intervention.

Nightingale entrusted nursing with two functions, 'nursing the room', or hygiene, and assisting the doctor:

Nursing is performed usually by women, under scientific heads — physicians and surgeons. Nursing is putting us in the best possible conditions for Nature to restore or to preserve health. The physician or surgeon prescribes these conditions — the nurse carries them out . . . . Sickness or disease is Nature's way of getting rid of the effects of con-ditions which have interfered with health. It is Nature's attempt to cure — we have to help her. Partly, perhaps mainly, upon nursing must depend whether Nature suc-ceeds or fails in her attempt to cure by sickness. Nursing is therefore to help the patient to live . . . . Nursing is an art, and an art requiring an organised practical and scientific training. For nursing is the skilled servant of medicine, surgery and hygiene . . . . Nursing proper means, besides giving the medicines and stimulants prescribed, or applying the surgical dressing and other remedies ordered: — 1. The providing, the proper use of, fresh air, especially at night, that is ventilation, of warmth and coolness. 2. The securing of the health of the sickroom or ward, which includes light, cleanliness of floors and walls, of bed, bedding and utensils. 3. Personal cleanliness of patient and nurse, quiet, variety and cheerfulness. 4. The administering and sometimes preparation of diet (food and drink). 5. The application of remedies. In other words, all that is wanted to enable Nature to set up her restoration processes, to expel the intruder disturbing her rules of health and life. For it is Nature that cures: not the physician or nurse (Nightingale, 1882).

This dual role corresponds to tasks related to a specific nursing practice — providing a clean and comfortable environment — and those arising out of the relationship between nursing and medicine.

However, this double role is united in, and structured by, the fact that medical dominance in health care manifests itself by limiting the access to patients of practioners in other health occupations by means of monopolising the initial intervention which designates the patient *qua* patient. Therefore both aspects of nursing care can be provided only after a medical diagnosis. Once the health care process is under way, nursing consists of a variety of tasks, some of which are ordered by the doctor, and others which reflect current ideas about providing a healthy environment. This conception of the function of nursing in health care prevailed throughout the period (and still exists today, though modified somewhat by the concept of the doctor as *primus inter pares* within a health care team). A 1904 *Hospital* editorial stated this succinctly:

The nurse has no certificate which entitles her either to diagnose cases, or to judge whether a patient is so seriously ill as to need to be received into the wards; and the public have a right to demand that cases sent to a hospital should be treated by a registered practitioner and not by a nurse . . . . The nurse cannot be too careful to keep a clear dividing line between her duties and those of the medical man, and she is culpable indeed if she rashly, and with her eyes

open, grasps at responsibilities which are beyond her limit
(26 November 1904, p. 121).

Nurse training was preoccupied with professional socialisation: teaching the limits of the role of the nurse in relation to
medicine within the overall structure and provision of health
care:

> Training is to teach a nurse to know her business, that is,
> to observe exactly, to understand, to know exactly, to tell
> exactly, in such stupendous issues as life and death, health
> and disease . . . . Training has to make her, not servile, but
> loyal to medical orders and authorities . . . . Training is to
> teach the nurse to handle the agencies within our control
> which restore health and life, in strict obedience to the
> physician's or surgeon's power and knowledge (Nightingale,
> 1882, p. 6).

> There is nothing to justify a nurse in going beyond her
> limit and diagnosing and treating patients . . . Her training
> ought to teach her above all things to keep within her own
> province (*Hospital*, 26 November 1904, p. 121).

Thus the division of labour between nursing and medicine
which mapped out nursing spheres of competence was not a
neutral division, based on equal contribution to, and participation in, the healing process. Instead it created stratified
health care and interprofessional inequality. The dominance of medicine in health care and its control over initiating
and directing the healing process relegated nursing practice,
in both its aspects, to a subordinate position. The nurse–
doctor relation determined the division of labour between
these two occupations.

The structure of the nurse–doctor relation was inferred
from alleged imperatives of medical science whose practice
depended upon a combination of diagnosis–prescription and
treatment–observation. This technological determinism
produced an unequal partnership in health care, locating
power and authority in medicine:

> A nurse should never diagnose. When required she should
> report clearly and concisely upon the symptoms she has
> been able to witness; but she should stop there. A nurse

who realises her part of the work may be of invaluable
service to the doctor and patient. She may by careful
watching and timely reporting save time, assist correct
diagnosis and thus facilitate a good result. We nurses are
and never will be anything but the servants of doctors and
good faithful servants we should be, happy in our dependence which helps to accomplish great deeds (*Hospital,*
7 April 1906, p. 11).

This conception of a proper division of labour, resting upon
work demands internal to the science, effectively obscured
professional inequality. The origins of the division of labour
were located in science rather than in the nurse–doctor relation. A doctor writes:

Once the great principle is established that nurses must not
usurp medical functions, their sphere of usefulness in relation to medical men is clear enough . . . . Nursing may be
roughly defined as the care of patients under medical control. Such care or treatment is subsidiary simply in the
sense that treatment is subsidiary to diagnosis . . . . This
definition of the status and function of nursing is only
another way of laying down a proper division of labour
. . . . This principle of the proper division of labour defines
the relation of medical men to nurses (*Hospital,* 8 June
1912, pp. 251–2).

The division of labour which designated nursing care as
subsidiary or secondary (that is, subordinate) could exist
only if based on power relations between the two professions
concerned. From the point of view of nursing the nurse–
doctor relation was encapsulated in 'obedience' to doctors.
Again, however, the need for obedience was located in the
structure of medical scientific practice (and in the urgency
characteristic of 'life and death situations'), but never in
interprofessional relations:

That duty [of the nurse] is to obey him and recognise his
sole responsbility for treatment, and her own responsibility
as an executive officer. Rightly or wrongly, we cannot
have every subaltern of genius discussing his superior's
orders. Only one battle has been won in a century by the
disobedience of orders. But let not the nurse think herself
a Nelson! (*Hospital,* 31 July 1897, p. 163).

Thus the obedience owed to doctors by nurses structured the nurse-doctor relation. Interprofessional relations reduced the nurse to a non-scientific aide, a technical assistant whose authority derived from her relation to medicine. Nursing became an occupation primarily defined by its responsibility for executing medical orders and directives:

> The nurse must recognise in the medical man her scientific chief, and it is only by assuming this view of her position that she will thoroughly understand the importance of the duties she has undertaken, and comprehend the necessity of that rigid discipline that should not be second even to that of the soldier . . . . A sense of duty, an absolute obedience to orders, a thorough comprehension of these orders, are the fundamental principles of nurses (*Hospital,* 14 April 1894, p. xxiii).

However, appeals to science which situated obedience within the division of labour inherent in the dual nature of medical science did not by themselves provide a sufficiently legitimate ideological basis for power relations between nursing and medicine. It was believed, moreover, that the healing process was dependent not only on obedience *per se* but also, more importantly, on the harmonious relations between the two health care occupations. An obedient but disloyal nurse could undermine the patient's confidence in the doctor and thus arrest or retard the healing process, which depended 'as much upon their confidence in their doctor as upon anything else' (*Hospital*, 23 January 1904, p. 231). Nevertheless, some doctors clearly perceived the sexual politics implied in these professional relations:

> My name and reputation as a man and surgeon depend on my ideas being carried out as I would have them carried out . . . . The nurse is not employed as consultant, as critic, as arbiter, she is strictly an executive officer (*Hospital*, 31 July 1897, p. 164).

The genderisation of the nurse-doctor relation and the allegedly scientifically determined division of labour provided another source for justifying interprofessional inequality. This genderisation was achieved by establishing an ideological equivalence between two sets of relations, nurse-doctor and female-male.

This ideological reconstruction of interprofessional relations and their transformation into male-female relations operated by representing the nurse–doctor–patient triad as essentially homologous to the family structure. Thus nurse-doctor relations came to be seen as basically male-female relations and the patient became the 'child'. The equation, patient = child, justified with reference to the childlike attributes and psychology of sick people in general, provided the ideological space for turning nurses into 'mothers' and doctors into 'fathers':

> In the bearing of a nurse toward her charge there must be something of the indulgence of a mother for her child; that is why women are better nurses than men . . . . It is astonishing what can be done with gentleness, especially when dispensed by a woman, and as the medical man is there, I think it would be well if the so-called firmness, when needed, were left to him. She can always invoke the physician's orders for the refusal of any unreasonable request (*Hospital*, 28 April 1894, p. xxxv).

The family analogy became a major *leitmotif* in nursing literature. Like patriarchal ideology, it too depended on 'naturalism' for its mode of operation, in that it divided all tasks into male and female ones. In nursing this was done by reference to the basic similarity between the tasks common to nursing and motherhood, to doctoring and fatherhood:

> Nursing is distinctly woman's work . . . . Women are peculiarly fitted for the onerous task of patiently and skilfully caring for the patient in faithful obedience to the physician's orders. Ability to care for the helpless is woman's distinctive nature. Nursing is mothering. Grownup folks when very sick are all babies (*Hospital*, 8 July 1905, p. 237).

This specific use of the family as a symbolic shorthand for describing the nurse–doctor–patient triad meant that there was no need to analyse further the content of the nurse-doctor relation. Instead the ideological representation of this latter relation depended on linking the social categories man-father and woman-mother with occupational divisions, doctor-father and nurse-mother. In this way the nurse-doctor relation was automatically subsumed under the rubric of female–male relations:

> The comfort and well-being of a ward largely depends
> upon whether the house surgeon and sister work well
> together or whether they swim in different currents. This
> will rest chiefly with the sister. Never assert your opinions
> and wishes, but defer to his, and you will find that in the
> end you generally have your own way. It is always easier
> to lead than to drive. This is a truly feminine piece of
> counsel, and I beg you to lay it to your heart (*Hospital*,
> 8 January 1898, p. 127).

This version of the 'power behind the throne' theory equated the nurse–doctor relation precisely with patriarchal marital relations. The subordination of nursing to medicine was therefore analogous to that of the wife–mother to the husband–father. This procedure ideologically transformed nursing; for its activities were not only seen to be 'like' family duties, but the material conditions under which these activities were performed also resembled those of the patriarchal family.

Moreover the patriarchal character of the ideological representation of family relations within health care relates to the fact that Nightingale and other nursing reformers, notably Louisa Twining and William Rathbone, established nursing as an occupation specifically for women. They were motivated by a desire to open up non-industrial occupations for women: at the time, teaching was the only 'respectable' job available to women of bourgeois and *petit bourgeois* origins who were forced, by adverse circumstances such as the lack or death of a husband or the lack of an inheritance, to earn their own living (Collet, 1902; Neff, 1929; Crow, 1971):

> It has become of late the fashion, both of novel and of
> sermon writers, to cry up 'old maids', to inveigh against
> regarding marriage as the vocation of all women, to declare
> that a single life is as happy as a married one, if people
> would but think so. So is the air as good an element for
> fish as the water, if they did but know how to live in it.
> Show us *how* to be single, and we will agree. But hitherto
> we have not found that young English women have been
> convinced. And we must confess that, *in the present state
> of things*, their horror of being 'old maids' seems perfectly

justified; it is not merely a foolish desire for the pomp and circumstance of marriage — a 'life without love, and an activity without aim' is horrible in idea and wearisome in reality. How many good women every one has known, who have married, without caring particularly for their husbands, in order to find — a nautral object — a sphere for their activity . . . . The want of *necessary* occupation among English girls must have struck every one . . . . In the middle classes, how many there are who feel themselves burdensome to their fathers, or brothers, but who, not finding husbands, and not having the education to be governesses, do not know what to do with themselves (Nightingale, 1851, pp. 6—7).

The reformers' goal was to create jobs for women in health care, not to intervene in the hierarchical structure of health care provision. The struggle thus centred on making nursing a paid job, that is, preventing it from becoming yet another form of Victorian female charity, performed on a voluntary basis:

Perhaps I need scarcely add that Nurses must be paid the market price for their labour, like any other workers, and that this is yearly rising. Our principle at our Training School at St Thomas's is to train as many women as we can, to certificate them, and to find employment for them, making the best bargain for them, not only as to wages, but as to arrangements and facilities for success (Nightingale, 1867, p. 2).

In a letter written to Dr Farr in 1866 Nightingale emphasised the importance of pay:

To make the power of serving without pay a qualification is, I think, absurd. I WOULD FAR RATHER THAN ESTABLISH A RELIGIOUS ORDER, OPEN A CAREER HIGHLY PAID. My principle has always been — that we should give the best training we could to any woman, of any class, of any sect, 'paid' or unpaid, who had the requisite qualifications, moral, intellectual and physical, for the vocation of a Nurse (quoted in Woodham-Smith, 1950, p. 483).

Nursing was therefore established as a paid job for women,

and open to women from all classes. This particular battle
for recognition was won relatively quickly. The secret of the
success of nursing reform lay in its objectives, creating jobs
for women without threatening medical control over health
care. Only 14 years after the opening of the Nightingale
Fund School the preface of Miss Lees's *Handbook for
Hospital Sisters* (1874) contained this categorical statement
by a medical man, Dr Henry Ackland; 'Nursing is the
MEDICAL WORK OF WOMEN . . . . It furnishes an outlet
for the tender power and skill of good women of almost
every class' (quoted in Woodham-Smith, 1950, p. 96).
Furthermore, the reformers were heavily influenced by a
proto-feminist theory (Delphy, 1977b) put forward by
Mrs Jameson in a lecture to the National Association for the
Promotion of Social Science in 1855. This theory, called the
'communion of labour', claimed that there were natural
spheres of activity for men and women, and demanded that
women be allowed to participate with men in non-domestic
work. Since this natural division of labour was rooted in the
family, women's work outside the home ought to resemble
domestic tasks, and complement the 'male principle' with the
'female principle':

> Is it not possible that in the apportioning of the work we
> may have too far surrendered what in God's creation never
> can be surrendered without pain and mischief, the mascu-
> line and the feminine influences? — lost the true balance
> between the element of power and the element of love? . . .
> It appears to me that the domestic affections and the
> domestic duties — what I have called the 'communion
> of love and the communion of labour' — must be taken
> as the basis of all the more complicated social relations,
> and that the family sympathies must be carried out and
> developed in all the forms and duties of social existence
> . . . . To enlarge the working sphere of woman to the
> measure of her faculties, to give her a more practical and
> authorised share in social arrangements which have for
> their object the amelioration of evil and suffering, is to
> elevate her in the social scale (Jameson, 1856, pp. 22—4).

Asserting the existence of a specifically female sphere in
health care had as its corollary not upsetting the power and

control of the medical profession. It was this initial power-lessness *vis-à-vis* medicine that resulted in a virtually all-women occupation. This situation formed the material basis for turning to the family, both to provide a justification for women's paid work and to establish a pattern of interprofessional interaction. But the family as a symbol for the nurse–doctor relation contained within it this contradiction: it gave women access to a non-industrial job, but at the same time deferred to medicine in setting it up and defining its limits.

In this situation, the anomalous position of women doctors and male nurses was simply glossed over or ignored in the conceptualisation of nursing and its relation to medicine. In a period which witnesses the entry of women into medicine, there are virtually no references to female doctors in nursing journals, even though Mary Scharlieb, one of the first woman doctors and a close friend of Florence Nightingale's, contributed regularly to the *Nursing Mirror* and the *Nursing Times*. Similarly, very little was written about male nurses. In the period between 1889 and 1923 the *Hospital* and the *Nursing Mirror*, both of which appeared weekly, featured only four articles on the subject. All of these addressed themselves to the question of a suitable health care role for male nurses. This was usually seen as consisting of mental nursing and tasks deemed inappropriate for women — shaving or male catheterisation. None of these articles acknowledged the contradiction evident in employing men to be nurses–mothers, given their biological, and thus — in the terms of a problematic which conflates the biological and the social — their social inability to perform these jobs.

Nursing was set up and defined as women's work, and a good nurse was seen as primarily a good woman. This 'de-professionalised' the relations between nursing and medicine, and situated the nurse–doctor relation, characterised by the subordination of nursing to medicine, within a patriarchal structure. The occupational ideology of nursing thus gendered the division of labour: it associated science and authority with doctors, and caring — putting science into practice — with women. In this way health care based itself on allegedly sex-specific personal qualities. Nurses were defined, in the first instance, by their personal qualities and virtues. Writers on nursing in this period were preoccupied with cataloguing long lists of individual and moral characteristics deemed necessary in a nurse. These reveal a preponderance of qualities relating not to skill and technical knowledge but to subordination and personality, including as they do references to virtues and qualities relating implicitly or explicitly to subordination (patience, endurance, forbearance, humility, unselfishness, self-control, self-sacrifice, self-abnegation, self-effacement, service orientation, self-surrender, devotion, loyalty, discipline, obedience); to personal qualities (orderly, neat, cleanly, strong, quiet, sober, punctual, dutiful, persevering, self-reliant, courageous, principled, chaste); to the manner of relating to others (cheerful, kindly, gentle, generous, courteous, discreet, grave, considerate, thoughtful, understanding, tactful, tender, calm, firm); to attitude to patients (goodwill, love, sympathy, pity, comforting, charitableness); to qualities relating to the nurse's role as observer and reporter of symptoms (guilelessness, sincerity, honesty, trustworthiness, truthfulness, reliability, accuracy, watchfulness, precision, observing); and to characteristics relating to skill and technical competence (ingenious, ready, quick, intelligent, skilful, competent, alert, practical, keen, sensible).

These qualities, selected from Nightingale's writings and *Hospital* articles, demonstrate the relative importance attributed to the nurse's ability to work in subordination to medicine and the relative absence of references to skill, competence, education and the like. It was *character* that mattered; and character was intimately linked with femininity. For Nightingale, femininity consisted primarily of moral attributes and qualities:

> To be a good nurse one must be a good woman, here we shall all agree . . . . What is it like to be 'like a woman'? 'Like a woman' — 'a very woman' is sometimes said as a word of contempt: sometimes as a word of tender admiration . . . . What makes a good woman is the better or higher or holier nature: quietness — gentleness — patience — endurance — forbearance, forbearance with patients, her fellow workers, her superiors, her equals . . . . As a mark of contempt for a woman, is it not said, she can't obey? — she will have her own way? As a mark of respect — she always knows how to obey? How to give up her own ways? . . .

You are here to be trained for *Nurses — attendants* on the Wants of the Sick — *helpers* in carrying out Doctors' orders . . . . Then a good woman should be thorough, thoroughness in a nurse is a matter of life and death in a patient or, rather, without it she is no nurse . . . . Now what does 'like a woman' mean when it is said in contempt? Does it not mean what is petty, little selfishnesses, small meannesses: envy, jealousy, foolish talking, unkind gossip, love of praise? Now, while we try to be 'like a woman' in the noble sense of the word, let us fight bravely against all such womanly weaknesses. Let us be anxious to do well, not for selfish praise but to honour and advance the cause, the work we have taken up (Nightingale, 1881).

In her writings Florence Nightingale frequently reiterated the equation good woman equals good nurse. She put it forward as a central criterion for selecting applicants, training future nurses, establishing professional relations with patients and mapping out the occupational sphere of competence of nursing. In 1882 she wrote that 'a woman cannot be a good and intelligent nurse without being a good and intelligent woman' (Nightingale, 1882, p. 2); in the 'Introduction' to Rathbone's *History and Progress of District Nursing* she stated that 'a good nurse must be a good woman with sympathetic insight' (Nighingale, 1890, p. xix). Thus Nightingale insisted on the existence of a close link between nursing and femininity, the latter being defined by a specific combination of moral qualities which differentiated men from women. The success of nursing reforms depended primarily, according to Nightingale, on cultivating the 'feminine' character, rather than on training and education.

From around the turn of the century there was a growing shift in emphasis from female moral qualities in general to a more specific consideration of characteristics of women-mothers and domestic workers. Since this represented a shift from virtues to tasks, femininity was more explicitly located within a patriarchal sexual division of labour: 'Ministering is certainly woman's vocation, be her talents what they may . . . . Self must be put entirely in the background, and patience, strength, gentleness and untiring energy must be brought forward' (*Hospital*, 17 Febuary 1894, p. cxcviii). Although *Hospital* still printed statements like, 'The best sort of nurse is merely the best sort of woman, the most unselfish, patient, gentle, cheerful and observant of her sex' (17 August 1895, p. cxxxviii), it became more common to draw links between nursing and other home and family based female occupations. Analogies were developed between nursing and motherhood: 'The best nurse is that woman whose maternal instincts are well developed . . . . The connection between mothering and nursing is very close' (*Hospital*, 27 March 1897, p. 232); and between nursing and housework: 'A good nurse must first be a good housemaid' (*Hospital*, 4 October 1902, p. 12).

The focus shifted from moral training in the family to domestic training of future nurses by their mothers. Maternal feelings and efficiency in domestic labour characterised both the good woman and the good nurse:

> The elements of making the true nurse must be in the woman. The bottom of the whole question is home train-ing; women who have had good mothers, who taught them obedience and self-discipline with a thorough domestic training, are the women who will make the best nurses (*Hospital*, 1 September 1917, p. 445).

The development of this ideological identification – good woman = good nurse – was evidently closely related to the use of the family as a symbol for nurse–doctor relations. The emphasis on femininity as a set of virtues and femininity seen in terms of motherhood and domestic labour provided the family analogy with content.

It is perhaps not surprising in relation to this particular ideological operation that the set of tasks in nursing which most closely resembled housework – those subsumable under the rubric of 'hygiene' – came to occupy a central and some-times problematic position. Nightingale treated as equivalent all health care sciences: hygiene was the nursing science and medicine and surgery belonged to the medical profession. She arrived at this notion of equivalence by attributing curing to nature aided by health care rather than to health care itself. Illness became identified with 'the reparative process which Nature has instituted' (Nightingale, 1883, p. 5). Thus the divisions in health care tasks were seen as ultimately rooted in nature and their distribution represented an historical accident. Hygiene was allocated to nursing because it was the only health care science available in 1860, when Nightingale opened the first nurse training school:

> [Nursing] ought to signify the proper use of fresh air, light, warmth, cleanliness, quiet, and the proper selection and administration of diet . . . . It is often thought that medicine is the curative process. It is no such thing; medicine is the surgery of the functions, as surgery proper is that of the limbs and organs (Nightingale, 1883, pp. 6 and 74).

This emphasis on hygiene as the specific scientific activity of nursing resulted in allotting most of the domestic work in hospitals to nurses, especially probationers. Ability and willingness to perform household tasks became the hallmark of good nursing: 'If a nurse declines to do these things for her patient, "because it is not her business", I should say that nursing was not her calling' (Nightingale, 1883, p. 13). More importantly, hygiene was singled out as the central element in health care, without which medicine and surgery were ineffective: 'The Life and Death, recovery or invaliding of patients depends generally not on any great and isolated act, but on the unremitting and thorough performance of every minute's practical duty' (Nightingale, 1886, p. 13).

It is clear, however, from articles and letters in nursing journals that the Nightingale position on the relationship between nursing, hygiene and housework did not pass unchallenged. Arguments about household tasks in nursing became debates about nursing itself:

> Now let me say a little on the subject of so-called 'menial' work. To my mind it is an incorrect term; no work is 'menial' that ministers to the comfort of the patient; and if a nurse is ambitious to be one day a ward sister, a thorough and practical knowledge of 'menial' work is essential . . . . You will frequently hear the opinion expressed that this sort of work is unnecessary for a nurse. Do not believe it (*Hospital*, 3 July 1897, p. 121).

Part of the debate about the function of hygiene in nursing centred on questions about whose province it was. Its importance was never disputed, but the issue at stake was the demarcation of household tasks, hygiene or menial work, scientific nursing or charring:

Scrubbing and cleaning used to be considered the very
lowest and least skilled class of labour. But the knowledge
of aseptics has changed this idea, and it is now understood
that the process of keeping things clean is one which
requires great accuracy, together with the use of proper
materials and methods (*Hospital*, 22 August 1908, p. 559).

However, the delegation to nurses of equally important medical tasks, such as the administration of treatment in the
doctor's absence, demonstrated the possibility of passing on
tasks to people with even less training, for example maids,
provided there was adequate supervision. At this point,
attempts were made to distinguish between cleaning — which
had to remain a nursing duty — and those tasks which could
be passed on to maids-cleaners:

What is Ward Work? In the usual application of the words
it means — all those duties, the performance of which is
essential to the good environment of patients, but which
in themselves form no part of medical treatment or nursing,
in strict terms, that is, sweeping, dusting, polishing, or
scrubbing of floors etc . . . . In some hospitals a large part
of a probationer's time is taken up with domestic duties —
sweeping, scrubbing of floors, lockers, tables, baths, cup-
boards, washing up of breakfast, tea, or supper crockery,
polishing of innumerable brass taps, cleaning of sinks,
washing of glass globes etc. In another institution some
only of these tasks are expected of a nurse. It would be a
distinct step in advance if matrons were to agree that the
majority of these duties should not be allocated to the probationers, exception perhaps being made in some particu-
lars for the operating theatre; a multitude would yet remain
that have close connection with nursing, for example,
brushing and carbolising of beds, cleaning of lotion bowls,
instruments, many and various, dusting etc. (*Hospital*,
16 November 1901, p. 98—9).

And so domestic tasks in nursing gradually became limited
to the sanitary aspects of patient care. This was a far cry
from Nightingale's grand notion of 'nursing the room'. As
nursing developed, hygiene remained part of its practice only
to the extent that it related to patient care. All other household chores were to be performed by maids under the super-

vision of nurses trained in the scientific principles of hygiene. The nurse–hygienist continued to exist in district and private nursing. But in the ideologically dominant form of nursing, voluntary hospital nursing, she was slowly supplanted by a nurse whose responsibilities were gradually confined to administering and supervising nursing care — that is, that part of nursing which related more directly to medical intervention.

This was a slow process, continuing well into the period between the wars. (Thus one of the recommendations of the Lancet Commission on Nursing, appointed in 1930, was that domestic work be removed from nursing: 'A redistribution between nurses and ward-maids of domestic work in the wards of hospitals is urgently required. We recommend the provision of sufficient ward-maids to relieve nurses of domestic duties not directly concerned with the patient' (Lancet Commission on Nursing, 1932, p. 171).) This process began at the same time as the ideological shift occurred in the definition of a good nurse, moving from good woman = good nurse to nurse = mother = housewife. There appeared to be a contradiction between nursing aspirations and material changes in the nursing labour process and the ideological representation of that labour process. The former oriented nursing more strongly towards patient care, whereas the latter intensified the patriarchal nature of the sexual division of labour in health care.

However, access to patients still depended on prior medical intervention through diagnosis. The primary identification of nursing with patient care rather than with hygiene contributed to the link between nursing and medicine. Nursing practice became even more closely subordinated to medicine. This was presented in ideology as motherhood and housework in nursing: tasks and duties were stressed in such a way that the relationship between nursing and medicine was mystified. In a sense, removing domestic tasks from nursing constituted the elimination of a relatively autonomous nursing practice from the overall functions of nursing. Thus the ideological equation of nursing with housework was in fact a statement about the patriarchal relation between nursing and medicine rather than about the division of labour in health care.

III

Nursing is a unique non-industrial female occupation. It was established and designed for women, and located within a labour process — health care — already dominated by doctors, all of whom were men. Success depended on both creating paid jobs for women who needed them and situating and defining these jobs in a way which would pose no threat to medical authority. The particular form of the sexual division of labour which resulted from this conjuncture is specific to nursing: it is vivid and precise. It represents the patriarchal nature of the sexual division of labour in relatively pristine form, especially in that in many ways it cuts across capitalist class boundaries. The analysis of the sexual division of labour in health care demonstrates that technological determinism, the ideological representation of the capitalist division of labour, was less crucial than the ideology of naturalism in situating nursing within health care. Thus emphasis was placed on the interconnections between femininity, mother-hood, housekeeping and nursing. Task division was circumscribed within the relationship between nursing and medicine. As such technological determinism was never the central issue.

The sexual division of labour is a patriarchal ideological structure in that it reproduces patriarchal relations in extra-familial labour processes. Thus women's labour in the family is based on the labour relations between husband and wife; in paid employment within capitalism her relationship to social production is on one level determined by the limits posed by the sexual division of labour. Any analysis seeking an explanation for the fact that women's work under capitalism is different from men's — both within marriage or the domestic mode of production and in wage labour in the capitalist mode of production — must unquestionably address itself to the pervasiveness of patriarchal relations. The form of these relations cannot be assumed to be self-evident, but must be analysed in their specificity.

References

Abel-Smith, B. (1975), *A History of the Nursing Profession*, Heinemann, London.
Beauvoir, S. de (1970), *The Second Sex*, Bantam Books, New York.

Braverman, H. (1974), *Labor and Monopoly Capital*, Monthly Review Press, New York.

Collet, C. (1902), *Educated Working Women: Essays on the Economic Position of Women Workers in the Middle Classes*, P. S. King, London.

Crow, D. (1971), *The Victorian Woman*, Allen & Unwin, London.

Delphy, C. (1977a), 'The main enemy' in *The Main Enemy: a Materialist Analysis of Women's Oppression*, Women's Research and Resources Centre, London.

Delphy, C. (1977b), 'Proto-feminism and anti-feminism' in *The Main Enemy: a Materialist Analysis of Women's Oppression*, Women's Research and Resources Centre, London.

Engels, F. (1970), 'Origin of the family, private property and the state' in K. Marx and F. Engels, *Collected Works*, Lawrence & Wishart, London.

Firestone, S. (1971), *The Dialectic of Sex*, Cape, London.

Gardiner, J., Himmelweit, S., and Mackintosh, M. (1975), 'Women's domestic labour', *Bulletin of the Conference of Socialist Economists*, vol. 4, part 2, pp. 1—11.

Gilman, C. P. (1966), *Women and Economics*, Harper & Row, New York.

House of Commons Select Committee (1904), *Report from the Select Committee on the Registration of Nurses*, HMSO, London.

Jameson, A. B. (1856), *The Communion of Labour*, Longman, London.

Johnson, T. J. (1972), *Professions and Power*, Macmillan, London.

Lancet Commission on Nursing (1932), *Final Report*, Lancet, London.

Maclean, U. (1974), *Nursing in Contemporary Society*, Routledge & Kegan Paul, London.

Marglin, S. A. (1976), 'What do bosses do?' in A. Gorz, *The Division of Labour*, Harvester Press, London.

Mathieu, N. C. (1977), 'Notes towards a sociological definition of sex categories' in *Ignored by Some, Denied by Others: the Social Sex Category in Sociology*, Women's Research and Resources Centre, London.

Marx, K. (1971), *Capital*, vol. I, Lawrence & Wishart, London.

Neff, W. F. (1929), *Victorian Working Women*, AMS Press, New York.

Palloix, C. (1976), 'The labour process: from Fordism to Neo-Fordism' in Conference of Socialist Economists, *The Labour Process and Class Strategies*, Stage One, London.

Parry, N. C. A., and Parry, J. (1976), *The Rise of the Medical Profession: a Study of Collective Social Mobility*, Croom Helm, London.

Pedinielli-Plaza, M. (1977), 'Sex differences and women's reality — the patriarchal chain', paper presented at the Anglo-French Seminar on Sexual Divisions, London.

Rathbone, W. (1890), *History and Progress of District Nursing*, Macmillan, London.

Schulman, S. (1958), 'Basic functional roles in nursing: mother surrogate and healer' in E. G. Jaco, *Patients, Physicians and Illness*, Free Press, Chicago.

Thorner, I. (1955), 'Nursing — the functional significance of an institutional pattern', *American Sociological Review* vol. 20, pp. 531—8.

Woodham-Smith, C. (1950), *Florence Nightingale*, Constable, London.

Florence Nightingale, some of her writings from the Nightingale Collection at the London School of Economics:
   (1851), 'Institution of Kaiserswerth'.
   (1867), 'Suggestions on the subject of providing, training, and
   organising nurses, for the sick poor in workhouse infirmaries', letter
   to the President of the Poor Law Board.
   (1874), 'Suggestions for improving the nursing service of hospitals
   and on the method of training nurses for the sick poor'.
   (1881), 'Letter to the probationer-nurses in the "Nightingale Fund"
   Training School, at St Thomas's Hospital', 6 May.
   (1882), 'Training of nurses and nursing the sick poor', reprinted
   from Dr Quain, *Dictionary of Medicine*.
   (1883; 1st ed., 1859), *Notes on Nursing: What It Is and What It Is
   Not*.
   (1886), 'Letter to the probationer-nurses in the "Nightingale Fund"
   Training School, at St Thomas's Hospital', 1 January.
   (1890), 'Introduction' in W. Rathbone, *History and Progress of
   District Nursing*. op. cit.
Hospital (journal):
   17 February 1894, J. L. J., 'The nurse's confessional'.
   14 April 1894, Louis Vintras, RMO at the French Hospital, 'The
   ethics of nursing'.
   28 April 1894, ibid.
   17 August 1895, 'Concerning nurses by one of their friends'.
   27 March 1897, 'Post-graduate clinics for nurses by a trained nurse'.
   3 July 1897, Sister Grace, 'Practical aspects of a nurse's life'.
   31 July 1897, G. A. Hawkings-Ambler, Hon. Surgeon at the Free
   Hospital for Women, 'The etiquette of nursing'.
   8 January 1898, Sister Grace, 'Practical aspects of a nurse's life'.
   16 November 1901, Late Matron, 'Necessary and unnecessary ward
   work as training for probationers'.
   4 October 1902, Esther H. Young, 'Words and advice to nurses'.
   23 January 1904, Sir William Bennett, 'On modern nursing in private
   practice'.
   26 November 1904, Nursing Outlook: 'The nurse's limit'.
   8 July 1905, Nursing Outlook: 'Three indispensable qualities'.
   7 April 1906, 'On practical nursing'.
   22 August 1908, Nursing Administration: 'The disappearance of the
   scrubber'.
   8 June 1912, Dr D. S. Davies, 'The relation of medical men to nurses'.
   1 September 1917, The Matrons' and Sisters' Department: Matrons
   in Council, 'The elements must be in the woman'.

6 Modes of appropriation and the sexual division of labour: a case study from Oaxaca, Mexico

Kate Young

The papers in the second half of this book are concerned primarily with the labour process, its relation to the class position of women, and the way in which the state and the education system intervene in the location of women in capitalist relations of production. Appropriately the first of these papers examines a Third World community currently undergoing changes in the form of capitalist relations. Drawing on ethnographic data from a community in a mountainous area in Mexico, Kate Young is able to compare the position of women over a relatively short period of time, but one which spans crucial changes in modes of production, by examining the specific conditions of sexual division of labour as affected by merchant and circulation capital. The way in which the 'complementarity' which exists between the sexes is altered to the detriment of women with the changes brought about in land usage and the introduction of 'free' labour is also demonstrated. It seems that what little power women previously held in regard to land ownership and control within their own communities has been eroded in this process. The 'effects of the intervention of differing types of capital on women's productive and reproductive roles' is, then, the central concern here. Although this paper is apparently limited in scope in that the data refer only to two small zones within a particular region in Mexico, it has a more general relevance in that it deals with the effect of changes in land usage on the sexual division of labour and the differentiation between fractions and strata which make any such changes operate in a complex and overdetermined way: for example, within groups such as those dealt with here, women do not comprise a homogeneous stratum as such, and understanding of their position needs to take cognizance of the different fractions and strata within the community.

It is fairly commonplace to hear the argument that the development of capitalism has brought a worsening of the position of women, whether in the advanced capitalist countries or those of the so-called Third World. At the same time, the apparent counter-argument, that only the capitalist mode of production has produced the necessary conditions for the liberation of women, is equally staunchly upheld. The two positions may not be as mutually exclusive as they seem, for it is possible to argue that it is precisely in the contradiction between the worsening conditions brought about by the development of class society, and the high level of development of the productive forces, which makes it technically possible for women to be freed from individual servicing and reproductive roles, that the potential for liberation lies. The changes now taking place in the Third World provide a unique opportunity to investigate both the forces underlying the development of class society and the specific ways in which conditions do (or do not) worsen for women.

This is clearly an enormous topic and a highly complex one. My aim in my work in Mexico was much more limited. I was concerned to investigate the interrelation between women's productive and reproductive roles since I hoped that this would provide an understanding of the means by which women have been excluded at the local level from positions of control over social resources and have been socialised to accept their subordinate position (or at best to regard it as complementary to that of their menfolk). In other words, I wanted to analyse the sexual division of labour, meaning by this the system of allocation of agents to positions within the labour process on the basis of sex, and a system of exclusion of certain categories of agents from certain positions within social organisation on the basis of sex, and lastly a system of reinforcement of the social construction of gender (cf. Edholm, Harris and Young, 1977). In this view the social construction of women (and men), and the roles attitudes and behaviours assigned to them have to be analysed as a process;

moreover a process which is historically specific. Underlying this process are changes derived from changing economic relations: during the historical period this article is concerned with these changes are the result of the laws of motion of capitalist development.

In this paper I describe the changes (primarily economic) that have taken place in some small agricultural communities in a fairly inaccessible, mountainous area of Oaxaca, Mexico, over the past 100 years. The object of the paper is to analyse these changes in terms of their effect on women. Although the timespan covered is relatively short in historical terms, I think it is possible to pick out the underlying tendencies and to show why the development of capitalist relations has such contradictory effects on women's position. The framework of the analysis is the intervention of two different types of capital — merchant capital and circulation capital — and the differing effects such intervention can have on women's productive and reproductive roles. The distinction between these two capitals is a fine one — Kay (1975) calls the one independent merchant capital and the other merchant capital as agent of industrial capital (for the sake of clarity I prefer to use the different terms for each type) — but I think it a useful distinction to make. I will briefly outline the differences between the two capitals and the reasons why their differences should be relevant to the analysis of the position of women.

Marx calls merchant's capital 'the oldest free state of the existence of capital' which requires no other condition for its existence than 'those necessary for the simple circulation of commodities and money' for 'the extremes between which merchant's capital acts as a mediator exist for it as a given' (Marx, 1970b, p. 325). His discussion in essence shows that merchant capital plays a very contradictory role in those economies in which it intervenes. In general it is strictly circulation capital and is indifferent to the products it circulates: that is, it circulates products in demand whatever the basis of that demand. The products it exchanges may be the surplus of independent producers' immediate needs or specifically produced for exchange under a variety of conditions such as slavery, petty commodity production and so on. But, as capital, it is driven to accumulate (that is,

M–C–M'), initially at least making its profits from unequal exchange, ensured by monopoly control of trade. But trade expansion gives equalisation of exchange rates: 'all development of merchant's capital tends to give production more and more the character of production for exchange value and to turn products more and more into commodities' (p. 327). Part of the merchants' surplus goes into the expansion of trade, not that of production, so with its expansion it 'encompasses no longer merely the profit of production but bites deeper and deeper into the latter and makes entire branches of production dependent on it' (p. 330). Hence eventually the necessity for increased productivity, the reorganisation of the labour process, the intensification of the social division of labour and restructuring of the social organisation of production itself, including the relations of production. This may, however, bring the interests of merchant capital into contradiction with those of the class it is politically dependent upon to control the labour process, and thus also with those of the producers. Where this contradiction is not resolved by the development of new relations such as the overthrow of the politically dominant class, the more merchant capital develops, the more enervating its effects: 'the independent development of merchant capital stands in inverse proportion to that of society so that wherever it still predominates we find backward conditions' (p. 327).

The important points to note are that merchant capital does not appropriate surplus labour through buying and selling labour but through its political control over the product of labour, ensured by its alliance with the locally politically dominant group.

Circulation or commercial capital, on the other hand, is the handmaiden of industrial capital according to Marx, who says that it functions only as the agent of productive capital, and serves to realise the capital invested in industrial production. Unlike merchant capital it is closely tied to the demands of industrial capital and in its search for new outlets for the products of industry it may undercut local domestic industries or destroy whole branches of production in competition with industrial capital. In so doing, it sets free the erstwhile producers' labour-time for investment in other activities. If such activities are absent locally, this free labour-time becomes expressed as the actual redundancy of individual labourers. In other words, a relative surplus population has been created. Industrial capital does appropriate surplus labour through buying and selling labour power. Thus where labour is freed in one geographical area it may be in demand in another, or where it is freed in one sector it may be absorbed by another.

If we look at one particular area that is of a geographical space and not at the system as a whole, in this case a largely self-provisioning agricultural area with a tradition of domestic manufacture which included cloth weaving, pottery, rope making, it is my suggestion that the intervention of these two types of capital will have differing effects on labour demand and the organisation of the labour force, and on the sexual division of labour. I would suggest that the intervention of merchant capital in areas where it stimulates production, because it does not become directly involved in production to raise productivity through new technologies, may create an increased demand for labour. On the other hand the intervention of commercial capital tends to bring about the opposite effect, not because it raises productivity but, as agent of industrial capital, it undermines many domestic manufactures and thus creates a relative surplus population.

To take the production of a surplus for merchant capital first, I am working with the supposition that the additional labour required to produce the surplus may initially be achieved by a reallocation of labour resources, a decrease in time allocated to leisure or the bringing into production of hitherto non-productive members such as children, the elderly and women. In other words, it does not, initially at least, immediately presuppose an increase in fertility rates. Clearly the reorganisation of labour resources must depend to some extent on the pre-existing division of labour and on the nature of the surplus extracted. None the less if merchant capital has the political ability to continue to expand and demand ever more increased production, this may affect fertility rates. The degree to which exactions of merchant capital may make larger families useful, so as to spread the tasks of subsistence and surplus production, must however depend on whether both men and women can collaborate with others in labour arrangements which permit the spreading of the total community labour over all households and thus allow individual households to acquire labour they themselves do not have. It must also depend on whether the surplus is appropriated at the household level, at the level of the village section (ward or quarter), or of the village itself. If the surplus is appropriated at the household level, and if the exactions of merchant capital demand an absolute increase in available labour, and immigration is not possible, then the individual household's labour requirements may be met only through larger numbers of children — this would be particularly so if children's labour is used in some part of the labour process, or to substitute for women's labour in household tasks. A sex specific demand for labour may influence not only the size but the sex composition of families. The effect of 'specialisation' in child production may then make it impossible for women to continue to be greatly engaged in other social roles, particularly those with an inflexible work schedule, which may lessen their control over certain social resources. In other words, the intervention of merchant capital may work upon an existing sexual division of labour and the social relations embodied in it in such a way that the relations between the sexes, whether relations of complementarity or of subordination/domination, may be changed in favour of the men because of their lesser role in reproducing the labour force. Lastly, one could expect that the rate of increase of the population might well come into contradiction with the rate of expansion of the resource base; that is, productivity in subsistence may lag behind productivity in human reproduction.

In the case of the intervention of industrial/productive capital the situation is typically quite different. The production process is not taken as a given but is that upon which industrial capital most powerfully operates: branches of production that can most profitably be reorganised are destroyed, production of needed raw materials and other commodities is fostered, and in large measure the labour process is restructured and the workforce itself transformed. The key distinction here is the capital–labour relation in which labour is 'free' that is, obliged by economic necessity to sell its labour power, as is capital to hire it and thereby appropriate surplus labour.

The intervention of productive capital in agriculture is, however, not an even process in Third World countries. In terrain where capital inputs can revolutionise production, or in areas which are relatively accessible and where investment in transport is not very costly, large-scale or highly intensive production units, based on the private appropriation of land and use of wage labour, develop. With the use of machinery, productivity is increased but the amount of labour needed on a permanent basis declines. With growing privatisation of land an ever larger category of landless families is created. Those who remain on the land come to depend on the wage, generally of the family head, for survival. The amount of the wage, as well as the possibilities for augmenting it by the sale of familial labour power, probably come to provide the boundary conditions for family size. Again with the increased complexity of agricultural operations, as well as the general rise in the level of development of the productive forces at a global level, children may have to acquire certain minimal skills such as the three Rs before they are employable. In this way the cost of raising children may rise substantially and restriction in family size become imperative.

In less fertile or accessible areas, such as the one under study, industrial capital may not, however, intervene directly. That is, there may be virtually no investment in land, machinery or other means of raising productivity. What does intervene is circulation capital although not directly in the productive process. None the less by undermining domestic manufacture and by encouraging the production of only certain products — raw materials for industry, foodstuffs for the urban proletariat — it brings about radical social transformation. The intervention of circulation capital clearly indicates the existence of an expanding industrial economy which is not necessarily domestic, and a situation where the industrial sector is looking for markets for its products. It thus draws within its orbit self-provisioning, or largely self-provisioning areas such as the one under study. This has a number of consequences: first, by restructuring local economies away from self-provisioning, primarily by destroying domestic manufacture rather than excouraging cash cropping, the connection between local resources and human population may well be broken. In other words, the community or local area is no longer the unit of reproduction, and structural constraints on rapid population growth may be removed. Second, by destroying some branches of production and fostering others, differentiation of the local community is encouraged. The differentiation is permanent in that there is an unequal access to means of livelihood whether land or marketing or employment. Third, it accelerates the 'freeing' of labour and thus the buying and selling of labour power is encouraged. One of the strata that develops is therefore composed of families dependent on selling their labour for survival. This may encourage large families, both because labour may be a family's only economic resource and it benefits from having as many labourers as possible to capture available employment, but also because the area of opportunities has greatly expanded. That is, if jobs become scarce locally, some of the wage earners can move away, temporarily or not, into other areas where employment is thought to be available. At the same time, for those families dependent on the wage, housework, child care, and general servicing activities may become even more rigidly the woman's province, while the man's familial responsibility may be thought to end with handing over some part of his wage packet. In cases where the man's wage is not even sufficient to maintain the family, the wife, too, may have to take on temporary labouring work, whenever it is available, in addition to her already heavy burden of tasks. The effect of this may be to reduce the number of children — not necessarily the number that are born but the number that are kept alive. These are the considerations encapsulated in the phrase: the differing effects of the intervention of differing types of capital on women's productive and reproductive roles.

The interplay between women's productive and reproductive roles is a theoretical problem which has already been touched on by a number of writers, but while some argue that women's reproductive roles determine the degree to which women can be committed to productive undertakings (Brown, 1970), others argue the reverse (Friedl, 1975; Draper, 1975). My own understanding of the situation is that one must look at the political and economic forces which may lead to either production or reproduction being given greater emphasis in any specific historical period. I have already suggested that the intervention of differing forms of capital will probably have quite differing effects on the extent to which women specialise in child rearing. Marxist theorists on the whole have not been especially interested in studying the particularities of workforce composition by sex, because in the main labour is viewed abstractly in terms of labour power. But we need to understand the mechanisms behind the construction of the sexual division of labour and the elaboration of the stereotype of 'women's work' and how such stereotypes change. It is also important to understand the relationship between the political and economic bases of the sexual division of labour and its ideological reinforcement; the degree of autonomy of ideology clearly makes the situation even more complex.

This paper will analyse the changes in the sexual division of labour and changes in relations between the sexes. I will not be able to do more than show how the economic changes that have occurred have limited or expanded women's access to economic roles. I will suggest how women's reproductive roles have also been affected: there are risks in such an enterprise, not the least of which is that in trying to theorise the relationship between women's productive and reproductive roles at an economic level there is a temptation to regard human beings at all times and in all circumstances as rational calculators of benefits — *homo economicus* — while left out are the constraints derived from underlying social forces.

The area under analysis is that of the Highland Zapotec region of Oaxaca: I shall for convenience refer to it as the Sierra, although this is not strictly accurate. It is a very mountainous area which divides roughly into two zones: a hot, humid zone of abundant rainfall, where today coffee is grown for export, and a drier, more temperate zone where avocados are grown for the domestic market. Of the two villages referred to, Copa Bitoo lies in the temperate zone while Telana lies in the coffee zone: both villages in the colonial period came within the administrative district of Villa Alta.

In the mid-nineteenth century the economy of the area was fairly self-contained: most villages produced enough maize, the staple, and other basic consumption necessities; most also specialised in some handicraft or agricultural produce for exchange within the zone. The only commodities which were regularly traded in any quantity outside the Sierra appear to have been cotton lengths and lamp/candle wicks made by the women. These were traded for cash which was used to pay taxes, or bartered for goods — such as salt, machetes, iron ploughshares, dynamite for fireworks, fish for Lent — not available in the area. Women appear to have controlled the local trade in cotton lengths and the proceeds from it and thus exerted some degree of economic power within the household, but only men undertook the longer trading journeys to acquire the raw cotton and sell larger quantities of lengths. There is some evidence that by the 1850s, in fact, the cotton trade was the concern of specialist traders from outside the zone.

The villages were not stratified internally according to permanent wealth difference, private appropriation of land and use of wage labour. Families were differentiated according to the prestige of the male head of the household, which depended on the number of ritual and administrative obligations the man had fulfilled, and this, to a certain extent, depended on his age. The older the household head, the more labour he could command from sons, daughters, husbands, godchildren, co-godparents and so on, the more foodstuffs he could cause to be produced on his own or on village land. Such surplus was spent on saints' day feasts or providing the food for the large labour parties required of those holding public office. Village government was in the hands of adult married men, the older the man in general the higher the post, and they also organised church activities especially in villages where there was no resident priest. Individual men annually sponsored the villages' saints' days festivities. While women held formal posts neither in the village government nor in the church, their participation with their husbands was essential in several important rituals. Such participation entitled the women, like the men, to public signs of respect such as bowing, and honarary terms of respect. The degree of control exercised by the Catholic Church seems to have varied greatly — it tended to be strongest in the larger market villages.

Land holding was *de jure* communal — that is, access to land was legally under the supervision of the village government, but customary practice meant that families had strong claims to use-rights in land they or their ancestors had cleared from the forest. Both sons and daughters could inherit claims to such virtually exclusive use-rights from either mother or father, but a woman's land was *de facto* under the control of her husband and he could dispose of it more or less as he wished. Land none the less was not alienable to anyone outside the community, and even within the community use-rights were rarely exchanged.

Labour was widely exchanged between households but each household organised the production of most of its basic needs and the locally specified required surplus. Part of that surplus was appropriated by the church in tithes, the state in taxes and the community through the feasts organised by the older males on saints' days. Only surplus destined for taxes had to be converted into cash. The economy was what most anthropologists would term a 'typical' peasant economy characterised by the household as a production unit initiating a distinct labour process but interlocked with others through the exchange of labour, little development of the productive forces, little potential for growth especially since even a limited degree of individual accumulation was prevented by the threefold appropriation of the surplus, and no permanent differentiation of the population but shifting grading of households according to the prestige and age of the household head.

Women, particularly older women, played important ritual roles as wives, had considerable authority in their household, and a certain degree of personal autonomy which derived from their activities as weavers. Many of them were respected, too, as healers and midwives, the most skilled of whom were sought after as godmothers which again entitled them to particular signs of respect and even a small degree of command over the labour of their godchildren. None the less their political power was negligible as they took no part in village government and thus in settling disputes over rights of land use or inheritance, or even conflicts of interest between men and women. Further, they were dependent on male outsiders for their supplies of cotton and for trading the cotton lengths outside the zone for the cash needed for taxes. To these men they were also politically and economically vulnerable for they dictated the terms upon which the women traded. Their

political and jural subordination to their menfolk was symbolically expressed by a father's right to give away his
daughters to other men as wives for their sons; their subordination within the ritual sphere was symbolically shown
by the fact that women sat together on the left of the
church, while in their relations with outside traders their menfolk were required to be intermediaries.

The following discussion covers the period 1870 to 1970,
which is divided into three sub-periods, a division which
imposes an arbitrary orderliness on a confusing and contradictory flow of events. In the first period (1870—1930)
independent merchant capital dominated economic activities
through its political alliance with local political leaders. Once
this alliance was broken, the inflow of new capital — circulation capital — and the monetisation of the local economy
became possible. In the second period (1930—55) the initial
response to the intervention of commercial capital brought
mobility and an apparent diversification of economic activity.
This expansion was, however, accompanied by the increasing
privatisation of land, the undermining of local small-scale
domestic manufacturing and the setting free of labour. In the
final period (1955—70) the effects of the restructuring of the
local economy become clearly apparent: the creation of a
relative surplus population leads to the redistribution of that
population through out-migration and the sharpening of
economic differentiation.

Cotton cloth production for exchange declined in the
latter part of the nineteenth century. In the 1860s supplies
of raw cotton dried up as cotton merchants turned to supply-
ing the more lucrative market in England as the American
Civil War had disrupted Manchester's traditional supplies.
Thereafter they were increasingly directed to the growing
Mexican textile industry which was dominated by French
and British capital. Women continued to weave for domestic
use but they had now to acquire manufactured yarn, yet
locally sources of cash were limited and barter was the
principal means of exchange. Although women could no
longer acquire cash or goods through selling their cotton
lengths, some village men had begun to take up seasonal wage
labouring in the expanding cotton plantations of the low-

lands. The plantations soon became known to be unhealthy (malaria was rife) and many villagers were reluctant to go there at the risk of their lives. Historians of this period note the great poverty of the *serranos* (people of the Sierra) and comment on the great numbers of men and women who came down during the slack agricultural months to Oaxaca City to beg (Iturribarria, 1955; Perez Garcia, 1956).

In the early 1870s, however, coffee cultivation was introduced by local political strongmen (*caciques*) into the hot region of the zone, and migration dwindled. The new crop was not grown on large-scale plantations (as in other parts of Mexico) but rather its cultivation was grafted on to the existing subsistence and petty commodity régime. It is not clear how willing the population was to accept the new crop. Perez Garcia suggests that there was some resistance which is apparent through the imposition of penalties in the form of fines imposed by the *caciques*. Each household used some of its land, particularly that near the village, for its coffee plots and both men and women were involved either in growing or harvesting the new crop. The staple, maize, was either relegated to slightly less favourable plots or the period of fallow was shortened.

Heads of households were not paid in cash for their coffee but in manufactured goods which included tools, soap and ornaments for the church. This was the result of a political alliance between the *caciques* and the coffee wholesalers (in effect there was only one) both of whom benefited from the large profits that could be made by procuring underpriced coffee beans for overpriced goods supplied, as well as from the state subsidies on coffee production, trade and export. The *caciques* themselves were men who initially became involved in the area as cotton traders providing such items as foodstuffs as well as other basic foodstuffs necessicities to nearby mining concessions. They had close connections with politically powerful people in the capital as well as loyal followings in the Sierra built up through patron-client ties and ties of fictive kinship (*compadrazgo*). Coffee produced as a petty commodity involved the traders in less risk, and production costs were kept low, the cost of the labour being borne by the household and its subsistence activities. At the same time households were placed in a competitive relation to each other as producers all serving a monopsonistic buyer, who could drive the price down by playing households off against each other and reward with better terms politically reliable households giving information on those working against the *caciques*, monopolistic control.

There appear to have been two main results of the introduction of coffee. At a zonal level the principal effect was the restructuring of economic flows: the non-coffee producing villages began to service the coffee producing ones, at first with muleteers who transported the coffee to the wholesalers' depots in the Valley of Oaxaca, and later with foodstuffs as their maize production dwindled. Second, at the village level, the immediate result of the alliance between merchant capital and the *caciques* meant that cash did not enter into productive relations to any great extent and there was thus little social upheaval within the communities in terms of differentiation on the basis of wealth. None the less, in the coffee zone, there was some illegal appropriation of land suitable for the new crop by those with political rather than economic power, generally the *cacique*'s henchmen. The selling of labour appeared on a small scale even though labourers were given goods or foodstuffs in return for their labour, not cash. Large-scale reciprocal labour exchanges between households, often within a village section, declined rapidly with the deepening of competition between households, and invididual households thus became more dependent on their own labour resources and more vulnerable to demographic hazards.

During and prior to this period the population of the area did expand rapidly. In Telana, a coffee producing village, the population grew between 1826 (the date of the Murgia y Galardi census) and 1883 (the date of the Martinez Gracida census) from 820 to 1,833 inhabitants. Unfortunately there is little hard data to go on as censuses were few and far between, and even their data are not always comparable. By 1900 the population again increased to 2,159. Copa Bitoo's population increased from 523 to 671 between the same dates, but between 1883 and 1910 it increased by 33 per cent, to 890. To what extent this increase can be accounted for by in-migration or by rising fertility rates is difficult to establish because of the poor census data. As far as Copa Bitoo is concerned, however, the increase was not due to in-migration.

Villagers remembered no tales of an influx of strangers into the village at this time and genealogical data would seem to confirm this. On the other hand baptisms for 1880 to 1910 do show a consistent decadal increase — from 215 to 360 to 416. It is worth noting that babies were frequently not baptised at birth, but only after they had survived the first two high-mortality months, so the increase may have come from a lowering of infant mortality, rather than increased birth rates *per se*.

Between 1910 and 1921 the population of the area declined as a result of the upheavals of the Revolution and its aftermath, particularly a flu epidemic in 1919. In fact the 1910 Revolution appears to have caused less disruption in the Sierra than a virtual civil war in Oaxaca itself, which lasted until 1925, between the supporters of foreign capital, primarily Spanish, French and British and their agents, and those in favour of the 'Mexicanisation' of the economy. In Mexico as a whole between 1920 and 1930 the power of local *caciques* was largely broken during internal struggles between factions of the Mexican bourgeoisie. This enabled the federal government by the 1930s to exercise greater control at the state level and opened the way for increased investment, primarily by US capital in Mexican industry. For the Sierra, the reorganisation of the state administrative apparatus made the area slightly less vulnerable to the domination of the old-style *caciques*, and the creation of a national banking system permitting freer access to credit by merchants inaugurated a new period of change.

This period was followed by an expansion of commerce. In the mid-1930s the barter economy of the Sierra, in which coffee and *ocote* (pitchpine) still served as media of exchange, was rapidly monetised as a result of the entry into the coffee trade of new investors, almost all of whom were Spaniards. These men were not constrained by the need to make alliances with local *caciques*, rather they entered the area with cash — silver pesos — and found the producers eager to trade with them. But not only was cash eagerly sought, so also were industrial products. Between 1938 and 1954 the world market price of coffee rose twenty-two-fold; as a consequence more householders in the hot zone dedicated more of their land to coffee, wage labouring became common as the land available for maize production declined or people preferred to work for cash and coffee growers' cash resources expanded. At roughly this same time the involvement of US industry in producing war goods for Europe gave the nascent Mexican industrial sector a boost because of both import substitution and production for the US market of certain consumer goods. The resumption of peace led to an aggressive expansion of commercial capital into the subsistence hinterlands of Mexico, in search of replacement markets to ensure the sale of goods from the still growing industrial sector. The Sierra was an obvious area for such expansion since its population was already involved in commodity production, and, especially after 1946 when coffee prices accelerated rapidly upwards, had the means to acquire industrial products. Both productive and consumption goods were in demand — tools, torches, kerosene lamps, hand-grinders, cloth, soap, beer, biscuits — many of which were more efficient and cheaper than local equivalents. The increased volume of trade made the archaic means of transport by mule trains no longer adequate; so commercial interests used their political power to push through the making of roads which lorries could use, using local, unpaid labour, to the principal coffee marketing villages. The first truck reached the chief coffee entrepôt village in 1952; by the end of the decade Telana was accessible by road and became in turn the premier entrepôt village, the former one now being characterised by bitter political strife and out-migration. By the mid-1960s Copa Bitoo had its own connecting branch road.

The immediate result of the intervention of commercial capital into the area was a blossoming of economic activity as people looked for ways to get cash income to meet their growing cash needs, or to take advantage of the new opportunities. The diversification led to increased women's involvement in extra-domestic activities but also to continued dependence on children's labour at a time when there was an expansion in schooling in the area. The population continued to soar: Telana from 1,223 to 3,126 between 1930 and 1960 and Copa Bitoo from 860 to 1,138 in the same period — although this last figure is artificially low because of heavy out-migration in the 1950s. While it is possible that some of the increase was due to declining mortality rates, particularly infant mortality, it should be noted that there had been no obvious improvements in standards of hygiene or supplies of medicines, and there were still no doctors or nurses permanently living in the area.

Once the roads were completed, the merchants were able to bring in ever larger quantities of consumption goods which further undermined local production and accelerated the restructuring of the local economy away from interzonal exchanges and self-provisioning. Many local trades — such as muleteering — vanished; production of locally exchangeable surpluses was made redundant by the truckers bringing in cheap foodstuffs produced under more highly capitalised conditions elsewhere or subsidised by the government. However, with the availability of rapid transport, some people were able to cultivate perishable fruits for the urban markets. The effects were thus uneven; while labour in some sectors was made redundant, in others more labour was required. In general, however, redundancy prevailed.

Once the growers had cash they also bought land, even though officially land was communally owned; land prices rose and a few of the richer families consolidated their control over the best cash cropping land. None the less holdings were not so unequal as in other areas of Mexico. A rapid process of differentiation divided the zonal population into, very crudely, a small number of people involved in the coffee business, either as producers on a commercial scale, traders or transporters; a small number of families without (coffee) land who worked as labourers; and a large number of families who both produced subsistence and a commodity, either agricultural or artisanate, on a small scale for the market.

The economic boom largely depended on the maintenance of high coffee prices, but in the mid-1950s they fell sharply. The result was that to maintain income levels people attempted to produce commodities in national demand, since many local trades had already disappeared through competition, or undertook seasonal migrant wage labouring. Thus, they began to feel the effects of fewer local opportunities, largely an effect of the intervention of commercial capital; they were in the process of being 'freed' for industrial capital.

After the slump in coffee prices in 1955, the increasing need to have cash to pay taxes, to acquire basic subsistence goods and labour, to pay for recently introduced services (electricity, running water, medical and postal services); the reduction in households' labour supply because children of both sexes between seven and fourteen were increasingly obliged to attend primary school; the constriction in the local economy — all led to the build-up of out-migration from the area. Increasing numbers of families found themselves in debt, in particular those who had lost their auxiliary livelihood, or who had little land and now depended on wage labouring. But the demand for labour was neither very great nor sustained — neither coffee nor avocados require a steady level of labour input throughout the year, maize production was declining (there being no market for local surpluses), and those who had hired labour were reverting to some extent to reciprocal labour exchange. In addition wages outside the zone were far higher than those offered within it. As a result both temporary/seasonal and permanent migration, relatively insignificant during the 1940s, augmented notably.

Initially the typical out-migrant was an unmarried person between ten and twenty-nine with girls providing the bulk of the youngest migrants, while adult men did seasonal migrant labouring. The disappearance from communities of a large proportion, sometimes as much as 70 per cent, of their young adults between fifteen and twenty-nine had repercussions on their productive capacity. Many individual households, no longer able to call upon the unpaid labour of their young adult members, had to rely more on cash to secure the labour they needed, yet ways of getting cash were limited. As a result, they were often forced to limit the amount of subsistence grown and to rely on selling labour to make up the deficit, but again local opportunities for employment were restricted. The result of these constraints was an increase in the absolute numbers of people leaving as well as a diversification of the migration pattern. By the 1970s people of all ages were leaving — married couples with or without children, elderly widows or widowers going to join their children, teenagers, unhappily married men and women. During the 1960s the out-migration rate was so high that the zone as a whole registered an absolute population decline by 1970.

I have specific details of the migration pattern only from Copa Bitoo (Young, 1976). There young girls were the principal victims of population redistribution: in the 1940s, 1950s and 1960s never less than 40 per cent of female migrants between ten and twenty-nine were under twenty years of age. The majority were under fifteen and had neither completed their schooling nor gained any specific skills. As a result they entered urban employment at the lowest level of pay and prospects, typically domestic service, with virtually no possibility of advancement or escape except through marriage, and even that for many is frequently little more than unpaid domestic service. Boys on the other hand tended to leave after completing primary schooling; in the 1940s, 1950s and 1960s only 28 per cent of male migrants between ten and twenty-nine were under twenty years of age. With primary education, they were eligible for some of the industrial employment possibilities open to males. Not only young people left, and migration was not necessarily long term: in fact every year a large proportion of the men of poorer families left the village on seasonal migration and others went for a year or so to the mines (often to earn a specific sum of money, sometimes to pay back a debt, redeem a piece of land or build a house). Of the total permanent as opposed to seasonal migration from Copa Bitoo between 1940 and 1970, 11 per cent took place in the first decade, 32 per cent in the second and 57 per cent in the third.

One of the effects of sex and age specific out-migration and school has been that many women are deprived of helpers in their domestic chores; mothers have to cope alone with the care of their young children, traditionally a task of older children, especially girls. Another is that women have had to take over many traditional children's tasks such as livestock grazing, fodder collecting, wood cutting, and some of those of men, too; weeding and mounding. Since many women have had to take on extra tasks, it might be thought that they would be eager to lessen their workload and perhaps primarily the burdens represented by motherhood and frequent childbirth. Girls do in fact now get married later than 30 years ago, now at around seventeen, then between eleven and twelve, but age at first birth may not in fact have changed greatly. Having a large family is still common, possibly because out-migration continually siphons off older children. The situation is both complex and contradictory: as a result, while many women are eager to know about modern contraceptive methods, others express the fear that the government is going to force them to have fewer children. It may be too soon to expect any significant decline in the birth rate, but the availability of modern medicines probably makes it more difficult for mothers to regulate family size by traditional methods of neglect, and at the same time contraceptives are not freely available.

I have indicated that during the period (1870–1970) a process of differentiation was taking place throughout the zone but at different rates. The 1955–70 period itself witnessed a dramatic restructuring of the economy away from zonal self-sufficiency towards integration with the national economy. Production in the area was directed to the national market and was dictated by the needs of that market. Constantly rising prices for manufactured goods, devaluations, as well as fluctuations in the price given for commodities, whether for export or for the national market, encouraged cultivators to diversify rather than specialise so as not to suffer hardship when prices fell. When profits were made, the larger coffee and avocado growers invested them in trade (and professional education for their children) while the smaller producers invested in expanding their capacity to produce for the market or diversifying into local marketing. Many families, however, failed and migrated, as did some of the very successful. While the principal effect of this restructuring has been the creation of a relative surplus population free to be drawn out of the area, at the same time within the area differences between families in terms of wealth, political power and size of land holdings became marked. Although the differentiation is less noticeable in Copa Bitoo than in Telana, the difference is more in degree than in kind, and I shall use Telana as my example. From this it follows that it is no longer possible to continue to talk of women as if they belonged to a homogeneous group or an undifferentiated category.

By 1975 differentiation in terms of wealth and land ownership was quite visible in Telana, that is, in the quality of housing, dress and diet of the families in the village. However, since the situation is highly complex and contradictory, and furthermore still changing, it is difficult to use terms such as class without falsifying the situation. The commonly used circumlocutions rich, middle and poor peasants I think obscure important structural differences between the categories which underlie the apparent differences in wealth. Thus I prefer to use the somewhat awkward classification of two categories but three strata: in the first category come two strata whose relationship was characterised by capitalist relations. In other words, those who employed labour both in agriculture, including coffee production, and in the home, whether permanently or temporarily, and those who provided such labour. These I shall call by the descriptive terms of *ricos* and *pobres* which correspond to local usage. In the second category come those families which owned land but neither employed nor provided labour regularly, but tended to use unremunerated familial labour or exchange labour. These I shall call *medios*. Some 20 per cent of families were in the *rico* category, 40 per cent in the *pobre* and the rest were *medios*.

Within the village — as within the area as a whole — there was a clearly defined sexual division of labour which anyone would describe without hesitation. Women do not work in the fields except at harvest or occasionally when their menfolk require a helping hand; they do collect water and wood, carry out all household maintenance tasks, care for children and the old, tend the family livestock and prepare food for eating. Men, on the other hand, do work in the fields but do not collect water or wood unless their womenfolk cannot for some reason, do not maintain the household on a day-to-day basis, nor do they cook or wash clothes. In fact, the women of each of the strata I have described were differently circumscribed in the work they carried out and had different employment or income earning opportunities available.

The *ricos* tended to own more coffee land than the majority, more than 5 hectares; many had occupations outside agriculture as well — they owned shops, trucks, bars, dressmaking enterprises or eating places. The women did no agricultural work, and at coffee harvest time organised the activities of the pickers rather than picking themselves. Many of them also worked in family enterprises, such as running a shop or mill; a few managed their own enterprise such as dressmaking, poultry keeping, or running a restaurant. As far as I could establish, women working in a family enterprise did not manage its finances but were consulted in most cases on important capital outlays, while women with independent enterprises did.

The *pobres* had no coffee land, many had no rights to subsistence land, others to very little (less than ½ hectare), and therefore had to rent land if they wished to produce any subsistence at all. Women worked both with their husbands in agriculture and independently as agricultural wage labourers for the wealthier families. Many had to work to repay debts contracted either when they had to borrow food to make ends meet during the hungry months, or when their husbands borrowed land against their wives' labour (in much demand at harvest). In addition to wage labouring in agriculture, poor women also took on paid chores for the *ricos* such as collecting wood, making tortillas and washing clothes. Without the women's financial contribution these poor families could not survive: their earnings were spent in buying basic necessities rather than on improving living standards. Wives were in charge of disbursements from household supplies, whether cash or foodstuffs, and therefore could, to some extent, restrain their husbands from squandering their small amounts of cash on alcohol, often at a cost of physical mistreatment. Some of the poorer men also worked on their own small plots which they had rented, or as labourers: but they did not have such a wide range of employment opportunities as the women because the sexual division of labour prohibited them from undertaking any domestic employment. Their wage earning opportunities mainly lay outside the village.

Almost all the *medios* grew some coffee, usually on holdings of under 5 hectares. Women did not work in the fields unless with their husbands or fathers — they provided unremunerated family labour; during the coffee harvest they worked as pickers, generally only on their household's land or that of their close kin. In some cases work for kinsmen was remunerated, in others it was reciprocated. *Medio* women appeared to be more constrained by the cultural requirement that married women should remain in the home and be entirely dependent on their husbands than women of the other two strata. Many

of them confessed to wanting to take up an occupation but
were forbidden to do so by their spouse. Roughly speaking
the younger the woman the more likely that she could only
undertake home based activities — as they got older and near
the menopause, some women did begin to take up independent economic activities which required a certain degree of
social visibility. *Medio* men also often had part-time specialisa-
tions such as carpentry, plumbing and housebuilding.

Economic roles thus differed according to the status of the
household: in part because some activities required initial
capital outlays, but in part social custom and the sexual
division of labour restricted the range of opportunities for
both men and women, but particularly for younger women.
Women who have fulfilled their maternal duties have more
time available for extra-domestic roles, but with the development of economic differentiation freedom from domestic
chores can also be bought.

If we were to ask, then, to what extent economic change
has bettered or worsened women's position, it would have to
be said that the situation is contradictory. In some ways
electricity, running water and so on have lightened women's
burdens; none the less while the richer women may work in
the family business, they are no longer as autonomous as their
weaver mothers. The poorer women today are clearly worse
off in that ever increasing poverty (amidst growing plenty
for others) can only be held at bay by increasing investment
of time and effort in poorly remunerated, labour intensive
jobs, many of which relieve the richer women of their household chores. Electricity and running water must also be paid
for, in cash, and these women whose mothers once enjoyed
the status of skilled workers (weavers) now have fallen to the
insecure status of non-skilled manual labourers. Their day has
become greatly extended as they struggle to cope with their
household tasks plus other economic activities which they
cannot organise to suit their own household schedule. They
have to bear the burden, in fact, of the double day. Better
off women can escape much of that burden: many in fact do
not have a second occupation, but those who do can afford
to offload some of their household chores onto other women.
Medio women are not exempt from the burden of the double
day, and many families with several young children depend

rather heavily on the wife taking on an additional remunerative occupation. The men's resistance to 'their woman' working outside the home in fact forces many of them to take up jobs at home which are not as profitable as less restricted ones. The double day does begin to tell during the coffee harvest which lasts up to three months, when *medio* women may work anything up to a seventeen-hour day; picking coffee for eight hours in addition to daily household chores plus helping with washing, depulping, drying and sorting the coffee beans.

For the poor women the double day is a reality most of the year through. They get up earlier than the *medios* and the *ricos* and their own menfolk so as to get some of their housework completed before going to work in the fields or taking on servicing tasks for the *ricos*, the most onerous of which is probably collecting wood. Many of them have to carry their youngest child round with them during the day for the two to three years that they breastfeed. In the coffee season when the majority of poor women hope to make enough money to cover the bulk of their annual outlay on staples and other necessities, the length of their working day frequently exceeds seventeen hours. Poor women often show signs of extreme physical exhaustion, especially in the child bearing and lactation years — they are prematurely aged, have few teeth and complain of back troubles from having to carry heavy loads of wood plus a nursing child. For this proletarian stratum, the transition to a class society has brought few benefits, for the women are not only over-worked but also socially disprized. Decent women don't work in the fields.

I have already emphasised that the poorer families in Telana are dependent on the women taking on wage labouring jobs — domestic or agricultural — throughout most of the year. I do not mean to suggest that such jobs are permanent or always available but rather that the women accept waged work whenever they can. The pay they receive is minimal: although men's rates are also well below the government established minimum, women's rates are between 40 and 60 per cent lower than men's. Even during the coffee harvest when women's labour is absolutely essential to the growers, for they are the pickers *par excellence*, their wages are lower:

in 1975, fifteen pesos a day as against twenty pesos for men. At other times of the year women were paid from five to ten pesos a day for agricultural work for which men were paid fifteen. Thus women were faced with the paradoxical situation that in order to earn the cash their family so badly needed, they had to work twice as long as a man — two days for a man's one. Domestic wage rates were also minimal and often women worked for piece rates which brought in an hourly return of only a few centavos.

There is another area in which the rights of men and women are markedly different: men can, and do, spend the product of their labours (and that of their wives) on a variety of personal consumption activities such as drinking, smoking, keeping two families and so on. In fact on any holiday or market day men could generally be found drinking in the bars with their male friends and relatives, while their women-folk were busying themselves with domestic chores or marketing. Alcohol dependence among men is high in the Sierra (as it is throughout Mexico) and a considerable proportion of a household's budget may be spent on drink. Women who protest are frequently met with verbal, if not physical, violence. In most of the Sierra it is not considered seemly for women to drink in public and few smoke; the socially approved of range of goods on which women may spend their earnings seems quite circumscribed — typically household consumption goods, or goods which enable them to be more productive, such as sewing machines. Few women wear jewellery but when bought it serves the function of a store of wealth rather than a means of beautification: it is frequently pawned to help out in a sudden cash crisis, and is in no way considered to be the exclusive possession of the woman herself.

I have previously made the point that economic changes in this area have transformed what was a relatively undifferentiated society based on a form of communal ownership of land, on exchange of labour between kin and neighbours and on non-productive investment of the surplus, to a stratified society based on private appropriation of land and other resources, and use of wage labour. Although there are variations in the degree to which individual communities are differentiated, the tendency is the same throughout the Sierra and reflects the increasing social division of labour in society.

At the same time it reflects the social transformations brought about by the intervention of two types of capital. I have argued that in the first period an alliance between merchant capital and local *caciques* ensured the production of a commodity for the international market. The mode of appropriation of surplus labour was not, however, through the buying and selling of labour, but through the political control over the product of labour. I have suggested that the substitution of coffee for cotton cloth weaving enabled the local populace to command the same sorts of goods that they had through the 'free' marketing of cotton cloth, and removed the necessity for seasonal migration. However, the new crop brought fundamental changes to women's lives which, I would argue, exacerbated their dependence on and subordination to their menfolk.

First, the labour process was completely altered and women could no longer organise their own work schedules so that household and other tasks could be neatly integrated. The disappearance of the domestic manufacture of cloth freed women from a time consuming activity, but it was replaced by coffee picking, in the hot zone. This crop depends on intensive inputs of female labour during a third of the year which, in restructuring women's annual rhythm, made child and house care more burdensome. In the non-coffee zone, the weavers were not able to invest their labour in extra-domestic economic roles, and in losing their ability to make a visible contribution to the household maintenance, they lost personal and public esteem.

Second, women's relation to the familial unit was changed: they lost their control over a vital input into the household budget. As weavers they controlled not only the labour process but also the proceeds of their work; as coffee pickers on the household plot their labour was unremunerated. Women who once enjoyed the status of skilled craftsmen fell to the insecure status of non-skilled manual labourers. The cash or goods paid for the coffee went to the person who initiated the labour process and controlled the land — the man; distribution of the proceeds was then made according to the prevailing cultural patterns of expenditure. I have suggested that, at least today, these patterns are different for men and women, and that there are no grounds for the common assumption that the familial budget is shared equally among all members of the family.

Third, I suggested that during this period households came to have to rely to a greater extent than previously on their own labour resources, thanks to the rapid contraction of reciprocal labour arrangements as well as the increased labour requirements and increasing competition between households. As a result more emphasis was given to women's generative capacities. Most of the labour involved in producing and maintaining more children falls upon women and I suggest that specialisation in reproduction inhibited them from taking up other available activities and increased their dependence on men. Although changes were made in the structure of village government after the Revolution, at least in this area women were given no roles within it, and were excluded from voting in village elections (as they are today) on the grounds that their place is in the home with the children.

The increased size of individual families, while beneficial for them (cf. Folbre, 1976; White, 1976), had, at the community level, quite harmful consequences — increased human pressure on non-expanding resources. This potential 'surplus' population was set free during the period of activity of the second type of capital mentioned. Commercial/circulation capital not only helped to create the relative surplus population, it augmented the speed of social differentiation on the basis of command over resources. One sector of the population became proletarianised and became wage labourers, and another developed into petty capitalist farmers producing mainly for the market but also hedging their bets by investing in trade.

For women the consequences of the development of capitalist relations have been quite contradictory. For those families with virtally no land, women's investment of their labour in labour intensive, poorly remunerated work in both the self-provisioning or subsistance sector and the commodity sector is absolutely essential for their survival. Women of this stratum are less dependent upon their husbands economically, and both men and women have little formal political power. None the less the men are enabled to borrow land against their wife's labour, or to ask for credit against it, and in this illegal proceeding they are given every support by men of other strata who do wield more formal political power — in other words those men who take positions in the village government. Again, the women's very active participation in the economic life of the village, which involves their increased social visibility, is not rewarded by a high degree of social esteem, but rather the reverse. The cultural prescription that a woman's place is the home ensures that those who have to work outside it to maintain it in existence derive no social benefit from their work.

Richer women in turn have been able to slough off many of the unrewarding tasks which go under the rubric of 'women's work' so as to enter into more managerial roles. These roles are generally associated with males and are prestigious because they conform to the valuation of mental, as against manual, work.

The women of the self-provisioning stratum are, unlike their counterparts of the other two strata, firmly enclosed within their domestic roles, and dependent upon their husbands not only for economic well-being but also their social status. Having lost the autonomy of their weaver grandmothers, they appear to be more firmly categorised as domestic slaves. None the less their contribution to the local economy is an important one, though it is submerged within the category of unremunerated familial labour. Without the labour of these women in the coffee harvest, these small-scale coffee producing families would not be able to produce. If low-cost coffee were to disappear, the Mexican economy would lose one of its principal exports and with it essential foreign currency. Yet these families are particularly at risk of losing their fragile self-provisioning status as economic forces constantly undermine their viability. It is these households which are in keen competition for scarce land and other social resources, thus the degree of mutual aid between them is slight, women's solidarity and co-operation with non-kin is equally slight, and interfamilial rivalry and strife is not infrequent.

Throughout Mexico this sector of the rural populace (and it probably represents about 50 per cent of the population of these partly self-provisioning areas) presents a serious political challenge to the government. If capital is allowed to undermine it further, to increase the rate of differentiation, an even greater flight to the cities will be provoked than has already occurred, and Mexico has one of the world's highest rural–urban migration rates. Pressure on the already strained urban resources, especially of Mexico City (which is not only the capital but the seat of government), may easily lead to an explosive social and political situation. To prevent this, the state, so as to maintain these families on the land, must intervene through a number of policies, including land reform, subsidised food stores, minimum guaranteed price for coffee, systems of credit, agricultural extension training, increasing educational facilities, augmenting investment in infrastructure – for example building roads, putting in electricity or running water. In part such intervention merely serves to facilitate the penetration of capital, but it also increases each household's cash requirements. The state must also make sure that women are maintained in their domestic roles, for without their hard work and unremunerated labour these families cannot survive, but at the same time it must discourage too abundant fertility, even though the household's survival may depend on a large amount of cheap unremunerated familial labour. So although the state may be pledged officially to helping women achieve equality with men, economic and political considerations make its stance highly ambivalent.

This ambivalence is echoed in the relations between men and women in the Sierra. Men will express the conviction that the women of the coffee zone are extremely hardworking and that without their help a man can never get ahead (*sin la ayuda de la mujer el hombre nunca se avanza*); none the less women are seen as dependents and as such deprived by the men of political and jural status. Furthermore there is strong resistance to women working as independent agents, outside the home. While the richer woman may run a familial business, remaining perhaps in the shop while the man goes out to oversee the hired labourers in the fields, a woman should not be an independent trader and thus socially visible. Again I have noted that the *medio* women often had to take on income earning employment, but within the home, which brought a lower return than other, more visible, work outside it. This taboo against women's independence underlies the lower wages that they receive: since women are not supposed to work or to support a family, their wage is considered to be additional to that of the man upon whom they depend, whether it is husband or father. In effect the taboo maintains such a dependence whether the woman is married or single, divorced or widowed. Furthermore it penalises those women who are the sole providers for their families whether they be single mothers, divorced or widowed women.

Older women do have more freedom to develop a degree of autonomy — they can develop their commercial capacities and be seen to be economically active. I would argue that this is a consequence of a male household head's need to ensure the production of a labour force adequate to his political and economic activities: once 'his' woman has done her duty in providing him with children, the degree of his control over her activities lessens. Clearly if the intervention of merchant capital and circulation capital has exacerbated inter-household competition such that each married couple is now more dependent on producing the labour it needs, then the position of all women must have deteriorated at least in this respect.

The sexual division of labour of the 'traditional' society has begun changing throughout the period; today socioeconomic status is as important a variable as sex in determining the division of labour. Thus women's extra-domestic occupations are largely correlated to the position of the household within the community. None the less women have not escaped from sex hierarchy, rather this has been replicated in the developing capitalist relations. I have tried to show that this is not merely a case of the perpetuation of the ideological system, but rather of women in this part of the world being more firmly locked into domestic and reproductive roles as a consequence of the type of economic change that has been fostered, and at the same time being compelled to enter into productive roles within a system which is based on the appropriation of a surplus through the buying and selling of labour. Their labour can thus be devalued both because of their 'real' role — that of mother and wife — and because that role itself places constraints on the type of work that they can in fact undertake.

Acknowledgements

In the introduction I indicated that my approach is limited and that much work remains to be done; I only hope that this article will stimulate some people to refine the concepts and ideas in it. Meanwhile I should like to thank Lourdes Arizpe, Carmen Diana Deere, Felicity Edholm, Diane Elson, Olivia Harris, Maxine Molyneux and Ingrid Palmer for their careful reading of preliminary drafts and their helpful and detailed comments.

References

Brown, J. (1970), 'A note on the division of labour by sex', *American Anthropologist*, vol. 72, pp. 1073—8.

Draper, P. (1975), 'Kung women: contrasts in sexual egalitarianism in foraging and sedentary contexts' in R. R. Reiter, *Toward an Anthropology of Women*, Monthly Review Press, New York.

Edholm, F., Harris, O., and Young K. (1977), 'Conceptualizing women', *Critique of Anthropology*, no. 9/10, pp. 101—30.

Folbre, N. (1976), 'Population growth and capitalist development', paper presented at the Annual Meeting of the Population Association of America.

Friedl, E. (1975), *Women and Men: an Anthropologist's View*, Holt, Rinehart and Winston, New York.

Iturribarria, J. F. (1955), *Oaxaca en la Historia*, Mexico.

Kay, G. (1975), *Development and Underdevelopment*, Faber, London.

Marx, K. (1970a), *Capital*, vol. I, Lawrence & Wishart, London.

Marx, K. (1970b), *Capital*, vol. III, Lawrence & Wishart, London.

Perez Garcia, F. (1956), *La Sierra Juarex*, Mexico.

White B. (1973), 'Demand for labour and population growth in colonial Java', *Human Ecology*, vol. 1, pp. 217—39.

White B. (1976), 'Production and reproduction in a Javanese village', unpublished Ph.D. thesis, Columbia University, New York.

Young, K. (1976), 'The social setting of migration', unpublished Ph.D. thesis, London University.

7 Women and production: a critical analysis of some sociological theories of women's work

Veronica Beechey

Within the framework of sociological discussion, feminist writing has struggled to bring to the fore descriptions of the conditions of women in relation to the occupational structure. To this extent it has been relatively successful, but much work has been located within an epistemology whose inadequacies have become increasingly evident. Veronica Beechey has provided, in a long-overdue exercise, a critique of this situation. Her starting-point is an analysis of Parsonian functionalism, on the grounds that in its theorizing on the family, it places women firmly within the family structure and ignores their role in the labour force (a point which is also taken up in Jackie West's paper). Anything other than their 'primary' task in maintaining the stability of the family and in this way contributing to the overall stability of society can, in Parsonian terms, be considered only as subsidiary. This has become part of conventional sociological wisdom and has been appropriated in an *ad hoc* manner, the extent of the influence of functionalism not always being fully recognized: for example, sociological work which has attempted to describe and analyse the role of women in the labour force in terms of their 'dual role' effectively adopts the terms of the functionalist problematic, and in particular ignores 'the economic role of female wage and domestic labour', the specificity of which is also unrecognized in the 'dual labour market' approach exemplified by the work of Barron and Norris. While a number of feminist writers had rejected the functionalist approach and its variants, no systematic alternative scheme such as that offered by Veronica Beechey had yet been published at the time when this paper first appeared. The arguments presented here were first given at a seminar of the Sexual Divisions and Society Study Group of the British Sociological Association in the summer of 1976, and they have subsequently been widely discussed. In confronting the issues that she has, the author has come to grips with many of the problems that had been the focus of attention, and the analysis put forward here is of direct relevance to other work which aims at the construction of a marxist feminism. The arguments about the position of women in the labour process are by no means devoid of controversy: one of the issues which will undoubtedly be taken up, for example, is the consistent observation that women wage workers are lower paid than men, and how this is to be explained. Here the argument is that women's wage rates are lower than the cost of reproduction of their own labour power, a phenomenon which is attributed to the family institution. Against this it may be argued that there is no absolute cost of reproduction of labour power. Any such arguments clearly hinge on the way in which value is to be considered, a question which will certainly be taken up in future work.

Despite the emergence of important new areas of theoretical discussion within the women's liberation movement, such as analyses of domestic labour and the concept of patriarchy, and despite the substantial growth of research by feminist historians into the history of women, relatively little attention has been paid to the problems involved in analysing the position of female wage labour in the capitalist mode of production.[1] In attempting to understand the material basis of women's position in the family at the same time as countering the view — certainly common within sociology — that women's position in the family is definable in cultural terms marxist feminists have tended to concentrate their work on the question of domestic labour and its productivity. One result of this concentration has been that the analysis of domestic labour has become isolated from the analysis of female wage labour, which has itself not been the subject of very much theoretical discussion either within the women's movement or within marxist theory.[2]

My purpose here is to discuss some of the problems involved in analysing female wage labour, through developing a critique of a number of approaches to the question; and the paper is divided into four sections. The first is a discussion of the conceptual framework for analysing the family which has been developed by Talcott Parsons. This constitutes the classic sociological analysis of the family, and provides the foundation for most subsequent sociological work on the family and the position of women. This is followed in the second section by a discussion of empirical studies of 'women's two roles' which have been developed within British sociology, and which combine a modified structural functionalist framework with empirical research on working women and the family structure. The third section considers the conception of a dual labour market which has been developed within economics as a radical critique of neoclassical economics and which Barron and Norris (1974)[3] have utilised to analyse the occupational position of women. The last section of the paper discusses albeit schematically, some of the problems which are raised for a marxist feminist analysis of female wage labour by Marx's analysis in *Capital*.[4]

The arguments which I attempt to develop in the course of this paper can be summarised as follows. First, I suggest that the domination of the structural functionalist problematic within sociology has led sociologists to divorce the family from an analysis of the forces and relations of production which are in capitalist societies class relations, and to underestimate the importance of both forms of female labour, domestic labour and wage labour. Furthermore, when empirical sociological studies have considered working women, they have reduced the question of the contradiction between women's position in the family and female wage labour to a subjective tension between two roles, which are defined in terms of different sets of normative expectations. While these sociological studies provide a great deal of valuable information (such as which women work, when in their life cycles they work, the problems they face when they work), they do not provide any analysis of the distribution of female labour among particular occupations and industries, nor do they consider the functions of the normative expectations they describe for the maintenance of the sexual division of labour or for the reproduction of the mode of production. More fundamentally, they fail to consider the ways in which the labour process structures the organisation of work in the capitalist mode of production and the relationship between the sexual division of labour and the labour process.

Theories of the dual labour market, in contrast, focus upon the fact that when they work, women are concentrated in unskilled, low-paid, insecure jobs in a secondary labour market, and locate the subordination of women in an analysis of the dynamics of the labour market, specifically its segmentation into primary and secondary sectors. Although the general thrust of these theories has been important in emphasising that the position of women results from discrimination within the labour market, I suggest that the dual labour market approach tends to be static and ahistorical, providing a loose classification rather than an explanation of the ways in which the labour process structures the organisation of work in particular historical circumstances; and further, that it fails to analyse the specificity of women's position because it ignores the importance of the sexual division of labour and the role of the family in structuring sexual inequality.

In the final section I put forward a schematic examination of Marx's analysis of the labour process and of the industrial reserve army as they are developed in the first volume of *Capital*, and suggest that these aspects of Marx's analysis of wage labour in the capitalist mode of production provide the basis upon which an analysis of female wage labour can be built. I argue, however, that Marx is unable to provide an adequate explanation of the specificity of female labour since his work lacks a theory of the family and the sexual division of labour, and hence cannot address the ways in which patriarchal ideology functions to reproduce the sexual division of labour within the capitalist mode of production. Marx is thus unable to relate his analysis of the forms of the labour process to an analysis of the sexual division of labour. It is a pressing task for feminists to integrate a feminist analysis of the sexual division of labour with a marxist analysis of the labour process, re-reading theorists such as Marx and asking specifically feminist questions. This paper comprises a very preliminary attempt to specify some of those questions.

I

In considering those aspects of Talcott Parsons's theory

which have been important in providing a framework for empirical sociological studies of the family and the differentiation of sex roles, I do not attempt to provide a comprehensive overview or critique of Parsons's work, but rather will refer to relevant and representative sections of that work. In *Essays in Sociological Theory* (1954) Parsons examines the relationship between the kinship system and the wider society, locating his analysis within a discussion of the problems involved in determining class status, which he defines as 'the status of any given individual in the system of stratification in a society may be regarded as a resultant of the common valuations underlying the attribution of status to him in each of . . . six respects' (Parsons, 1954, p. 76) — membership in a kinship unit, personal qualities, achievements, possessions, authority and power. Parsons focuses on the ascription of status through membership in a kinship unit, and the achievement of status through position in the occupational structure. Although he is inconsistent in that at times he regards kinship as the primary determinant of social status while at others occupational position is presented as determinant, the overall thrust of Parsons's argument suggests that the dominant patterning of the occupational system in an industrial society requires a high degree of social mobility and equality of opportunity in order that individuals can attain their 'natural levels' within the occupational structure:

> We determine status very largely on the basis of achievement within an occupational system which is in turn organised primarily in terms of universalistic criteria of performance and status within functionally specialised fields. This dominant pattern of the occupational sphere requires at least a relatively high degree of 'equality of opportunity' which in turn means that status cannot be determined primarily by birth or membership in kinship units (pp. 78–9).

However, Parsons continues, such an occupational system coexists with a strong institutional emphasis on the ties of kinship since 'the values associated with the family, notably the marriage bond and the parent–child relationship, are among the most strongly emphasized in our society' (p. 79). This suggests a contradictory relationship between the occupational system and the kinship system which is a potential source of disharmony. However, Parsons argues that this contradictory relationship has been largely resolved within the industrial societies, since the family has developed in such a way as to minimise the strain between the kinship system and the occupational system:

> The conjugal family with dependent children, which is the dominant unit in our society, is, of all types of kinship unit, the one which is probably the least exposed to strain and possible breaking-up by the dispersion of its members both geographically and with respect to stratification in the modern type of occupational hierarchy (p. 79).

This is because it has developed an internal structure which is adapted to the functional requirements of the occupational system.

The key to this internal structure lies in the segregation of sex roles. For, Parsons argues, if all members of the family were equally involved in competition within the occupational structure, there might be a very serious strain on the solidarity of the family unit. Thus a segregation of sex roles has emerged to ensure that their respective incumbents do not come into competition with each other. Parsons defines this sex role differentiation, which corresponds to the differentiation of family and economy in industrial societies in *Family: Socialization and Interaction Process* (Parsons and Bales, 1956), in terms of a structural differentiation between instrumental and expressive roles. The instrumental role involves goal attainment and adaptation and is basically concerned with the relationship between the family and the wider society, while the expressive role involves integration and is defined in terms of the internal structure and functions of the family. Parsons's analysis of the structural differentiation of sex roles is underpinned by the evidence from Bales's analysis of small groups, from which it is argued that there exists a tendency for all small groups to be structurally differentiated so that some persons take on leadership roles while others take on subordinate roles. For Parsons the conjugal family is no exception. While it is in principle possible for either men or women to hold expressive or instrumental roles, Parsons argues that men fulfil instrumental ones while women fulfil expressive ones. The reason he gives is that women are involved in the bearing and early nursing of children, and are therefore best adapted to performing internal expressive roles, while the absence of men from these activities makes them best adapted to instrumental ones. Since the tension between the kinship system and the occupational system requires a clear segregation of sex roles, the man is ascribed the instrumental role while the woman is removed from competition within the occupational system by her confinement within the family.

Since Parsons's definition of class status is defined in terms of social evaluations and since sex roles are defined in normative terms, it follows that his analysis precludes consideration of economic factors. Thus the woman's role in the family is portrayed in cultural terms, and the question of the economic role of the woman's domestic labour which has been emphasised by many feminist writers is ruled out by a theoretical sleight of hand. This has led Middleton to state that 'in academic sociology the view that female activity in the home is essentially cultural has often been associated with a denial of the proposition that women to in fact constitute a subordinate group at all' (1974, p. 180). Although the fact that women work outside the home is acknowledged by Parsons, the economic implication of women's wage labour is ignored, since the role of women continues to be defined in expressive terms. This is because, according to Parsons, the number of women in the labour force with young children is small and is not increasing, and the kind of job which the woman does 'tends to be of a qualitatively different type and not a status which serious competes with that of her husband as the primary status-giver or income-earner' (Parsons and Bales, 1956, p. 14). He can therefore conclude that

It seems quite safe in general to say that the adult feminine role has not ceased to be anchored primarily in the internal affairs of the family, as wife, mother and manager of the household, while the role of the adult male is primarily anchored in the occupational world, in his job and through it by his status-giving and income-earning functions for the family. Even if, as seems possible, it should come about that the average married women had some kind of job, it

seems most unlikely that this relative balance would be
upset; that either the roles would be reversed, or their
qualitative differentiation in these respects completely
erased (Parsons and Bales, 1956, pp. 14—15).

Parsons is aware in *Essays in Sociological Theory* that such
sex role segregation presents problems for the egalitarian
system of values within American society. Even though
women's status is evaluated on a different basis from men's,
however, Parsons insists that the status of women is equal to
that of men. He states, somewhat ambivalently, in his essay
'An analytical approach to the theory of stratification' that
members of kinship groups are

> in certain respects treated as 'equals' regardless of the fact
> that by definition they must differ in sex and age, and very
> generally do in other qualities, and in achievements, author-
> ity and possessions. Even though for these latter reasons
> they are differently valued to a high degree, that is still an
> element of status which they share equally and in respect
> of which the only differentiation tolerated is that involved
> in the socially approved differences of the sex and age
> status (Parsons, 1954, p. 77).

He furthermore argues that the marriage pattern is a relationship of equals, and does not involve structural superordination
and subordination, because the wife's status is ascribed on
the basis of her husband's, which in turn derives from his
occupational position: 'in a system not resembling the caste
type, husband and wife need not be rigidly equal by birth,
although they *become* so by marriage' (p. 78, my emphasis).
Thus inequalities between men and women disappear, for
Parsons, because the woman's social status is ascribed on the
basis of her husband's. The married woman, by definition,
has an equal social status to her husband. In his 'A revised
analytical approach to the theory of social stratification',
Parsons does in fact recognise more explicitly the contradiction between the dominant egalitarian values and sex role
segregation, and ultimately accepts some degree of inequality
as being functionally necessary:

> it follows that the preservation of a functioning family
> system even of our type is incompatible with complete

equality of opportunity. It is a basic limitation on the full implementation of our paramount value system, which is attributable to its conflict with the functional exigencies of personality and cultural stabilization and socialization (1954, p. 422).

Parsons recognises that such a situation is unstable, since the wife is denied any occupational definition of her role, and suggests that the housewife may try to modify the domestic role by adopting what he describes as the 'glamour pattern' (which attempts to emphasise feminine values), or the 'common humanistic element' (emphasising 'civilised' values), instead of adhering to domestic values in defining her status. Parsons's version of the feminine dilemma is described as follows:

> In our society, . . . occupational status has tremendous weight in the scale of prestige values. The fact that the normal married woman is debarred from testing or demonstrating her fundamental equality with her husband in competitive occupational achievement creates a demand for a functional equivalent. At least in the middle classes, however, this cannot be found in the utilitarian functions of the role of housewife since these are treated as relatively menial functions . . . it may be concluded that the feminine role is a conspicuous focus of the strains inherent in our social structure, and not the least of the sources of these strains is to be found in the functional difficulties in the integration of our kinship system with the rest of the social structure (1954, pp. 193–4).

In *Family: Socialization and Interaction Process* (Parsons and Bales, 1956) this analysis had undergone a number of modifications, several of which are of relevance to the present discussion. First, in his essay on 'The American family: its relations to personality and to the social structure', Parsons adds an evolutionary component, arguing that the family has become more specialised as a result of industrialisation, having lost some of the functions which it used to exercise on behalf of society, such as its role as a unit of economic production, its significance in the political power system, and its functions as a direct agency of integration within the wider society, while gaining new functions on behalf of personality (namely as an agency for the primary socialisation of children, and for the stabilisation of adult personalities). A second modification is discernible in his more clearly developed theory of socialisation, which draws heavily from psycho-analytic insights: in contrast with the earlier *Essays* in which the social differentiation of sex roles is located in an analysis of the contradictory tensions between the occupational system and the kinship system, Parsons argues in *Family: Socialization and Interaction Process* that it is primarily on account of the socialisation functions of the family that there is a social, as distinct from a purely reproductive, differentiation of sex roles. One consequence of this increased emphasis on socialisation is that the tensions between the occupational system and the kinship system and the resulting strains on the woman's role which Parsons discusses in the *Essays* assume a lesser importance. He is no longer concerned primarily with the structural sources of tension which would be dysfunctional for the social system, but with equilibrating processes, the most important of which, so far as the family is concerned, is socialisation. Parsons appears not only to regard socialisation as the principal function of the nuclear family, but also to regard the isolated nuclear family as the social institution which is best adapted to the socialisation process, as this quotation from *The Social System* suggests:

> The important point is the near universality of the limita-tion of variability to such narrow limits both with respect to function and to structural type. Why is not initial status-ascription made on the basis of an assessment of individual organic and personality traits? Why is not all child care and responsibility sometimes placed in the hands of specialised organs just as formal education is? Why is not the regulation of sexual relations divorced from res-ponsibility for child care and status ascription? Why are kinship units not patterned like industrial organisations? It is, of course, by no means excluded that fundamental changes in any or all of these respects may sometimes come about. But the fact that they have not yet done so in spite of the very wide variability of known social systems in other respects is none the less a fact of considerable importance (quoted in Morgan, 1975, p. 35).

The explanation Parsons offers for the apparent universality of the nuclear family is threefold. First, it is an adaptive response to the functional prerequisities of tension management and pattern maintenance. Second, it is best adapted to fulfil the psychoanalytically defined needs of the individual in the process of socialisation. And third, it results from the biological fact that women bear and nurse children. Thus both the structure of the nuclear family and the sex role divisions within it, within Parsons's analysis, are overdetermined by a combination of social, psychological and biological elements.

What I am suggesting, then, is that in *Essays in Sociological Theory* Parsons places the position of women within an analysis of the contradictory demands of the occupational system and the kinship system in industrial societies; and I have criticised this mode of conceptualisation for its concentration upon evaluative and normative factors, a preoccupation which has led Parsons to ignore the economic role of women within the home as domestic labourers and also to ignore the significance of women's wage labour. Parsons's conceptual framework necessarily excludes the possibility of any analysis of the sources of sexual inequality which locate it in terms of the organisation of the capitalist mode of production. In the next section I shall discuss the conceptual framework which has been developed by sociologists to analyse 'women's two roles', and here I argue that empirical sociological studies have adopted some of Parsons's major assumptions in an *ad hoc* way, but that whereas Parsons's analysis contains a theory of the functions of the family and of sex role differentiation for the maintenance of society as a whole, empirical sociological studies have reduced Parsons's analysis of sex roles to a descriptive level. Sex roles, defined in terms of different sets of normative expectations, are taken as given. These empirical studies thus reduce the 'feminine dilemma' to a subjective tension between two normatively defined roles, those of housewife and mother, and thereby fail to provide any analysis of female labour, paid and unpaid, in relation to the occupational structure.

II

There has emerged in postwar Britain a fairly coherent body

of sociological studies which have been concerned with
married women working, and with the implications of this
for relationships within the family. The pioneer study, Myrdal
and Klein's *Women's Two Roles*, first appeared in 1956. This
has been followed by other similar studies (such as Klein's
Britain's Married Women Workers (1965) and Yudkin and
Holme's *Working Mothers and Their Children* (1969)), some
of which — for example Fogarty, Rapoport and Rapoport's
Sex, Career and Family (1971) — have restricted themselves
to women engaged in professional occupations. Other studies
have considered the impact of women working on the structure of the family (Rapoport and Rapoport's *Dual Career
Families* (1971) and Young and Willmott's *The Symmetrical
Family* (1975)). Most of these investigations have been policy
oriented — written with the objectives of investigating barriers
against women working, of influencing social policies which
would make it easier for women to work (policies concerning
nursery provision, maternity leave and so on) and advocating
the reorganisation of working in order that women's labour
can increasingly be drawn upon, (for example, by developing
more flexible hours of work, part-time work). Recognising
the shortage of labour which existed during the postwar
period in Britain, the studies have shared the assumption
that married women are an important source of labour at all
levels of the occupational structure, and have investigated
the social characteristics of women who work, when in their
life cycles they work, what problems they face when they
work and so on, amassing a considerable amount of evidence
on these questions. I am not concerned with their particular
empirical findings here, but rather with an examination of
the theoretical framework within which these studies have
been undertaken, and I shall attempt to show how their focus
upon what economists call the 'supply' of labour has led
them to ignore some important questions concerned with the
structuring of women's employment.

These studies have accepted elements of Parsons's functionalist framework, but in an *ad hoc* way, and since they are
formulated as empirical studies their functionalist assumptions
are not always explicit. Such assumptions become evident,
however, in the central place occupied in these analyses by
the concept of sex roles: the position of both men and

women within the social structure is defined in terms of the
social expectations of a person holding a particular role,
social positions being defined in normative terms. While these
studies share with Parsons a notion of sex roles understood in
terms of normative expectations, they lack the macrosocio-
logical analysis which Parsons provides, in his early *Essays*, of
the tensions between the demands of the occupational system
and the kinship system in industrial societies. Thus, instead
of providing an analysis of tensions whose roots are located
at a societal level, the empirical studies locate tensions for the
individual women as resulting from the existence of different
sets of normative expectations. The basis of women's social
position is therefore defined, as in the title of Myrdal and
Klein's book, precisely as a tension between two roles, housewife and worker, a tension which does lead the authors to
speak of a 'feminine dilemma' determined by the 'typical'
conflicts which women subjectively experience between their
career and familial roles. No analysis of the social/historical
foundations of these conflicts is provided.

Where these studies do depart from Parsons, however, is
in their recognition that many women go out to work, and
they furthermore advocate changes in social policies which
would make it easier for women to work outside the home,
especially when they do not have young children. Women's
position is therefore not defined in terms of the Parsonian
expressive-instrumental dichotomy, since the studies recognise that many women fulfil aspects of both roles. Klein
argues that 'the number of . . . social roles has . . . been increased and the forum on which they are enacted been
widened' (1965, p. 18). However, the studies do accept the
fundamental Parsonian functionalist thesis that industrialisation has modified the functions of the family by removing
production to factories, which employ individuals and not
families, and which supply goods and services outside the
home. And they agree with Parsons that the family, shorn of
many of its economic and educational functions, has been
left with two major functions: socialisation, and providing a
focal point for lasting affections. However, they then develop
what might be described as a reformulated functionalist
thesis, by which I mean a thesis that there has emerged in
postwar Britain, as a response to a demand for labour, a

further development involving the re-entry of women into
the world of work, and the subsequent combination of
family and work life. The effects of women performing 'two
roles', it is argued, may lead to the emergence of new forms
of family: the dual career family described by Rapoport and
Rapoport (1971), and the symmetrical family described by
Young and Willmott (1975). Thus Klein (1965), for example,
argues that there has been a tendency for the traditional
patriarchal family to be replaced by a new, more democratic
family form characterised by a relationship of partnership
between husband and wife, which among other things en-
courages the relative independence of children.

One of the problems with this reformulated functionalist
approach is that no adequate explanation of these changes is
offered. This point has in fact been made by Barron and
Norris in their paper, 'Sexual divisions and the dual labour
market':

> Sociologists who have looked at the position of women in
> the labour market have traditionally assumed the general
> subordination of women in the family and society and
> have then gone on to consider the factors underlying the
> decisions of women to participate in the labour market.
> Thus they have stressed the role conflicts that a working
> wife may experience, the importance of the household
> structure and the stage of the life cycle, and the family
> income position. In doing so, they have taken for granted,
> for example, the fact that men can go out to work without
> experiencing role conflicts (indeed, men will experience
> them if they stay at home) and that men will be considered
> the primary breadwinner. In other words, they have set
> aside some of the more important sociological puzzles
> by concentrating on the movement of women into and out
> of the labour force. By focussing attention on the crucial
> decision about labour force participation, they have to
> some extent diverted attention from the question of which
> jobs are filled by men and which jobs are filled by women
> — and more importantly, from the difficulty of explaining
> why it is that there are these pronounced differences be-
> tween men's and women's jobs (1974, pp. 1—2).

The change which these empirical studies document are

ascribed in twin sources: the impact of industrialisation and the normative march towards democracy. These factors, either alone or taken together, do not provide a satisfactory explanation, however. The studies first of all posit industrialisation as a kind of *deus ex machina*, without specifying which elements of industrialisation bring about particular changes. Capitalist industrialisation involves a process of uneven development, and the labour process is transformed in different ways in different branches of production. Thus some industries (for example, the sweated or domestic industries which arose as a consequence of the development of modern industry, forming an underbelly of the industrial revolution, and providing an extremely important locus of female labour) remain relatively labour intensive (Alexander, 1976), while others undergo rapid mechanisation (for example, first spinning and then weaving in textiles, the latter remaining an important area of women's employment in nineteenth-century Britain). An adequate explanation of the impact of industrialisation would require an analysis of the development of modern industry and the relationship between changes in the labour process and the employment of women in different branches of production. Likewise, any analysis couched in terms of the demand for labour would have to explain why in some conditions and not in others there is a demand for female labour (for example, in weaving, but in large numbers of mills not in spinning as industrialisation proceeded), and how this demand is related to the organisation of the labour process in particular industries as well as to the availability of other sources of labour. It is inadequate to postulate industrialisation *per se* as an explanatory factor without specifying which elements of the development of industrial capitalism bring about particular changes, and without showing how these changes affect the demand for female labour.

A second problem with these studies is that their analysis is founded on various taken-for-granted assumptions the bases of which themselves require explanation. Thus the increased employment of married women is ascribed by Klein to the expansion of administrative, education, welfare and other services, which she describes as 'the very types of work which women are thought to be particularly well fitted to perform'. Myrdal and Klein likewise provide no explanation of the re-establishment of pre-war conditions after the Second World War, but merely describe the closure of day nurseries and the cutting down of part-time jobs as part of the urge to go 'back to normal'. An adequate explanation of these phenomena, however, would have to consider why women are brought into employment in some conditions of labour scarcity — for example, during both world wars — to analyse the extent to which the sexual division of labour was modified under the impact of women working, and to examine its subsequent restructuring as after both wars women were excluded from employment in many industries and occupations. This would involve an analysis of a number of different levels: changes in the labour process, state policies, trade union agreements, values and beliefs around the family and women working. The authors of the empirical sociological studies are evidently aware of the importance of ideological factors in influencing the employment of women, but any such awareness tends to take the form of the kind of broad generalisations about the advance of progress, affluence and so on common in the postwar period in which they were writing. Thus Myrdal and Klein speak of the long march of social progress in the following terms:

> Social progress always proceeds at an unequal pace in diff-
> erent fields of human activities. It has, as a rule, followed
> roughly the same pattern, namely that new scientific inven-
> tions lead to technical advances which, in their turn, are
> followed by social adjustments and reorganization; changes
> in general attitudes and opinions usually bring up the rear.
> There is no reason to suppose that in the sphere of women's
> employment, which has been facilitated, and also made
> necessary, by contemporary technical developments, the
> succession of phases could be different or that prejudices
> should be allowed to block the road to social advance. . . .
> Attitudes and ideologies are gradually being brought into
> line with technical and social developments and tend to-
> wards greater participation of married women in the econ-
> omic, political, administrative and cultural activities of the
> community (1970, pp. 195—6).

A similar tone of optimism pervades Young and Willmott's

book, *The Symmetrical Family* (1975), in which the consequences of the increasing numbers of married women working
for the family structure are analysed. The authors argue that
there have been three stages in the development of the family,
from the pre-industrial family through the family of individual wage earners to the symmetrical family. In the symmetrical family, the former unity of husband and wife is restored
around the functions of consumption, the couple is privatised
and home centred, the nuclear family is more important than
the extended family and sex roles are less segregated. The
concept of the symmetrical family preserves the notion of
differentiated sex roles, on a 'separate but equal' basis. Young
and Willmott argue, on extremely flimsy evidence, that the
symmetrical family enjoys more equality since there is increased financial partnership, more work sharing (their criterion
for this being that men help with one task once a week!), and
men work less while women work more — hence the symmetry.
Thus 'a partnership in leisure has . . . succeeded a partnership
in work'. Like the Rapoports, Young and Willmott assume
that this new form of family, the harbinger of the future,
will be diffused from the middle to the lower classes. A major
problem with *The Symmetrical Family*, as with the optimistic
beliefs of Myrdal and Klein, is that it is based upon an article
of faith, upon a general optimistic belief in the long march
towards democracy which is presumed to emerge as a natural
outgrowth of a broad evolutionary process. Instead of taking
such optimistic beliefs as given, however, it is necessary to
explain why women were for so long excluded from the
extension of democratic rights, and to show how their gradual
inclusion within the body politic so far as legal and political
rights are concerned has resulted not from an evolutionary
process but from feminist struggle. Furthermore, it is important to explain why, even when some political and juridical
rights have been achieved, the economic position of women
has remained subordinated to that of men.

I have, in the preceding pages, suggested a number of
criticisms of empirical sociological studies of 'women's two
roles'. First, I have argued that they share the functionalist
preoccupation with normative expectations. One result of
this has been the obliteration of the economic role of female
wage labour and domestic labour; a further consequence has

been the pervasive optimistic belief in the long march of progress, which the studies accept as an article of faith. Second, I have suggested that the tensions which Parsons locates *structurally* within the organisation of society have become reduced to individual role conflicts, and no explanation is provided of the foundations of these role conflicts within the organisation of society. Third, no analysis is provided of the conditions which gave rise to the sexual division of labour, the existence of which, in fact, the studies take for granted. Finally, no analysis is provided of the labour process. One result of the fact that these empirical studies offer no analysis of the ways in which the capitalist labour process structures the organisation of work and the demand for labour on the one hand, nor the basis of the sexual division of labour and its relationship to the labour process on the other, is that no explanation can be provided for the concentration of women in unskilled occupations in certain branches of manufacturing industry and in service occupations, nor for the fact that much 'women's work' is part time and low paid. In the next part of this paper I turn to the dual labour market approach which claims to constitute such an explanation.

III

Unlike the empirical sociological studies which I have discussed above, dual labour market theories locate the subordination of women within an analysis of the labour market. Barron and Norris describe their departure from conventional sociological accounts in these terms:

> To borrow the terminology of economics, the sociologists have concentrated upon the supply side of the situation and have paid less attention to the demand side. Although they have pointed out that demand factors are important (for example, by showing that female labour force participation rates have shown sharp upsurges in times of high demand for labour) they have been less observant about the structure of the labour market into which women have been drawn and have had little to say about the forces which maintain that structure (1974, p. 2).

Their objective is therefore to suggest a framework by means of which the nature and causes of occupational differences between the sexes can be approached, drawing on the concept of the dual labour market.

The dual labour market approach grew from studies of local labour market situations in the USA, originally emerging in the 1960s from attempts to understand the problems of poverty and underemployment and the position of blacks in the American occupational structure. It involves, through its emphasis on a segmented labour market, a critique of the neoclassical economic assumption of a unitary labour market and of the 'human capital' theories which link occupational positions to educational background and qualifications. The dual labour market approach has since taken a variety of forms. I shall mainly concentrate here on the version of the theory which Barron and Norris adopt in their paper, 'Sexual divisions and the dual labour market' (1974), since this explicitly attempts to apply the concept to the employment of women in Britain.

Essential to the notion of the dual labour market is the assumption that the labour market is segmented into a number of structures. The most common approach differentiates two sectors, primary and secondary labour markets, and Barron and Norris describe the differences between these sectors:

> Primary sector jobs have relatively high earnings, good fringe benefits, good working conditions, a high degree of job security and good opportunities for advancement, while secondary jobs have relatively low earnings levels, poor working conditions, and negligible opportunities for advancement, and a low degree of job security. . . . The difference between the opportunities for advancement offered by jobs in the primary sector and those in the secondary sector is usually related to the existence of structured internal labour markets to which primary jobs are attached. A highly structured internal labour market contains a set of jobs organised hierarchically in terms of skill level and rewards, where recruitment to higher positions in the hierarchy is predominantly from lower positions in the same hierarchy and not from the external labour market. Only the lowest positions in the firm's job hierarchy are not filled from within the organisation

by promotion. Secondary jobs, on the other hand, are not part of a structured internal market; recruits to these jobs tend to come from outside the organisation and will go back outside the organisation onto the open labour market when they leave the job. Furthermore, because of the low skill level requirement for most secondary jobs, training is non-existent or minimal, so that secondary workers rarely acquire skills which they can use to advance their status on the open market (Barron and Norris, 1974, pp. 12—13).

Not only, therefore, is there a segmentation of labour markets: there is also a segmentation of workers into primary and secondary sectors. As Gordon points out (1972, p. 52), one problem with the dual labour market approach arises in differentiating between characteristics of occupations in different sectors and their holders, which frequently become conflated. This problem becomes apparent in the last section of Barron and Norris's paper, where they describe the characteristics of secondary occupations and then examine the 'fit' between common 'female' characteristics and these occupations, yet never actually demonstrate that in concrete situations women are employed in particular secondary occupations for these reasons.

The dual labour market approach claims that there is a restricted movement of workers between the two sectors of the labour market and that mobility in the hierarchically organised primary labour market tends to be upward, while in the secondary labour market it is horizontal. Thus primary employees are more likely to be mobile within hierarchically organised career structures in the firm, while secondary employees tend to move between industries and occupations (for example, in and out of unskilled and semi-skilled jobs). It postulates the existence of a division also among employers into primary and secondary groups. Some theorists (Bluestone, 1970; Edwards, 1975) assume that employers in the monopoly sector of the economy act as primary employers, utilising an internal labour market in monopolistic enterprises; while employers in the competitive sector adopt a secondary strategy. Edwards attempts to tie the distinction between primary and secondary employers into distinction (as used by O'Connor in *The Fiscal Crisis of the State* (1973), for example) between monopolistic, competitive and state sectors of the economy. Barron and Norris do not tie primary employers into the monopoly sector in this way, however, but rather assume that primary employers can exist in different sectors of the economy. Various explanations have been advanced as to why employers adopt different recruitment strategies. Gordon (1972) argues that the division between primary and secondary labour markets stems from employers' reactions to two problems: first, the need to promote employee stability in certain jobs; and second, the need to prevent the growth of class consciousness among certain sectors of the working class. However, Barron and Norris modify these arguments, suggesting that the attempt to create a primary labour market arises from the need to tie skilled workers into the firm and thus to reduce labour turnover among groups of workers with scarce skills, and from the need to buy off groups of workers in the face of demands for improved pay and working conditions. The strategies adopted by employers in the primary sector to reduce turnover and buy off sectors of workers have important implications for the structure of jobs in the secondary sector, particularly as far as levels of security and earnings are concerned. It therefore follows that 'in so far as it is in the interests of employers to maintain and expand the primary sector, it is also in their interest to ensure that instability and low earnings are retained in the secondary sector' (Barron and Norris, 1974, pp. 23–4). This becomes easier, Barron and Norris point out, if there exists a readily available supply of labour which is prepared to accept the inferior pay, job security, job status and working conditions which are offered by the majority of employers in the secondary sector: a reserve army of labour.

Having characterised the primary and secondary labour markets as emerging from strategies adopted by employers to cope with labour market and consumer market fluctuations, Barron and Norris attempt to demonstrate that the female labour force can be characterised in terms of the concept of the secondary labour market. They argue that women's pay is significantly lower than men's, and that there is a high degree of occupational segmentation between male and female workers; that there is some evidence that women are more likely to be made redundant than men and thus to have a higher degree of job insecurity; that men are more likely to be upwardly mobile than women; and finally that women have limited opportunities for advancement, tending instead to be horizontally mobile. In this way it can be argued that women workers conform to all the criteria of secondary labour market employees. The concluding part of Barron and Norris's paper is concerned with the question of *why* women are confined to the secondary labour market. They argue that there are five major attributes which make a particular group likely to be a source of secondary workers, and that women possess each of them. These attributes are:

(1) workers are easily dispensable, whether voluntarily or involuntarily;
(2) they can be sharply differentiated from workers in the primary labour market by some conventional social difference;
(3) they have a relatively low inclination to acquire valuable training and experience;
(4) they are low on 'economism' — that is, they do not rate economic rewards highly;
(5) they are relatively unlikely to develop solidaristic relations with fellow workers.

This part of the analysis is problematic, partly because little evidence is offered that these attributes actually are significant in concrete situations: the suggestion that women possess them relies heavily upon inference from stereotypical assumptions, and such a suggestion also casts doubt on their general claim that women's position can be explained in terms which are internal to the labour market. However, before discussing this particular problem, which is concerned with the application of the dual labour market approach to women, I first want to make some general comments about the dual labour market approach's characterisation of the labour processs.

The principal advantage of this approach is its emphasis that where women are employed it is in unskilled and semi-skilled jobs in particular occupations and industries, many of which provide little job security and are poorly paid. Thus Barron and Norris provide evidence to demonstrate that the employment situation of women is not equal to that of men (especially of white men), although it may share characteristics with those of certain other groups of workers, for example immigrant, Asian or black workers. In locating the reasons for this inequality within different employer strategies which are *de facto* discriminatory, the approach counters the view derived from neoclassical economics that individuals are allocated to occupational positions purely by the play of market forces. It also counters technological determinism by analysing the role that management plays in structuring the labour process. Nevertheless dual labour market theories do encounter a number of problems, especially at the level of explanation. Some of these are general difficulties which exist independently of whether the approach is being used to analyse the position of women workers, while others apply specifically to the attempt to extend dual labour market analysis to women's employment. The first problem is suggested by Edwards when he argues that 'while the dual labor market theory may allow us to classify market behaviour, it does not necessarily explain it. . . . We must return to the sphere of production for an adequate explanation' (1975, p. 99). As it stands the dual labour market approach is generally descriptive and taxonomic: it does not adequately explain the growth of the segmented labour market. This is because it abstracts the question of employers' behaviour in the labour market from an analysis of the labour process, specifically from an analysis of the productive forces as they are manifested in technological developments, and of the relations of production as they are embodied in class struggle.

Gordon suggests that the dual labour market approach is not inconsistent with a class analysis:

> The dual labor market theory offers a specific analysis of the labor market which can be interpreted in class terms, but the dual labor market theory itself does not rely on the concept, does not link the distinction between primary and secondary markets to other potential class divisions, and does not consistently base its hypotheses on evaluations of the group interests of employers or employees in either market (1972, p. 88).

But Barron and Norris's explanation is only a partial one, for two reasons. First, it only makes sense to talk about employer strategies in the context of a concrete analysis of the organisation of the labour process. Braverman (1974) attempts to do this by tying the question of the different strategies adopted by capital and its representatives for organising the labour process into an analysis of capital accumulation. The question of capitalist control over the labour market and the labour process is extremely important, but an adequate analysis needs to be far more specific than Barron and Norris's discussion. The second reason why their explanation is partial is that Barron and Norris, like Braverman, ignore the fact that the organisation of trade unions and other forms of shop floor organisation can be an important constraint upon capital's capacity to pursue a rational labour market strategy in terms of its interests. Apprenticeships regulations, for example, or trade union practices may impose constraints upon employers' decisions. A clear example of this is to be found in arguments concerning the recent British equal-pay legislation. The Confederation of British Industries had for some time been in favour of such legislation so long as it was linked with a package which would abolish protective legislation for women, presumably because this would enable employers to develop a more rational labour market strategy without restrictions upon the mobility and use of labour. The Trade Union Congress successfully resisted this demand, however, and an Equal Pay Act was passed in 1970 which retained protective legislation for women (although the Equal Opportunities Commission has a statutory duty to review the protective laws and to advise the government as to whether they should be repealed, amended or left as they are, so the future of these laws is by no means guaranteed). Any analysis of capital's labour market strategies, whether on a national or a local level, must consider the ways in which organised labour, both formally and informally (through custom and practice and shop floor organisation), may in certain circumstances impose constraints upon capital's ability to pursue its interests. Such an analysis must also consider the ways in which organised labour fails to represent the interests of its membership – or certain sectors of it – by adopting policies which do not challenge capital's domination of the labour process. The forms of struggle between capital and labour over the organisation of the labour process, and the implications of different forms of struggle for the position of female wage labourers within the labour process, are important questions to be investigated.

Having pointed to some of the problems involved in the dual labour market approach in general, I shall now consider further problems which arise from its application to female employment. My first point is that the major concentrations of female employment exist in different sectors of the economy, women being distributed horizontally — employed in particular industries and occupations — and vertically — employed mainly as unskilled and semi-skilled workers. In the conflation of the multifarious forms of employment into a heterogeneous category of secondary sector workers, the important differences between these predominantly female occupations become submerged. My second point is that much of the postwar expansion of women's employment has taken place in the state sector (nursing, teaching, cleaning and catering, clerical work and social work, for example). It is not clear from Barron and Norris's paper, however, how the dual labour market analysis might apply to the state sector in terms of changes in consumer demand, and employers' strategies in response to these changes. If state sector workers are categorised merely as secondary workers in the economy and the dynamics of their employment are seen to follow from employers' attempts to create a stable primary labour market, the important questions of the determinants of the demand for female labour in the state sector and the specificity of the position of employees in that sector are ignored.

A third, and crucial, problem concerns the fact that the dual labour market approach relegates the sexual division of labour to the status of an exogeneous variable, while the dynamics of the labour market are assumed to be the determinant factor in explaining the position of female labour. Barron and Norris's conceptual framework is essentially Weberian in this respect:

> The question of women's place in the family — the household sexual division of labour — will be relegated to the status of an explanatory factor which contributes to, but does not of itself determine, the differentiation between the sexes in their work roles . . . . The approach adopted in this paper . . . emphasises the importance of considering the structure of the labour market and women's place

within it as one cause among several of women's overall social position. Indeed a degree of causal circularity is assumed in the discussion which follows; ideological factors are seen as contributing to the preservation of the existing job structure for women, while the job structure is seen as a principal determinant of the inferior status of women as a social group and of the sexist ideology which helps to maintain their position (1974, p. 1).

The list of attributes which Barron and Norris provide in the final part of their paper exactly indicates the importance of the family and of assumptions which justify the sexual division of labour in determining the attributes with which women enter the labour market. In fact, only one of the five attributes which Barron and Norris list arises intrinsically from the labour market situation of women (this is the lack of solidarism, which is ascribed to the fact that many women work in small establishments, work part time and so on). Given the salience of extrinsic criteria which derive from women's role in the family and from ideological representations of this role, it is difficult to understand why Barron and Norris attempt to locate their explanation solely within the internal dynamics of the labour market. They describe a 'vicious cycle' between ascriptive characteristics, such as sex, and the labour market:

> When ascriptive characteristics like sex are used as selection criteria this will have the effect of confining the groups so delineated to the secondary sector over the whole of their working lives. . . . The actual confinement of particular groups to the secondary sector will result in their having higher rates of labour turnover and job mobility. Thus a 'vicious cycle' is created which reinforces the discriminating power of the trait which was made the basis of the selection criterion, and the labelling process becomes self-fulfilling (p. 39).

But the failure to analyse a situation in which criteria like sex or gender become socially significant results in the 'vicious cycle' approaching a tautological explanation. What is in fact required is a theory which links the organisation of the labour process to the sexual division of labour; it is of fundamental importance to analyse the relationship between the family and the organisation of production in the process of capital accumulation. In the next section I discuss relevant sections of Marx's analysis in *Capital*, the main project of which is a critical analysis of capitalist production.

IV

In this part of the paper I shall discuss two aspects of Marx's analysis in volume one of *Capital* which are in my view essential for understanding the position of female wage labour in the capitalist mode of production.[5] The first is Marx's analysis of the labour process, and specifically his discussion of the transition from manufacture to modern industry. The second is his concept of the industrial reserve army.

For Marx, manufacture and modern industry are two forms of organisation of the labour process, which is defined in *Capital* as a relationship between the labourer (who has nothing to sell but his/her labour power), the object of labour and the instruments of labour (such as tools and machinery). The labour process in any period is a product of the development of the forces of production, and embraces both the forces and relations of production. Manufacture, according to Marx, is the characteristic form of labour process throughout the manufacturing period of the capitalist mode of production, before this mode of production has taken hold of all branches of production and drawn them into the system of commodity production. Its basis lies in handicrafts, and production takes place in the workshop. As far as the actual organisation of the labour process is concerned, the important characteristics of manufacture are twofold. First, traditional handicrafts are broken down into a succession of manual operations in the workshop, such that 'each workman becomes exclusively assigned to a partial function, and that for the rest of his life, his labour-power is turned into the organ of this detail function' (Marx, 1967, p. 339). That is, there is a specialisation of functions, or a developed division of labour based upon co-operation among those working in a particular workshop, among the detail labourers who together comprise the collective labourer. Second, these different functions are arranged according to a hierarchy of concrete labours with a corresponding scale of wages. At the bottom of this hierarchy emerges a class of unskilled labourers. Marx argues that since manufacture adapts detail operations to varying degrees of maturity, strength and development of labour power, this is in theory conducive to the employment of women and children, but that 'this tendency as a whole is wrecked on the habits and the resistance of the male labourers' (p. 367), who jealously insist on maintaining apprenticeships even when these become unnecessary.

This system of production, with its hierarchy of concrete labours and subjective division of labour, gives way to modern industry, to 'real' capitalist control, Marx argues, when machines are created which can make machinery. In modern industry the instruments of labour, the workman's tools, are converted into machines, and there emerges a new form of division of labour in which the worker becomes a mere appendage of the machine. The most important characteristics of modern industry as far as the present discussion is concerned are first of all that, since the worker's skill has been handed over to the machine, the use of machinery provides the precondition for the abolition of the division of labour which was based on manufacture:

> Along with the tool, the skill of the workman in handling it passes over to the machine. The capabilities of the tool are emancipated from the restraints that are inseparable from human labour-power. Thereby the technical foundation on which is based the division of labour in Manufacture, is swept away. Hence, in the place of the hierarchy of specialised workmen that characterises manufacture, there steps, in the automatic factory, a tendency to equalise and reduce to one and the same level every kind of work that has to be done by the minders of the machines; in the place of the artificially produced differentiations of the detail workmen, step natural differences of age and sex (Marx, 1967, p. 420).

That is, the manufacturing division of labour with its hierarchy of concrete labours is no longer inherent in the labour process as it was in manufacture. However, Marx argues that the division of labour hangs on through what he calls traditional habit, and becomes in modern industry a way of intensifying exploitation through fostering competition. Thus there exists a contradiction between the technical necessities of modern industry and the social character inherent in its capitalist form, such that 'the life-long speciality of handling one and the same tool, now becomes the life-long speciality of serving one and the same machine' (p. 422).

Second, Marx argues that there exists a tendency in modern industry towards the substitution of unskilled labour for skilled, female labour for male, young labour for mature. He ascribes this tendency to the fact that machinery dispenses with the need for muscular strength, an argument founded upon naturalistic assumptions that women's physical strength is less than men's:

> In so far as machinery dispenses with muscular power, it becomes a means of employing labourers of slight muscular strength, and those whose bodily development is incomplete, but whole limbs are all the more supple. The labour of women and children was, therefore, the first thing sought for by capitalists who used machinery. That mighty substitute for labour and labourers was forthwith changed into a means for increasing the number of wage-labourers by enrolling, under the direct sway of capital, every member of the workman's family, without distinction of age or sex (p. 394).

Third, Marx argues that the excessive employment of women and children serves to break down the resistance which male operatives had to the development of machinery in the manufacturing period; that is, the existence of female labour is used by capital to foster competition.

Fourth, Marx argues that modern industry gives rise to intensified production outside factories, in the form of outwork, sweating, and so on, a new form of domestic industry in which women and children are extensively employed.

Finally, Marx argues that the more extensive employment of women and children gives rise to a new form of family and relations between the sexes:

> However terrible and disgusting the dissolution, under the capitalist system, of the old family ties may appear, nevertheless, modern industry, by assigning as it does an important part in the process of production, outside the domestic sphere, to women, to young persons, and to children of

both sexes, creates a new economic foundation for a higher form of the family and of the relations between the sexes (pp. 489–90).

This becomes a central tenet of Engels who argues in 'The origin of the family, private property and the state' that:

since large-scale industry has transferred the woman from the house to the labour market and the factory and makes her, often enough, the bread-winner of the family, the last remnants of male domination in the proletarian home have lost all foundation (1968, p. 508)

and thereby concludes that 'the first premise for the emancipation of women is the reintroduction of the entire female sex into public industry' (p. 510). It is important to emphasise that both Marx and Engels constitute the form of the labour process and also the form of the family as matters for historical investigation.

Although Marx does not discuss in any detail the advantages to capital of employing female labour, it is possible to cull a number of arguments from his discussion at different points in *Capital*. These hinge, in one way or another, on the theory of value. Jean Gardiner (1975) and others, including Paul Smith in his contribution to this volume, have pointed to the ways in which women's domestic labour can lower the value of labour power by producing use values which contribute to the reproduction of labour power in the home. It is also important to consider the relationship between female wage labour and the value of labour power, and to show how capital utilises female wage labour in ways which are economically advantageous to it. The first advantage to capital of the tendency for modern industry to employ all the members of the workman's family is that the value of labour power tends to be lowered since the costs of reproduction are spread over all the members of the population. Thus the portion of the working day in which the labourer works for himself is lowered, and more surplus value is thereby extracted.

The value of labour-power was determined, not only by the labour-time necessary to maintain the individual adult labourer, but also by that necessary to maintain his family. Machinery, by throwing every member of that family on to the labour-market, spreads the value of the man's labour-power over his whole family. It thus depreciates his labour-power. To purchase the labour-power of a family of four workers may, perhaps, cost more than it formerly did to purchase the labour-power of the head of the family, but, in return, four days' labour takes the place of one, and their price falls in proportion to the excess of the surplus labour of four over the surplus labour of one. In order that the family may live, four people must now, not only labour, but expend surplus-labour for the capitalist. Thus we see, that machinery, while augmenting the human material that forms the principal object of capital's exploiting power, at the same time raises the degree of exploitation (Marx, 1967, p. 395).

This tendency is generalised from Marx's analysis of the textiles industry in which men, women and children were extensively employed in the early stages of modern industry.

Marx also suggests at various points in his argument that while the value of labour power is theoretically assumed to be averaged for a given society, in practice labour power will have different values. As determinants of these concrete differences in the value of labour power he cites a number of factors, including the expenses involved in training, natural diversity and the part played by the labour of women and children. This raises the question of whether female labour power has a lower value, and if so, why. One reason might be that women have less training, and therefore the costs of re-producing their labour power are lower; a second that, by virtue of the existence of the family, women are not expected themselves to bear the costs of reproduction. Since male wages are paid on the assumption that men are responsible for the costs of reproduction, and since it is generally assumed that women have husbands to provide for them and their children, the value of labour power can be lowered since it is assumed that women in the family do not have to bear the costs of reproduction.

The advantage of capital of female labour power having a lower value parallels the tendency, noted by Marx, to pay wages below the value of labour power. This is commonly the case with female wage rates, which can be lower because of the assumption that women are subsidiary workers and

their husband's wages are responsible for the costs of reproduction. Marx states that the

> Forcible reduction of wages below . . . [the] value [for
> labour power] plays . . . in practice too important a part
> . . . . It, in fact, transforms, within certain limits, the
> labourer's necessary consumption-fund into a fund for the
> accumulation of capital (p. 599).

As far as women are concerned, it is only possible to pay
wage rates below the value of labour power because of the
existence of the family, and because of the assumption that a
woman is partly dependent upon her husband's wages within
the family. It is this tendency to pay women wages below the
value of labour power which is responsible for the plight of
single, working-class women, widows and female-headed,
single-parent families — the impoverished needlewomen and
shopworkers of the nineteenth century, many of whom were
forced into prostitution, and the single-parent family of
today. The point is that even where women do not have
husbands — or fathers — to support them, in patriarchal
ideology their social position is defined in terms of the family
as a patriarchal structure. A fourth advantage to capital of
female labour concerns the circulation of commodities. Marx
suggests in a footnote that the employment of women leads
to an increased demand for ready made articles, and hence
speeds up the circulation process. He states that when

> certain family functions, such as nursing and suckling
> children, cannot be entirely suppressed, the mothers con-
> fiscated by capital, must try substitutes of some sort.
> Domestic work, such as sewing and mending, must be re-
> placed by the purchase of ready-made articles. Hence, the
> diminished expenditure of labour in the house is accom-
> panied by an increased expenditure of money. The cost of
> keeping the family increases, and balances the greater
> income (p. 395, footnote).

This theme is taken up by Braverman (1974) in his chapter
on the 'The universal market' in which he discusses how
capital took over tasks such as food production and processing,
clothes production, and so on, which were formerly undertaken within the domestic economy at the same time as

employing women as wage labourers to perform these tasks. That is, women's work leads to an increased demand for consumer goods, while the demand for female wage labour historically has been linked to the development of consumer goods manufacturing industries, according to Braverman. (It should perhaps be noted, however, that Braverman does not sufficiently link his discussion of the universal market with his analysis of the labour process; and thereby loses sight of the fact that it is because of the family that capital is able to draw on female labour in particular ways as a form of industrial reserve army.)

A final advantage to capital of employing female wage labourers which is discussed by Marx in his chapters on the labour process is that it breaks down male workers' resistance to capitalist development which had existed in the manufacturing period. He states that 'by the excessive addition of women and children to the ranks of the workers, machinery at last breaks down the resistance which the male operatives in the manufacturing period continued to oppose to the despotism of capital' (p. 402). One implication of this is that the introduction of women and children, while being advantageous to capital, is at the same time resisted by the male workers who struggle to maintain their position of privilege. That is, it suggests that the introduction of women and children into modern industry is a source of class struggle. This can itself be an important source of divisions within the working class.

Before returning to discuss some of the problems which this analysis raises, I shall now turn to the second aspect of Marx's analysis which is relevant to an analysis of female wage labour, the concept of the industrial reserve army. For Marx an industrial reserve army[6] or relative surplus population is both a necessary product and a lever of capital accumulation, a condition of the existence of the capitalist mode of production:

> It forms a disposable industrial reserve army, that belongs to capital quite as absolutely as if the latter had bred it at its own cost. Independently of the limits of the actual increase of population, it creates, for the changing needs of the self-expansion of capital, a mass of human material always ready for exploitation (Marx, 1967, p. 632).

This is not the case in the early stages of capitalism where capital composition changes slowly, but rather emerges in the transition of modern industry where capitalist control of the labour process is generalised. At this point an industrial reserve army becomes a permanent feature of capital accumulation. Thus:

> The course characteristic of modern industry . . . depends on the constant formation, the greater or less absorption, and the re-formation, of the industrial reserve army of surplus-population. In their turn, the varying phases of the industrial cycle recruit the surplus population, and become one of the most energetic agents of its reproduction (p. 633).

When accumulation develops in old branches of production, or penetrates new branches of production, 'there must be the possibility of throwing great masses of men suddenly on the decisive points without injury to the scale of production in other spheres' (p. 632). This requires a relative surplus population which is independent of the natural limits of the population. In the discussion below I shall concentrate upon three questions which are raised by Marx's analysis. First, how is the concept defined? Second, what are the functions of the industrial reserve army? And third, can female labour be described in terms of the concept of the industrial reserve army?

The concept of the industrial reserve army, or relative surplus population, is not very precisely defined by Marx, and this imprecision has given rise to various interpretations in subsequent marxist writings. At some points Marx distinguishes between the active labour army and the industrial reserve army, implying that these are mutually exclusive categories, while at others he describes the major forms of the industrial reserve army as all being part of the active labour army. Marx further distinguishes between three forms of industrial reserve army:

(1) the floating form, whereby labourers are sometimes repelled and sometimes attracted into the centres of modern industry. This is linked to the argument that the demand for labour in the centres of modern industry tends to substitute unskilled for skilled labour,

women for men, and youths for adults;

(2) the latent form, which exists among the agricultural population which is displaced by the capitalist penetration of agriculture;

(3) the stagnant form, comprising labourers who are irregularly employed, for example, in domestic industry, whose members are recruited from the supernumerary forces of modern industry and agriculture.

Below these are the categories of pauperism and the 'lazarus layers'.

Marx's analysis contains two elements. There is first of all a theory of the tendency for capital accumulation both to attract and to repel labour which suggests that the structuring of the working class by the labour process is a dynamic process, and that the process of capital accumulation generates considerable amounts of underemployment. The tendency towards attraction of labour resulting from capital accumulation in particular branches of production then raises the question of the sources of labour which become part of the working class, while the tendency towards repulsion raises the question of the destiny of the labourers, whether employed or unemployed (for example, the tendency towards marginalisation of certain groups of workers in Latin America suggested by Obregon (1974), and the tendency discussed by Jean Gardiner (1975–6) for women rendered unemployed in manufacturing industry in Britain to be absorbed into the service sector). The second element of Marx's analysis is a theory of the functions of the industrial reserve army. He argues that it provides a disposable and flexible population. That is, it provides labour power which can be absorbed in expanding branches of production when capital accumulation creates a demand for it, and repelled when the conditions of production no longer require it. It is therefore a crucial component of capital accumulation, as Obregon (1974) points out, essential to the analysis of economic cycles (the industrial reserve army being disposable in the recession) and to the analysis of the penetration of the capitalist mode of production into new branches of production. It is also seen as a condition of competition among workers, the degree of intensity of which depends on the pressure of the relative surplus population. This competitive pressure has two consequences. It depresses wage levels: Marx argues that the general movements of wages are regulated by the expansion and contraction of the industrial reserve army, which in turn corresponds to periodic changes in the industrial cycle. It also forces workers to submit to increases in the rate of exploitation through the pressure of unemployment. Finally, it counteracts the tendency for the rate of profit to fall. The sources of reserve labour which Marx mentions are modern industry itself, which tends to repel labourers as machinery is introduced, and agriculture, which repels labourers as capitalism develops. Clearly women can be repelled, alongside men, in either of these ways — whether they are is, of course, a matter for concrete investigation. The question which I want to raise here, however, is whether the family is *per se* a source like any other of the industrial reserve army or whether married women drawn into production from the family constitute a specific form of industrial reserve army which is different from the forms described by Marx. I have already suggested certain advantages to capital in employing female labour, and will now consider whether further advantages accrue if married women constitute an industrial reserve army.

I would argue that married women function as a disposable and flexible labour force in particular ways, and that the specificity of the position of women arises from their domestic role in the family and the prevalent assumption that this is their primary role. There are several ways in which married women can more easily be made redundant — disposed of — than men. They are less likely to be strongly unionised than men; if made redundant, they are less likely to be in jobs covered by the Redundancy Payments Act; in Britain at the moment married women paying a married woman's national insurance contribution receive less state benefits; and unless they register as unemployed, women do not appear in the unemployment statistics, which accounts for a massive undernumeration of female unemployment. Thus women who are made redundant are able to disappear virtually without trace back into the family. I would also argue that women are more likely to be a flexible working population, being horizontally mobile and willing to take on part-time work. This relates to the assumption that their primary place is in the home, an assumption actually embodied in state policies which, as Mary McIntosh argues elsewhere in this volume, virtually compel women to accept movement into and out of jobs at different periods of their life cycle. Female employment also poses particular pressure on wages since women's wage rates are substantially lower than men's. The fact that women's wages can be paid below the value of labour power means that women, as part of the industrial reserve army, constitute a particularly intense pressure on wage levels. It appears, therefore, that women form a specific element of the industrial reserve army by virtue of the sexual division of labour which consigns them to the family and inscribes a set of assumptions about women's roles. While they can occupy Marx's floating, latent and stagnant categories, married women also have a position which derives specifically from their role in the family.

It is, of course, a matter for concrete historical analysis to establish which sources of industrial reserve army are at various conjunctures drawn upon by capital, this being determined by the availability of various sources of reserve labour and by political expediency, as well as by the relative economic advantages offered by different groups of labour, such as married women and migrant workers, who are partially dependent upon sources other than their own wages for the costs of reproducing their labour power. In the last instance, the question of who actually comprises the industrial reserve army of labour turns on class relations, as two examples from Britain indicate. First, during the First World War, because trade unions objected to the employment of coloured labour, women, drawn mainly from the family and from domestic service, as well as from sweated trades, became a significant reserve for the war effort. After initial objections to dilution and to the employment of women, especially on non-munitions work, a number of agreements were reached between the Amalgamated Society for Engineers and the government, and the Trades Union Congress and the government, which while granting women equal piece rates refused them equal time rates, and moreover ensured that jobs would be vacated for men at the end of the war. The employment of women as a reserve thus offered advantages both to capital, since lower wages could be paid (both by not paying equal time rates and by *de facto* not paying equal piece rates), and also to skilled workers, who could secure the return to the *status quo ante* after the war, at least as far as the exclusion of women from skilled jobs was concerned. A second example emerged during the 1960s when it became politically expedient to restrict immigration to Britain from the Commonwealth to particular occupational groups, thereby rendering women an important source of the industrial reserve army.

I have in this section of the paper attempted to point out the ways in which Marx's analysis of the labour process in the transition to modern industry and his theory of the industrial reserve army can be used to analyse female wage labour in the capitalist mode of production. I have also tried to show, at each point in my argument, how the existence of the sexual division of labour which consigns women to the family and the patriarchal ideology embodied in it must be presupposed in order that female labour can constitute these advantages to capital. This suggests that it is the sexual division of labour and the family rather than women's 'natural' lesser physical strength (the explanation which Marx actually resorts to) whose existence must be assumed if the specificity of the position of female wage labour in the capitalist mode of production is to be understood.

It is important to assess the limitations of the marxist analysis discussed here, and to put forward some questions which require further consideration. My basic argument at this point is that a marxist explanation which considers the family–production relationship to be central is able to explain the vertical division of labour: that is, it can explain the tendency for women to be employed in unskilled and semi-skilled jobs in the centres of modern industry and for women to be employed in the sweated trades which flourished as an outgrowth of capitalist industrialisation. It cannot, however, explain the horizontal division of labour: that is, it cannot adequately explain why there has emerged a demand for female labour in some centres of modern industry — such as textiles, clothing and footwear, leather goods, food, drink and tobacco production, as well as certain sectors of engineering (electrical engineering and instrument engineering, for example) — but not in others, such as shipbuilding and machine engineering, mining and quarrying, construction and metal manufacture. The tendency has been for analyses of female wage labour to focus upon the appropriation of women's domestic labour into factories with the development of capitalist commodity production, and to show that women perform similar tasks in the factories to those which they perform in the home. Thus Braverman, for example describes how women were drawn into employment in food processing, clothes manufacture and so on, as these activities became appropriated from the family by capitalist commodity production. And the apparent symmetry between women's wage work and domestic labour has led the Power of Women Collective to conclude in *All Work and No Pay* (1975) that all forms of women's work are really housework. A glance at the principal occupations of women in nineteenth-century Britain does indicate some symmetry between women's domestic labour and other forms of female wage labour, the major occupations for women in 1851 being domestic servant, milliner, worker in cotton manufacture, washerwoman, mangler and laundrykeeper. It is important to emphasise, however, that the view that women's work is a kind of extension of domestic labour is too simplistic (Taylor, 1975–6). While women's wage labour may seem to mirror domestic labour in particular periods, it is essential to penetrate beneath surface appearances and to recognise that wage labour has a different relationship to the organisation of production than does domestic labour. As well as analysing the organisation of the labour process along the lines already suggested, the analysis of the horizontal division of labour, in order to try to explain why at certain moments some industries and trades have generated a demand for female labour, would also have to consider alternative sources of labour (were women the only available reserve army?), trade union policies relating to the recruitment of women, state policies towards both the employment of women and the family, and attitudes towards women working in particular kinds of occupation. Since the thrust of my argument here has been to emphasise the necessity of integrating an analysis of the sexual division of labour which consigns women to the family into an analysis of the capitalist labour process, I shall conclude by outlining, very briefly, how I see the relationship between the two spheres of production and family in the capitalist mode of production. Prior to the development of industrial capitalism, production took place in the household alongside reproduction and consumption. One of the consequences of the development of modern industry has been that production was largely removed from the family to the factory (although in practice many women continued to work in the home and in small workshops attached to the home). The sphere of production thus became separated from the family, which retained 'functions' which can be discussed by reference to two sets of concepts, reproduction and consumption.

As production moved to the factories with the development of modern industry, a new form of family emerged to fulfil the function of reproducing the commodity labour power, on both a generational and a day-to-day basis. Generational reproduction involves biological reproduction, the regulation of sexuality, and the socialisation of children, while day-to-day reproduction involves numerous tasks of domestic labour such as shopping, cooking meals, washing, cleaning and caring. The two forms of reproduction of labour power inscribe biological, economic and ideological components, which are the tasks of domestic labour. The family is furthermore involved in the reproduction of the social relations of production which are in capitalist society both class relations and gender relations. The specific role of the family here involves, on one hand, the transmission of property/ propertylessness (the major functions of the family in class societies according to Engels (1968)) and, on the other, the reproduction of patriarchal ideology (see Annette Kuhn's contribution to this volume). Like the reproduction of labour power these take place on both a generational and a day-to-day basis. The family also operates as a primary locus of consumption, which is essential to the circulation of commodities in the capitalist mode of production. The relationship between the three elements — production, reproduction and consumption — changes historically, the forms of reproduction and consumption, and therefore the forms of the family and of the sexual division of labour within it, being determined in the last instance by changes in the mode of production. According to this mode of analysis, therefore, the sexual division of labour in the family, which Parsons explains in purely normative terms, is ascribed a material basis. An adequate analysis of the family and of the position of women both as domestic labourers and as wage labourers must provide a theory of the relationship between these elements, which functionalist sociology fails to do. Furthermore, an analysis of female wage labour must integrate an analysis of the labour process with an analysis of the family which defines the specificity of the position of female wage labour, which Braverman and Marx fail to do. It has been the object of this paper to point to some of the problems involved in this task through discussion of a number of approaches to the analysis of women's wage labour. Clearly much more work needs to be done on the subject. My purpose here has been simply to attempt to clarify some of the questions involved in providing a marxist feminist analysis of female wage labour.

Notes

1 This paper was written in June 1976 and slightly revised in September 1977 for publication. I am grateful to many feminists, friends and colleagues, especially in the Coventry—Birmingham area and at the University of Warwick for helpful discussion of the issues raised in the paper, and in particular to Colleen Chesterman, Annette Kuhn and AnnMarie Wolpe for detailed comments on the original version of the paper.
2 Since this paper was first written, the paper by Adamson *et al.* (1976), 'Women's oppression under capitalism', has been published. This emphasises the interrelationship between women's wage labour and domestic labour.
3 All references are to an unpublished version of Barron and Norris's paper 'Sexual divisions and dual labour market' presented at the annual conference of the British Sociological Association in 1974. A slightly revised version is published in Diana Leonard Barker and Sheila Allen (eds), *Dependence and Exploitation in Work and Marriage*, Longman, London, 1976.
4 My own ideas on the relevance of Marx's analysis in *Capital* for an understanding of female wage labour have developed since I first wrote this paper. See my 'Female wage labour in capitalist production' (1977).
5 This section relies heavily upon collective discussions within the Women and Labour Process Group, of which I am a member.
6 I develop the analysis of women as an industrial reserve army and the question of the similarities between married women and other groups in the industrial reserve army (e.g. immigrants and migrant workers) in 'Female wage labour in capitalist production' (1977).

References

Adamson, O., Brown, C., Harrison, J., and Price, J. (1976), 'Women's oppression under capitalism', *Revolutionary Communist* no. 5, pp. 2—48.

Alexander, S. (1976), 'Women's work in nineteenth-century London: a study of the years 1820—50' in J. Mitchell and A. Oakley, *The Rights and Wrongs of Women*, Penguin, Harmondsworth.

Barron, R. D., and Norris, G. M. (1974), 'Sexual divisions and the dual labour market', paper presented at the BSA Annual Conference.

Beechey, V. (1977), 'Female wage labour in capitalist production', *Capital and Class*, no. 3, pp. 45—66.

Bluestone, B. (1970), 'The tripartite economy: labor markets and the working poor', *Poverty and Human Resources Abstracts*, July—August, pp. 15—35.

Braverman, H. (1974), *Labor and Monopoly Capital*, Monthly Review Press, New York.

Edwards, R. C. (1975), 'The social relations of production in the firm and labor market structure', *Politics and Society*, vol. 5, pp. 83—108.

Engels, F. (1968), 'The origin of the family, private property and the state' in K. Marx and F. Engels, *Selected Works*, Lawrence & Wishart, London.

Fogarty, M. P., Rapoport, R., and Rapoport, R. N. (1971), *Sex, Career and Family*, Allen & Unwin, London.

Gardiner, J. (1975), 'Women's domestic labour', *New Left Review*, no. 89, pp. 47—58.

Gardiner, J. (1975—6), 'Women and unemployment', *Red Rag*, no. 10, pp. 12—15.

Gordon, D. M. (1972), *Theories of Poverty and Underemployment*, D. C. Heath, Boston.

Klein, V. (1965), *Britain's Married Women Workers*, Routledge & Kegan Paul, London.

Marx, K. (1967) *Capital*, vol. I, International Publishers, New York.

Middleton, C. (1974), 'Sexual inequality and stratification theory' in F. Parkin, *The Social Analysis of Class Structure*, Tavistock, London.

Morgan, D. H. J. (1975), *Social Theory and the Family*, Routledge & Kegan Paul, London.

Myrdal, A., and Klein, V. (1970), *Women's Two Roles*, Routledge & Kegan Paul, London.

Obregon, A. Q. (1974), 'The marginal pole of the economy and the marginalised labour force', *Economy and Society*, vol. 3, pp. 393—428.

O'Connor, J. (1973), *The Fiscal Crisis of the State*, St Martin's Press, New York.

Parsons, T. (1954), *Essays in Sociological Theory*, Free Press, New York.

Parsons, T., and Bales, R. F. (1956), *Family: Socialization and Interaction Process*, Routledge & Kegan Paul, London.

Power of Women Collective (1975), *All Work and No Pay*, Falling Wall Press, Bristol.

Rapoport, R., and Rapoport, R. N. (1971), *Dual Career Families*. Penguin, Harmondsworth.

Taylor, B. (1975–6), 'Our labour and our power', *Red Rag*, no. 10, pp. 18–20.

Young, M., and Willmott, P. (1975), *The Symmetrical Family*, Penguin, Harmondsworth.

Yudkin, S., and Holme, A. (1969), *Working Mothers and Their Children*, Sphere, London.

8 Domestic labour and Marx's theory of value

Paul Smith

Juliet Mitchell's article 'Women: the longest revolution', first appearing as it did in 1966, came somewhat before its time, not only in attempting to deal with the oppression of women in its historical specificity, but in even initiating treatment of the issue in analytical terms. Much of the early theoretical work of the post-1968 women's movement 'forgot' Mitchell's intervention and tended instead to mobilize concepts which were readily appropriated to a universalistic account of women's oppression. (Indeed, Mitchell, in drawing in a particular way upon the notion of patriarchy, may herself be seen as guilty of such universalism in some of her subsequent work, as McDonough and Harrison have argued in Chapter 2.) In such a situation domestic labour was seized upon as the key to an historically concrete understanding of women's oppression, in that housework could be thought as the central point at which women's specific subordination in capitalism is articulated. The 'domestic labour debate' as it has taken place hitherto may be usefully if simplistically characterized in terms of two main tendencies. The 'orthodox' tendency approaches domestic labour in terms of its relationship to the capitalist mode of production, and in analysis draws on Marx's expositions in *Capital* of value, surplus value, productive labour, and so on. The 'unorthodox' position also adopts the terms of the marxist problematic, but from the prior point of view of a consideration of the position of women with regard to domestic labour, and how such a consideration might relate to feminist political practice. Two early analyses of domestic labour in capitalism illustrate these tendencies in a particularly clear-cut way. John Harrison's paper on

'The political economy of housework' (1973) comes out of the Conference of Socialist Economists, a group whose primary interest is in
marxist analysis rather than in feminism, in spite of an evident awareness of the potential intersection of the two problematics. Harrison
argues — and this is characteristic of the orthodox position — that
domestic labour constitutes a mode of production quite distinct from
the capitalist mode, describing it as a client mode 'created or co-opted
by the dominant mode to fulfil certain functions within the economic
and social system' (p. 40). Dalla Costa in *The Power of Women and the
Subversion of the Community,* which first appeared in English in 1972,
argues that domestic labour, as well as being socially necessary labour,
is productive in the sense that it contributes to the exchange value of
the commodity labour power, and hence to the creation of surplus
value. Paul Smith's contribution to the debate, in stressing the distinction between productive labour and socially necessary labour, in arguing
that it is the capitalist mode of production and not marxist analysis
that marginalizes domestic labour, and above all in suggesting that
activities (such as domestic labour) which secure the conditions of
existence of capital 'are external to it, however functional they may be
for it', may be read as inscribing an orthodox position. It is probably
true, at least on a theoretical level, that the disparity between these
positions rests simply on a conflation in the unorthodox argument of
productive and socially necessary labour, but none the less the differences in the conclusions which result have important implications for
practice, which is why the 'domestic labour debate' is more than merely
a doctrinal squabble. The argument that domestic labour, by being
'indirectly' productive, is central to the capitalist mode of production
leads Dalla Costa and others to argue that women as a class can usefully
organize around their specific relationship to housework, the point of
their common oppression, and possibly to demand 'wages for housework' as a basis of linking, presumably at the level of consciousness,
women's subordination with its material foundation. Although the
orthodox position generally tends to make its implications for practice
less explicit, to the extent that it argues that the domestic mode of
production is not only external to the capitalist mode of production
but is fundamentally pre-capitalist in structure, it would point either,
pace Engels, to the progressive character of the proletarianization of
women, that is that a prior condition for their emancipation is their full
entry into capitalist relations of production; or perhaps to the evident
contradiction involved in the specific character of women's relationship
as wage workers and houseworkers to two distinct modes of production,

with the implication that it is this very contradiction which constitutes the terrain of feminist struggle.

Discussion of domestic labour in social formations dominated by the capitalist mode of production has focused on its role in producing the commodity labour power, and hence on the question of whether or not such labour contributes to the value of labour power, and the related question of whether it is productive or unproductive labour, or neither. The case for 'domestic labour as value producing' has not been well argued — rhetoric often substituting for understanding of Marx's theory of value — and this has allowed the 'orthodox' marxist response to rely on mere assertion to dismiss, rather than refute, the case.[1] However, the question of whether domestic work contributes to the value of labour power does present a real problem for marxism, primarily because Marx gives two distinct, and apparently inconsistent, definitions of the value of labour power:

> The value of labour-power is determined, as in the case of every other commodity, by the labour-time necessary for the production, and consequently also the reproduction, of this special article. So far as it has value, it represents no more than a definite quantity of the average labour of society incorporated in it. . . . Given the individual, the production of labour-power consists in his reproduction of himself or his maintenance. For his maintenance he requires a given quantity of the means of subsistence. Therefore the labour-time requisite for the production of labour-power reduces itself to that necessary for the production of those means of subsistence; in other words, the value of labour-power is the value of the means of subsistence necessary for the maintenance of the labourer (1974a, p. 167).

However, the labour time necessary for the production of labour power clearly does not reduce itself to that necessary for the production of the means of subsistence since, as Seccombe points out, 'an additional labour — namely housework — is necessary in order to convert these commodities into regenerated labour power' (1974, p. 9). When the housewife works upon wage purchased goods and alters their form, her labour becomes part of the congealed mass of past labour embodied in labour power and so, Seccombe continues, contributes to its value. Seccombe claims that all this

> is merely a consistent application of the labour theory of value to the reproduction of labour power itself — namely that all labour produces value when it produces any part of a commodity that achieves equivalence in the marketplace with other commodities (1974, p. 9).

However, it is not 'all labour' that produces value, but labour performed within the social relations of commodity production which takes the form of socially necessary, abstract and social labour, and it is necessary to examine to what extent domestic labour in social formations dominated by ‚the capitalist mode of production conforms to this.

There are essentially two ways of viewing domestic labour: either as a set of services which are partly themselves consumed (immaterial production) and partly produce use values (such as cooked meals) for immediate consumption; or as activities with a definite product, labour power, which, under capitalist relations of production, is a commodity. There is no obvious reason for assuming one of these models rather than the other. Thus the objection to Seccombe that domestic labour is merely a concrete labour producing use values for consumption and not for exchange (Coulson *et al.*, 1975, p. 62; Adamson *et al.*, 1976, pp. 11 and 12)[2] merely proposes the alternative assumption without critically examining Seccombe's. However, it will be argued here that in the light of serious examination Seccombe's position is ultimately untenable — not as a consequence of Marx's definitions but as a consequence of the nature of commodity production and exchange.

Seccombe himself is in some confusion and offers a variant of the opposing model when he claims that housework is unproductive labour since it is exchanged with revenue — wages or profits. He thus equates it with the hired labour of a domestic servant or similar, and the domestic labourer is seen as having exchanged her (typically) labour for her means of subsistence.[3] But since this type of unproductive worker simply consumes revenue and creates no value, this analogy is inconsistent with Seccombe's main thesis that domestic labour produces value: as Marx points out, 'the cook does not replace for me (the private person) the fund from which I pay her, because I buy her labour not as a value-creating element but purely for the sake of its use-value' (1969, p. 165).

However, the strength of the case for 'domestic labour as value producing labour' lies not in the view that it is the domestic *labour* that enters exchange, but its *product*, the commodity labour power. Thus the analogy is not with the unproductive worker hired out of revenue but with the simple commodity production of 'independent handicrafts-men or peasants who employ no labourers and . . . confront me as sellers of commodities, not as sellers of labour, and this relation therefore . . . has nothing to do with the distinction between productive and unproductive labour' (Marx, 1969, p. 407).[4] Thus, for Seccombe 'domestic labour . . . contrib-utes directly to the creation of the commodity labour power while having no direct relation with capital. It is this special *duality* which defines the character of domestic labour under capitalism' (p. 9); and for Dalla Costa and James, 'the family under capitalism is a center . . . essentially of *social production* . . . . Labor power is a commodity produced by women in the home' (1975, pp. 10 and 19). Labour power is, then, seen as the result of a production process in which the depleted wage labourer and his means of subsistence enter as means of pro-duction to be transformed by domestic labour into the replen-ished labourer and his labour power. (That domestic labour does not physically transform a raw material to produce a new use value is not a problem for this subsumption under commodity production, just as Marx includes under produc-tive labour[5] the labour of certain managers and engineers and transport workers.) This commodity is then sold and its value determined, 'as in the case of every other commodity', by the labour time necessary for its production. Far from being a mere application of Marx's theory of value, as Seccombe claims, this represents a serious challenge to it in that it suggests one commodity, labour power, is always sold below its value, since this would be equivalent to the value of the means of subsistence bought with the wage *plus* the value said to be created by the domestic labour. (Seccombe attempts to get round this discrepancy with the following nonsense: 'domestic labour figures substantially in the relative value of labour power, but is no part at all of its equivalent, expressed in the wage. Of course the wage and labour power are of equal value, and so abstractly, equal amounts of social labour are expended on each side of the equation, but this equivalence is not an identity, concretely' (p. 10).)

If labour power is seen as a commodity produced outside the capitalist mode of production and then exchanged like any other product of simple commodity production, then most of the objections advanced against Seccombe are invalid. It is insufficient to assert, as Adamson *et al.* do, that 'domestic work is carried out by women outside social production'; since it produces a definite use value, why is it not a branch of social production, albeit one not taken over by capital? Similarly, it is insufficient to point out that 'domestic work is privatised, individual toil. It is concrete labour which lies outside the capitalist production process and therefore cannot produce value or surplus-value' (Adamson *et al.*, 1976, p. 8).[6] Not only does this completely neglect the value production of non-capitalist commodity production, but it ignores the fact that *all* commodity production is private, individual and concrete labour which through exchange manifests itself as social, socially necessary, and abstract labour: '*Labour-products* would not become *commodities* if they weren't products of *private-labours* which are plied independently of one another and stand on their own' (Marx, 1976c, p. 57; see also Marx, 1974a, p. 49). As Seccombe notes, in anticipation of this objection, 'it matters not at all that the concrete conditions of domestic labour are privatized.' It will be shown that it is not because domestic labour is private that it cannot become abstract labour but, on the contrary, it is because it cannot become abstract labour that it remains private.

If domestic labour contributes to the production of a commodity then it would seem that, like any other commodity-producing labour, it too is reduced to abstract labour and so is value-creating, and constitutes a branch of social production. The problem for marxism is not dogmatically to assert that this is not the case but to show why it cannot be the case: to show why this particular concrete, private and individual labour cannot manifest itself as its opposite, as abstract, social and socially necessary labour, and hence why it must be seen as simply a concrete labour producing use values for immediate consumption.

Two preliminary points must be made to situate this discussion in a wider theoretical framework. First, while the discussion will concentrate largely on commodity exchange, it must be remembered that the existence of the market is dependent on certain relations of *production* – in particular, that labour power is a commodity at all is, of course, an effect of a certain social distribution of the objective conditions of production. Second, Marx's theory of value is treated as dealing with one type of production relation, that between commodity owners, in abstraction from the other types of production relations of the capitalist mode of production, particularly that between capital and wage labour in the process of production. This is in opposition to Engels who claimed it dealt with precapitalist commodity exchange. Thus Marx's order of presentation in *Capital* is seen as primarily logical rather than historical, in opposition, for example, to Mandel and Engels.[7] For Marx 'it would therefore be unfeasible and wrong to let the economic categories follow one another in the same sequence as that in which they were historically decisive. Their sequence is determined, rather, by their relation to one another in modern bourgeois society ...' (1973b, p. 107).

The first reason that domestic labour cannot be subsumed under commodity production is a consequence of the fact that in a commodity economy labour is allocated between branches of production by the law of value, and equilibrium between branches consists in their products exchanging at value.[8] When exchange ratios diverge from relative values, a movement of labour and means of production is provoked which establishes a tendency towards (constantly disturbed) equilibrium, that is to say, exchange at value (Marx, 1974a, p. 336; Marx, 1974c, p. 880). The first way in which domestic labour cannot be subsumed under commodity production, then, is that fluctuations in the price of labour power do not affect the performance of domestic labour – indeed, it is performed when its product, labour power, cannot be sold at all. When the process of capital accumulation draws women into capitalist production as wage workers, this is not instead of, but in addition to, their performance of domestic labour. This banal point is significant because it means that domestic labour is performed independently of the social allocation of labour through the value of its product and is in this sense qualitatively different from the labour embodied in the wage labourer's means of subsistence which is reallocated with fluctuations in the price of labour power. (Although this is not, of course, to say that domestic labour is unaffected by the process of capital accumulation — in periods of recession women, as a relatively weak section of the working class, are the first to be laid off, they are heavily employed in the state sectors which are cut back, they are also the main consumers of these services, and domestic labour may be intensified to compensate for reduced real wages.) The fact that the specificity of women's oppression in social formations dominated by the capitalist mode of production consists in their dual role as domestic labour and wage labour (Coulson *et al.*, 1975, p. 60; Adamson *et al.*, 1976, p. 7), or, as Beechey argues in her contribution to the present volume, as members of the industrial reserve army, is not suppressed by the view of domestic labour as productive of value: on the contrary, it subverts that view. It is precisely because domestic labour is not labour which is allocated by the law of value, but is performed independently of such allocation, that it does not constitute a branch of the social division of labour producing just another commodity.

The second way in which domestic labour cannot be subsumed under commodity production derives from the fact that exchange is not simply a phase of the process of reproduction but is also a definite social form of the production process (Rubin, 1972, p. 149). Labour is socially regulated through exchange in its methods, technology and productivity. Private labour takes the form of social labour not simply because independent producers are related to each other through exchange of their products but because this exchange influences their productive activity — not only their exchange is a social act but also their labour, because it is socially regulated. Abstract labour, the specific form of social labour under commodity production, develops to the extent that exchange becomes the social form of the production process, transforming the production process into commodity production: for Marx abstract labour develops 'in the measure that concrete labour becomes a totality of different modes of labour embracing the world market' (1972, p. 253). It is not simply in exchange, but in production itself, in production for exchange, that abstract labour is established as the form of social labour. Marx makes this clear:

> This division of a product into a useful thing and a value becomes partically important, only when exchange has acquired such an extension that useful articles are produced for the purpose of being exchanged, and their character as values has therefore to be taken into account, beforehand, during production. From this moment the labour of the individual producer acquires socially a two-fold character (1974a, p. 78).

While the commodity labour power can be seen as the product of domestic labour, it cannot be said that the commodity form of the product impinges on the domestic labour process, that its character as value is taken into account — this is clear from the fact that domestic labour does not cease to be performed when there is relative overproduction of its particular product. Without this indifference to the particular concrete form of labour, the domestic labourer does not assume the economic character of commodity producer. Consequently, domestic labour cannot be seen as abstract labour, the substance of value.

There is another sense in which domestic labour cannot manifest itself as abstract, and in that form social, labour which does not depend on the 'purpose' of the domestic labourer. Every system of social production must establish qualitative equivalence between the various concrete forms of labour. In a socially organized economy this equalization is a conscious process, but in a commodity economy it is carried out unconsciously through exchange. The reduction, in exchange, of different use values to their common quality as values entails the simultaneous reduction of the different forms of concrete labour that produced them to their common quality as abstract labour:

> Whenever, by an exchange, we equate as values our different products, by that very act, we also equate, as human labour, the different kinds of labour expended upon them.

> We are not aware of this, nevertheless we do it (Marx, 1974a, pp. 78–9).

Thus, as Rubin points out, the concept of abstract labour expresses the specific historical form of equalization of concrete labours as homogeneous labour that occurs under commodity production. Because domestic labour is performed in addition to labour performed in capitalist production, and so is performed independently of the regulation of labour through the value of its product, it is not equal and interchangeable with other concrete labours and so is not abstract (value creating) labour, the historical form of equal labour under commodity production. For Marx:

> [Abstract labour] is not merely the mental product of a concrete totality of labours. Indifference towards specific labours corresponds to a form of society in which individuals can with ease transfer from one labour to another, and where the specific kind is a matter of chance for them, hence of indifference. Not only the category, labour, but labour in reality has here become the means of creating wealth in general, and has ceased to be organically linked with particular individuals in any specific form (1973b, p. 104).[9]

According to Marx, it was the absence of this historical condition which 'prevented Aristotle from seeing that, to attribute value to commodities, is merely a mode of expressing all labour as equal human labour, and consequently as labour of equal quality' (1974a, p. 65). It is precisely because the capitalist mode of production leaves the 'maintenance and reproduction of the working-class . . . to the labourer's instincts of self-preservation and of propagation' (Marx, 1974a, p. 537),[10] and that this falls in particular to the female section of the proletariat, that domestic labour does not become equal with other concrete labours and so is not expressed as abstract labour. Here we see again that it is the specific oppression of women in capitalist social formations – as the main bearers of the domestic work burden and as occupying an inferior position in social production, aspects which are mutually reinforcing – that is not simply an addition to Seccombe's framework of analysis of domestic labour, but completely undermines it.

Having established that domestic labour does not achieve equivalence with other forms of labour qualitatively, as abstract labour (substance of value), we can now see that it cannot achieve equivalence quantitatively, as socially necessary labour (magnitude of value). There is no mechanism whereby individual domestic labour can be expressed as socially necessary labour; there is no competition between 'domestic units' (Seccombe) to minimize the labour time embodied in their products; inefficient households do not fail to sell their commodity. There are two aspects to this. First, there is no social mechanism which defines the necessary tasks which are supposed to contribute to the value of labour power — if cooking meals is necessary for its production, why not eating them?[11] One might as well argue that since sleeping is necessary for the replenishment of the capacity to labour, it too is value creating labour. Second, there is no mechanism which ensures individual labour time tends towards socially necessary labour time, or which relates the value of labour power to the average level of productivity of domestic labour. Without this dual reduction of individual labour to socially necessary labour, there can be no measure of the magnitude of value produced by domestic labour. While traditionally the qualitative aspect (value form) of Marx's theory of value has been neglected, in favour of treating it in a Ricardian manner merely as a theory of price determination, the quantitative aspect (magnitude of value) cannot be discarded or treated as separate since for Marx 'What was decisively important, however, was to discover the inner, necessary connection between value-*form*, value-*substance*, and value-*amount*' (1976b, p. 34). While '*Ricardo's* mistake is that he is concerned only with the *magnitude of value*' (Marx, 1972, p. 131) to the neglect of the social form in which the social character of human labour is expressed as the value of its product, the opposite error of the 'restored mercantile system (Ganilh, &c.), which sees in value nothing but a social form, or rather the unsubstantial ghost of that form' (Marx, 1974a, p. 85n), similarly breaks the 'inner, necessary connection' between magnitude of value, substance of value, and value form. Individual, concrete labour cannot become abstract (value creating) labour without simultaneously being reduced to socially necessary labour — the qualitative and quantitative aspects of the equivalence established in exchange are inseparable. Thus although the commodity labour power achieves equivalence with all other commodities through its sale, domestic labour does not become equalized with all other forms of labour and so is not reduced to socially necessary and abstract labour. Since, under commodity production, abstract labour is the only form in which private labour becomes social labour, domestic labour, despite being materialized in a social use value, remains private. It is not because domestic labour is private that it cannot become abstract labour; it is because it cannot become abstract labour that it remains private.

To argue that domestic labour is value producing implies that it is abstract labour, and therefore indirectly social labour, under the capitalist mode of production through its contribution to the production of the commodity labour power. It follows from this that to posit domestic labour as directly social labour, a socialist social formation would not need to collectivize the domestic labour process. Thus the apparent radicalism of Seccombe and Dalla Costa and James in their attempts to 'complement' Marx is quite spurious in that it obscures the historical specificity of the private domestic labour process. Similarly, the associated demand of 'wages for housework', despite its proponents' intentions, can only serve to legitimize privatized domestic labour.

Returning to the point that domestic labour does not achieve quantitative equivalence with other concrete labours, it is true Seccombe recognizes that 'whether a domestic task is completed in one hour or four has no effect on capital', but he fails to see the significance of this for the magnitude of value that domestic labour is supposed to produce. This value he simply assumes to be equivalent to the value of the domestic labourer's means of subsistence. The assumption of equal exchange between wage labourer and domestic labourer — and it can only be assumption since there is no mechanism which ensures equality — obscures the domestic labourer's legal-economic dependence on the wage labourer. Furthermore, Seccombe himself quotes Marx's point that 'if we now compare the two processes of producing value and of creating surplus-value, we see that the latter is nothing but the continuation of the former beyond a definite point'

(Seccombe, 1974, p. 12), but he does not recognize that this is inconsistent with his own point that the duration of domestic labour is unregulated. Thus he argues, in effect, that there is no way of measuring the magnitude of value supposed to be created by domestic labour but it just happens, fortuitously, to be equal to that borne by the domestic labourer's means of subsistence.

Because, as we have seen, domestic labour does not constitute a branch of social production and is not expressed as abstract labour, it does not enter into society's labour-totality. This cannot be regarded as some empirical aggregate (such as, working population multiplied by normal working day) but must, for a commodity economy, refer to that labour which is socially allocated by the law of value since, as Marx says, 'the standard of "socialness" must be borrowed from the nature of those relationships which are proper to each mode of production, and not from conceptions which are foreign to it' (1976b, p. 32). Labour is social if it is part of the total homogeneous labour which, in a commodity economy, is abstract labour. In a consciously regulated economy, domestic labour, as socially useful labour, can be incorporated into the social process of production and thus constitute a branch of the social division of labour. (This, of course, is not automatic: direct social regulation of production is a necessary condition for, not a guarantee of, this incorporation.) Marx's theory of value explains how the capitalist mode of production distributes its total labour without planning, without conscious regulation – if domestic labour is included in this total labour, despite its performance independently of the operation of the law of value, then the allocation of the labour-totality becomes inexplicable. For the capitalist mode of production, social labour can only be that which is socially regulated in a reified form, through the value of its product – abstract labour.[12] Here again we see the close connection between magnitude of value and substance of value, socially necessary labour and abstract labour since 'magnitude of value expresses a relation of social production, it expresses the connexion that necessarily exists between a certain article and the portion of the total labour-time of society required to produce it' (Marx, 1974a, p. 104). Without a means to enforce socially necessary labour, domestic labour cannot be expressed in a definite magnitude of value and does not constitute a portion of society's total homogeneous labour, does not constitute social labour in a commodity economy.

Marx's analysis of the commodity and its production revealed three aspects of value — its form, substance and magnitude. While the product of domestic labour, if it is viewed as producing the commodity labour power rather than use values for immediate consumption, assumes the value form — since 'social form of the commodity and value-form or form of exchangeability are thus one and the same thing' (Marx, 1976b, p. 29) — domestic labour cannot be subsumed under either abstract labour or socially necessary labour. Thus Marx's two definitions of the value of labour power, with which this paper started, are seen to be consistent since domestic labour cannot form part of 'the average labour of society' and so cannot be seen as contributing to this value.

In terms of Marx's theory of value, domestic work has the property, along with all other forms of concrete labour acting on commodities, of *transferring* value piecemeal by transforming the material bearers of a definite magnitude of value. As Marx points out,

> the labourer preserves the values of the consumed means
> of production, or transfers them as portions of its value to
> the product, not by virtue of his additional labour, ab-
> stractedly considered, but by virtue of the particular useful
> character of that labour, by virtue of its special productive
> form (1974a, p. 194).

Thus, domestic labour, by working on the means of subsistence in a useful way, transfers their value to the replenished labour power but does not add to that value. This reconciles the necessity of domestic labour in the reproduction of the commodity labour power with the purely private and individual character of that labour.

Domestic labour is, then, not problematic for Marx's theory of value because it is not part of its object, the production and exchange of commodities. Consequently, it does not form part of the capitalist mode of production of commodities, but is rather one of its external conditions of existence which it continually reproduces: 'This incessant reproduction, this perpetuation of the labourer, is the *sine qua non* of capitalist production' but 'his private consumption, which is at the same time the reproduction of his labour-power, falls outside the process of producing commodities' (Marx, 1974a, p. 536; 1976a, p. 1004). The domestic labour debate, and the wider discussion of productive and unproductive labour, has been characterized by a lack of rigour in the use of the concept of a mode of production such that anything connected with the capitalist mode of production is subsumed under it. With respect to domestic labour, this procedure neglects Marx's simple point about the circulation of capital:

> Within its process of circulation, . . . industrial capital, whether as money-capital or as commodity-capital, crosses the commodity-circulation of the most diverse modes of social production, so far as they produce commodities. No matter whether commodities are the output of production based on slavery, of peasants . . ., of communes . . ., of state enterprise . . . or of half-savage hunting tribes, etc. . . . The character of the process of production from which they originate is immaterial (1974b, p. 113).

The scientific analysis of the capitalist mode of production and of social formations dominated by it, requires that it is clearly distinguished from other forms of production to which it relates in such social formations. Domestic labour and state enterprise, for example, need to be distinguished from the capitalist mode of production if their determination by it is to be understood,[13] whereas their subsumption under it constitutes a rejection of Marx's theory of capitalist development for a sociologistic and empiricist conflation of mode of production and social formation.

The expansion of the concept of the capitalist mode of production is evident, for example, in Ian Gough's (1975) attempt to squeeze the various expenditures of the 'capitalist state' into the departments of capitalist production. Capital, it would seem, is superfluous to capitalist production. The theoretical assimilation of the social formation into the mode of production has resulted in the conflation of productive labour and labour which is necessary for the capitalist mode of production.

For example, for Dalla Costa and James 'the entire female

role' is 'essential to the production of surplus value' and so the 'passivity of the woman in the family . . . becomes productive for capitalist organization' (1975, pp. 33 and 42); for Gough, circulation workers are 'essential for the smooth functioning of commodity production' and hence 'indirectly productive'[14] despite being employed by the surplus value produced by productive labour; housewives too are, for Gough, 'indirectly productive for capital' and state expenditure is seen as increasingly 'productive' because 'more and more it is a necessary precondition for private capital accumulation' (1975, p. 80). This identification of 'necessary' and 'productive' would mean that, for example, the police, technological innovation, natural forces, are all 'productive'. This confusion ignores Marx's warning that 'there are works and investments which may be necessary without being productive in the capitalist sense' (1973a, p. 531). While productive labour is internal to the capitalist mode of production in that it is necessarily exchanged against capital, activities which secure its conditions of existence are external to it, however functional they may be for it. This confusion of productive labour and necessary functions, evident in Gough's work, rests on a confusion of the concrete, useful form of labour and its social form, determined by the relations of production. This is further expressed in Gough's claim that the growth of products designed to meet consumer needs which may be regarded as 'unnecessary' or 'inessential' has a bearing on Marx's theory of productive and unproductive labour. Consequently, for Gough,

> The principal ambiguity in Marx's theory of productive and unproductive labour . . . is the use of a historical perspective to distinguish the labour necessary to produce a given use-value, whilst rigorously denying the use of such a perspective to determine the 'necessity' of the final 'use-value' itself. The productiveness of labour depends on the former, but not the latter, according to Marx (1972, pp. 61–2).

Gough ignores the fact that Marx's definition of productive labour in the capitalist mode of production is made from the standpoint of capital, not from the point of view of Gough's blueprint for socialist production. Marx's 'ambiguity' consists in 'rigorously denying' the subjectivism and utopianism evident in Gough. It is not Marx who is indifferent to the use values produced, but *capital* (see, for example, Marx 1976a, pp. 1045 and 1046).

The position of privatized domestic labour as an external necessity for the capitalist mode of production is clear from the separation of domestic labour from social production as the specifically capitalist mode of production developed. For Marx 'there is immanent in capital an inclination and constant tendency, to heighten the productiveness of labour' in order to produce relative surplus-value (1974a, p. 303), and so 'the conditions of production, . . . and the labour-process itself, must be revolutionised' (1974a, p. 298). The first step in this process is the destruction of domestic industry, the gathering of workers together under one roof: 'A greater number of labourers working together, at the same time, in one place . . . constitutes, both historically and logically, the starting-point of capitalist production' (Marx, 1974a, p. 305). By transforming the economic basis of the family from productive property to the wage, the development of the capitalist mode of production transforms it from a productive unit to a centre of consumption. It is only by recognizing that the reproduction of labour power takes place outside the capitalist mode of production, although of course in a manner determined by it, that the relative technological backwardness of the domestic labour process can be understood – the alternative is to separate technical change from the social relations of production.

Both sides in the domestic labour debate recognize that it was the establishment of the capitalist mode of production that brought about the privatization of domestic labour, its exclusion from social production, yet both sides attempt to include this excluded sector within the capitalist mode of production. Thus for Seccombe 'the division of the capitalist mode of production into domestic and industrial units removes the housewife from any direct relation with capital' (1974, p. 7), and yet he wants to 'situate the housewife accurately in the capitalist mode of production' (p. 11n) – it is a strange conception of the capitalist mode of production in which capital is absent from what is regarded as one of its two sectors. It is absurd, then, for Seccombe to note that the capitalist mode of production creates the division between domestic labour and social production and then to bemoan marxists' 'failure to consider domestic labour within the capitalist relations of production'. Similarly, Zaretsky notes that 'with the rise of industry, capitalism "split" material production between its socialized forms (the sphere of commodity production) and the private labour performed predominantly by women within the home' (1976, p. 29), and yet complains of writers who share 'the idea of a split between the family and the economy' (p. 23). Marx ridiculed this sort of argument: 'As if this rupture had made its way not from reality into the textbooks, but rather from the textbooks into reality, and as if the task were the dialectic balancing of concepts, and not the grasping of real relations' (1973b, p. 90).

It is not Marx's theory of value which marginalizes domestic labour, but the capitalist mode of production. The separation of the worker from his or her labour, and its absorption into capital as its variable component, entails the separation of individual consumption (the production of labour power) from productive consumption (the consumption of labour power): the reproduction of capitalist relations of production, then, entails the reproduction of the privatized, technically backward nature of domestic labour. The abolition of this separation, of the commodity form of labour power, is, therefore, a necessary condition for the socialization of domestic labour.

Notes

1 The proponents of this case are taken to be Wally Seccombe (1974) who argues that domestic labour produces value but is unproductive labour, and Mariarosa Dalla Costa and Selma James (1975) who argue housework 'is *productive* in the Marxian sense, that is, producing surplus value' (p. 53, note 12). Seccombe is taken as the main exponent as his position is the least extreme of the two and the least dependent on rhetoric. The marxist response has come from Jean Gardiner (1975), Coulson *et al.* (1975), and Adamson *et al.* (1976). The last is taken as the main reply in that it is the most comprehensive of the three and takes the others into consideration. While it makes many correct points against Seccombe, these are not proved but remain at the level of dogmatic assertion.

It has since transpired (see *Revolutionary Communist Papers*, no.

1, 1977, p. 48) that the relevant section of this last article (Adamson *et al.*, 1976, pp. 7—14) was written by David Yaffe. It seems appropriate, then, to acknowledge the influence of Yaffe's earlier work, in particular 'Value and price in Marx's *Capital*' in *Revolutionary Communist*, no. 1, 1975, pp. 31—49.

2 The point that the *immediate* products of the various tasks which constitute domestic labour are use values not commodities, and that this differentiates housework from commodity production, could just as well be applied to each branch of the technical division of labour within capitalist enterprises. Coulson *et al.* would not, however, claim this meant their final products were not commodities.

3 This approach, despite Seccombe's intentions, shifts the problem to intrafamilial relations and particularly the distribution of the wage.

4 Without this analogy, value is identified with labour, that is to say, seen as independent of the social relations within which labour is performed. This is the case with the view, held for example by Gardiner, that 'domestic labour does not create value, on the definition of value which Marx adopted, but does nonetheless contribute to surplus value by keeping down necessary labour, or the value of labour power, to a level that is lower than the actual subsistence level of the working class' (1975, p. 58). While domestic labour certainly contributes to workers' standard of living it does not thereby indirectly create surplus value. This view confuses the magnitude of the value of labour power (a definite portion of society's homogeneous labour) with a set of use values (workers' standard of living). However, necessary labour and surplus value are a function of the former, not the latter.

5 Throughout, Marx's definition of productive labour from the standpoint of capital is adhered to — that is, labour exchanged against capital in the sphere of production and producing surplus value. Productive labour is, then, labour which transforms money and commodities into capital. It is in this sense that productive labour produces capital, and not by reference to whether the particular use values produced can re-enter production. Thus workers engaged in luxury production and immaterial production can be productive.

An excellent discussion of the theory of productive and unproductive labour, pointing up its crucial importance in Marx's work and charting the 'dour and dismal progress of contemporary revisionism', is to be found in Peter Howell's (1975) article.

6 Similarly, this article repeatedly asserts that it is crucial that there is an absolute limit to the extent to which capital can socialize domestic labour, which is doubtless correct, but without any genuine demonstration of why this is so. Coulson *et al.* make the same assertion and yet claim that at the peak of the industrial revolution 'in many areas of Britain domestic work was commercialized, in a haphazard sort of way' resulting in the 'disappearance of privatized housework' (1975, p. 66).

7 E. Mandel, Introduction to Marx, *Capital*, vol. I, Penguin, Harmondsworth, 1976, p. 14; Engels, 'Law of value and rate of profit', supple-

ment to Marx (1974c, pp. 891–907), pp. 899–900. Thus Engels arrived at the astonishing view that Marx's 'theory of value and of money . . . [is] on the whole, immaterial to what we consider the vital points of Mr Marx's views on capital' – review of first edition of *Capital*, vol. I, reprinted in Engels, *On Marx's Capital*, Progress Publishers, Moscow, 1976, p. 29.

A lucid exposition of Marx's theory of value which emphasizes the point made in the text is to be found in Rubin (1972).

8 This paragraph follows Rubin (1972, pp. 63–7). Abstraction is made here from differing organic compositions of different branches of capitalist production – at a lower level of abstraction, where differing organic compositions are considered, equilibrium consists in exchange at prices of production and the establishment of a general rate of profit. However, this is not a problem here since we are examining the possibility of subsuming domestic labour under simple, not capitalist, commodity production.

9 This reveals the close connection between the concepts of abstract labour and alienated labour. But note that the movement 'with ease' between branches of production refers to 'indifference' towards the particular use values and concrete labours because exchange, hence value and not utility, provides the purpose of production. It is not the case that this 'ease' of movement refers to the 'de-skilling' of labour under the specifically capitalist mode of production – that is, the result of capital's continual transformation of the labour process in order to produce relative surplus value – described in Part IV of *Capital*, vol. I, and in H. Braverman, *Labor and Monopoly Capital*, Monthly Review Press, New York, 1974. While this latter process will facilitate the movement of labour, the view that this 'de-skilling' process means abstract labour increasingly becomes a social reality represents the common confusion of abstract labour (the opposite of concrete labour) with simple labour (the opposite of skilled labour). Abstract labour emerges with production for exchange, while the reduction of complex labour to simple labour becoming increasingly a social reality is contingent upon the development of the specific mode of capitalist production and so presupposes generalized commodity production.

10 Although the notion of 'instincts' is perhaps foreign to historical materialism, the point is that the reproduction of labour power is external to a mode of production directed towards the production of surplus value.

11 Marx ridicules the view that 'the labour of eating . . . produces brain, muscles, etc.' which stems from 'the stupidity that consumption is just as productive as production' (1969, pp. 185–6).

12 'The total labour power of society, which is embodied in the sum total of the values of all commodities produced by that society . . .' (Marx, 1974a, p. 46). Thus non-commodity producing labour organized by the bourgeois state is also excluded from the capitalist mode of production's labour-totality. The sociologistic identification of the capitalist mode of production and state economic activity

facilitates the confusion of 'full' employment with the absence of
Marx's industrial reserve army and the obscuring of the production
of relative surplus population in the capitalist mode of production.
The labour-totality, moreover, consists of socially necessary labour.
This refers both to the labour embodied in an individual commodity
such that any excess of individual labour time over that socially
necessary is wasted, from the point of view of value (Marx, 1974a,
p. 196), and to the total labour employed in a given branch of
production such that labour is wasted when its product is dispro-
portionately produced relative to other branches of production,
when the total labour employed in it exceeds the socially necessary
(Marx, 1974c, p. 636).

13 The basis of an explanation of the role and limits of state expenditure in terms of Marx's theory of value and capital accumulation is
laid in D. Yaffe, 'The Marxian theory of crisis, capital and the state',
Bulletin of the Conference of Socialist Economists, winter 1972,
pp. 5—58, reprinted in *Economy and Society*, no. 2, 1973, pp.
186—232, and P. Bullock and D. Yaffe, 'Inflation, the crisis and the
post-war boom', *Revolutionary Communist* no. 3/4, 1975, pp. 5—45.

14 The view that commercial workers are productive, deriving from
Adam Smith, expresses the viewpoint of the individual capitalist —
see Howell (1975, p. 62) and Marx (1974c, p. 43).

References

Adamson, O., Brown, C., Harrison, J., and Price, J. (1976), 'Women's
oppression under capitalism', *Revolutionary Communist*, no. 5,
pp. 2—48.

Coulson, M., Magaš, B., and Wainwright, H. (1975), ' "The housewife
and her labour under capitalism" — a critique' *New Left Review*, no.
89, pp. 59—71.

Dalla Costa, M., and James, S. (1975), *The Power of Women and the
Subversion of the Community*, Falling Wall Press, Bristol.

Gardiner, J. (1975), 'Women's domestic labour', *New Left Review*, no.
89, pp. 47—58.

Gough, I. (1972), 'Productive and unproductive labour in Marx', *New
Left Review*, no. 76, pp. 47—72.

Gough, I. (1975), 'State expenditure in advanced capitalism', *New Left
Review*, no. 92, pp. 53—92.

Harrison, J. (1973), 'The political economy of housework' in *Bulletin
of the Conference of Socialist Economists* vol. 4, pp. 35—51.

Howell, P. (1975), 'Once again on productive and unproductive labour',
Revolutionary Communist, no. 3/4, pp. 46—68.

Marx, K. (1969), *Theories of Surplus Value*, part I, Lawrence & Wishart,
London.

Marx, K. (1972), *Theories of Surplus Value*, part III, Lawrence &
Wishart, London.

Marx, K. (1973a), *Grundrisse*, Penguin, Harmondsworth.

Marx, K. (1973b), '1857 introduction' in Marx (1973a), pp. 81—111.
Marx, K. (1974a), *Capital*, vol. I, Lawrence & Wishart, London.
Marx, K. (1974b), *Capital*, vol. II, Lawrence & Wishart, London.
Marx, K. (1974c), *Capital*, vol. III, Lawrence & Wishart, London.
Marx, K. (1976a), 'Results of the immediate process of production' in Marx, *Capital*, vol. I, Penguin, Harmondsworth, pp. 948—1084.
Marx, K. (1976b), 'The commodity', vol. 1, chapter 1 of the first edition of *Capital*, in *Value: Studies by Marx*, New Park Publications, London.
Marx. K. (1976c), 'The form of value', appendix to first edition of *Capital*, in *Value: Studies by Marx*.
Mitchell, J. (1966), 'Women: the longest revolution', *New Left Review*, no. 40, pp. 11—37.
Rubin, I. (1972), *Essays on Marx's Theory of Value*, Black & Red, Detroit.
Seccombe, W. (1974), 'The housewife and her labour under capitalism', *New Left Review*, no. 83, pp. 3—24.
Zaretsky, E. (1976), *Capitalism, the Family and Personal Life*, Pluto Press, London.

9 Women, sex, and class

Jackie West

The question of 'class' is a vexed one within sociological debate, in which it tends to be raised as a central concept in analyses concerned with 'inequalities' in contemporary societies. In terms of such 'conventional' analyses the specific class position of women can never be considered, for a social category defined in terms of the theoretical framework adopted relegates women to 'second-hand' status. Bearing in mind that this is a 'legitimate' area of study, its impact must obviously be very great, particularly when it is considered how much funding is received by sociological work on stratification. In this paper Jackie West exposes the inadequacies of a functionalist approach which, starting as it does with the family as the basic unit in class allocation and locating the position of the family in the class hierarchy as derived from the status of the male head of the household, can in no way account for the specific position of women in a class society. The argument put forward here is that the starting-point for an analysis of women's class position lies in the transformations which have occurred within the division of labour, and that it is the question of the proletarianization of certain sectors in the economy which needs to be addressed. The way in which the distinction between productive and unproductive labour is conceptualized, for instance by Poulantzas, is questioned here. On this issue there is certainly no consensus amongst marxist scholars: here it is articulated in the question of whether the increased proportion of white-collar workers in the occupational structure is resulting in an increased 'proletarianization'. The importance of this analysis to the location of women with regard to class relations stems precisely from the fact of their widespread employment in the white-collar sectors of the workforce, and a consideration of the specificity of the sexual division of labour is predicated in an examination of the implications of this situation. West considers the way in which the family institution structures the sexual division of labour, and poses the problem of why it is that women — and not immigrants or school leavers or unemployed men — are recruited for employment, an issue which, she argues, tends to be overlooked by writers such as Poulantzas and Braverman. However, while the conclusion here is that the only basis for analysing the class position of women is through capitalist labour relations and the specificity of women's position within them, the problem of how to deal with married women who are not paid workers, the topic precisely of the 'domestic labour debate' addressed in the previous paper, is left unresolved.

It is no longer unusual to note that the relationship of women or sex to certain basic sociological phenomena has tended to be regarded as irrelevant or non-problematic. 'Women and class' is no exception. As recently as 1972 a respected sociologist was able to make, merely in passing, the following unqualified remark:

> Let me, in a higgledy-piggledy way, list some obvious points. Women are ambiguous: they may do more than men to sustain the ideology of class, and yet it is clear that they are, even when 'gainfully employed' less central to social classes than are men (MacRae, 1972, p. 209).

And yet reference is often made in the conventional social science literature to women or sex in order, for example, to justify a concentration on men, to distinguish class or stratification from social differentiation or to highlight significant features of the class structure. Indeed the position of women is frequently 'used' to substantiate other arguments. Exclusion has never been complete but has rather coincided with a belief in the marginality of female labour and sexual divisions with regard to class analysis, although the reasons for this cannot be examined here. Some recent marxist contributions challenge, more or less indirectly, the prevailing image of marginality in according the place in the class structure occupied by women a critical significance in understanding contemporary class relations (Braverman, 1974; Poulantzas,

1975): but a concern with sexual divisions as such is far from central to this work, the limitations of which will be considered later in this paper. Sociological conceptualisations have been based on notions of 'second-hand status' or derived class, and on various views on the irrelevance or otherwise of sex to class and of women's occupations to the class system (Parkin, 1971; Hamilton, 1972; Giddens, 1973). These contributions are frequently brief, which may account for the fact that their problematic nature has gone largely unnoticed. Underpinning most analyses of this type have been two basic and related assumptions, namely that women's place is in the family, and that the family — apart from its (male) breadwinner linkage to the economy — is outside class analysis. Women have been confined chiefly to their position as housewives and female employment has been theoretically subordinated to the claims of domesticity. These assumptions, however, have not prevented the family from being seen as the crucial, if not the only, determinant of women's class position.

The aim of this paper is to consider the implications of female employment for women's class position. I believe it is essential to deal with this before we can adequately integrate the two facets of women's position as housewife and paid worker: it is necessary before we can break down the polarity between the two and arrive at an understanding of women in the class structure. To focus exclusively on the 'dual role' of women is to suggest more ambiguity and complexity in the position of women than may in fact exist. Without an adequate theoretical appreciation of women's direct relationship to and experience of productive and market forces, we continue the mistaken tradition of allocating women to a wholly special place in our society which so easily becomes a 'problem' area requiring entirely different tools of enquiry. Special concepts and methods must have their place alongside those modes of analysis which we use to understand the class structure in general. The first part of this paper is concerned essentially with how one theorises — or rather should not theorise — women and class. The second part is primarily an examination of analyses which, by being centred around female labour, begin to overcome problems in conceptualising women's class position: it is also an attempt to move towards some substantive conclusions about women's white-collar work and its location in the class structure.

I

The conventional argument on women's class position, which in effect accords women class by proxy, revolves around the old 'truth' that the family is the unit of the class system; it concerns the implications of marriage and assumptions about both the critical significance of male as opposed to female labour and the shared class position of women and their men. Now, whatever the basis for the view that the family is the unit of the class system, and however acceptable it is to use an argument about shared class to disprove the notion that women are a class, it does not follow — as is often assumed — that women do not occupy an independent or indeed particular place in the class structure, nor that sexual divisions make no contribution to this. Women, or for that matter any other group, do not need to constitute a separate class in order to have a class position in their own right or having their own specificity, as they might, for example, within classes. Even though the assumption about the family unit has already come under severe attack, it still remains the most prevalent. General texts on class theory and empirical studies continue to maintain its validity (Parkin, 1971, p. 14; Giddens, 1973, p. 301 note 5; Hamilton, 1972, pp. 153 and 188–9; Anderson, 1974, p. 317). Its continued uncritical acceptance doubtless lies partly in the lack of serious attention given to feminist critiques within sociology; but also, I believe, in a tendency for the critiques themselves frequently to bypass some of the central issues, for example by concentrating on questions of ranking rather than objective class positions. It should be noted that even if the family is the unit of the class system, this does not necessarily entail the notion that women's class position is determined through their families. In the conventional literature the two assumptions are seen as integrally related, mutually reinforcing, yet it is the latter which is the most theoretically problematic.

First, the family is seen as the unit of the class system because it acts as a 'placement agency' ensuring continuity in the reward position of family units and thus stratification rather than just inequalities *per se*; it is the family which is the major unit of reward and, for example, it is families and not individuals which have a life cycle and a standard of living. Second, the allocation of economic and social rewards, though in general deriving from the occupational order, in the case of women, however, is seen to be determined primarily by the position of their families, and in particular by the occupations of their husbands or fathers, not their own. This is supposedly due to the fact that men are the main breadwinners — women's paid employment is intermittent (and may involve less commitment) because of marriage and child care, and is apparently secondary since women's earnings 'only supplement' those of their husbands. Thus since class or even stratification analysis is concerned with the relationship of groups to the productive and market system but women have only a secondary link to those systems, women's class position is seen to be mediated by or through their husbands and the latter's involvement in work. Hence, also, wives and daughters generally identify their position and interests, not in opposition to, but with, those of their male kin, and they are likely to share beliefs and values. In other words women are thought to lack a common condition and interests, or at least that any shared interests are insufficient to override their common class position and interests as identified with those of their menfolk (Parkin, 1971, ch. 1; Hamilton, 1972, p. 153; Anderson, 1974, pp. 315–19; Szymanski, 1976, pp. 105–6 and 108). Finally, the family's role in the placement of women to positions in the class hierarchy has been seen — for example by Parkin — as especially critical. But it should be noted that, in view of the above arguments, the family is conceptualised not simply as placing (allocating) *women* to positions in the same general way as men, but as accounting for a special position in the social system, a class position which derives from men and marriage. That is, even allowing for the fact that references to the placement of women in the class system 'through membership of a kin group' refer to the recruitment of women to class positions, the determination of those positions is seen to lie in the positions of husbands (or fathers) through marriage (or paternity). Within this problematic, the only other possibility is that women do not have a position in the class system at all, but merely a position in the *social* system defined by family relationships.

Criticisms of these approaches have emphasised the significance of three issues: first, unattached and/or non-dependent women whose social position is not derived from their families or male heads of households; second, stratification by gender (Acker, 1973), and third, stratification within the family (Gillespie, 1972; Middleton, 1974; Whitehead, 1976; Bell and Newby, 1976). However, gender stratification, though often conceptualised as separate from class, simply provides an additional criterion to the existing analyses, and stratification within the family does not go beyond locating women *in* the family. Discussion of the sources of women's position has tended to emphasise that of housewives and to deal with status rather than class (Oakley, 1974, pp. 9 and 13; Marceau, 1976; Acker, 1973; Hutton, 1974). The conventional belief that men are the main breadwinners has not, however, gone unchallenged. While the questions arising from this are more important than the data themselves, it is worth pausing to consider the relevant British evidence. At least one in six households are substantially or solely supported by women. However, this is only the tip of the iceberg. This figure (of chiefly or exclusively female breadwinners) excludes pensioner households and, more significantly, those where there is a man in full time work, for in such cases the man is automatically counted as the chief breadwinner whether he is or not (Land, 1976, p. 119). Women now comprise over 40 per cent of the employed population and at least 43 per cent of women are in the labour force. Contrary to prevailing myth, only between one in three and one in two women workers are part timers, and the proportion of married women workers falling into this category is less than half.[1] Furthermore, by 1971 almost as many as two out of five married women with two dependent children were counted as officially 'economically active'.

This immediately suggests, first, that the notion of the family as the unit of the class system must precisely take into account women's economic role. More significantly it raises the question of the determination of women's class position by indicating women's particular place in the general division of labour. How are we to interpret this? What class place is indicated by women's occupations?

The family's status as unit of the class system rests on the notion that what we should have in mind is the material life experience of its members, and the family as the unit of reward. But once the contribution made by women's earnings is recognised, we cannot ignore women's occupations as if they had no influence on their own or their family's well being, particularly when it is suggested that it is the family's position which determines that of the woman. Such considerations importantly do not only apply to households headed by women (although it is here most of all that the composition of the domestic unit does not correspond to conventional ideas on the family unit). There are many families whose material standard of living is maintained or increased through the contribution made by working wives;[2] although this is not to deny that in many cases women are economically dependent on their husbands – or to be more precise that families are often more materially dependent on men (who generally earn more) than women.

The second major question that arises here concerns the conceptualisation of class position. There are theoretical as well as empirical objections to the notion of derived class. The determination of class lies in the mode of production to which women have a relationship, as do men. If married men and women share broadly similar class positions by virtue of their relation to the mode of production, then women as such do not constitute a class. They do not have class interests opposed to men. Assumptions about derived class are unnecessary as well as questionable. Whether women are the main breadwinners or not we must also consider the experience women have as workers, that experience from which stems their direct economic contribution to the family and, more realistically, their class position. Now of course, as a whole, women's place in the division of labour, as opposed to their relation to the mode of production, may be a specific one, particularly once account is taken of the material (as well as ideological) relationships of domestic work. Arguments to this effect, although examining the relationship of women to the class structure in terms of women's position in the family, have, however, also directly confronted the assumption of women's derived class by focusing on the material nature of women's labour (Middleton, 1974; Seccombe, 1974;

Gardiner, 1975; Coulson *et al.*, 1975). The arguments focus on a level of material relationships 'separate' from those affecting male labour and occupations. They are concerned with the material contribution of female labour to the position of the family and of consequence to the class structure as a whole, in particular the working class, and with the significance of female labour to the specific class position of women. This is the case even when domestic labour is not seen as itself productive, nor even contributing to the cost of labour power, but related to wage levels through the creation of use values which reduce the necessary amount of the ready-made or finished consumer goods that enter into the average subsistence level of the working class. It is not my purpose here to develop these arguments (see the contributions to the present volume by Veronica Beechey and Paul Smith) but merely to emphasise that women's place in the division of labour is specific not *only* because of female domestic labour, but is to an extent specific within the general division of labour *outside* the home. However, we can only adequately understand this by also recognising that women's position in the class structure (as that of any other group) is, at one level, given independently of women's relationship to the family, however the latter is conceptualised, and, perhaps paradoxically, that this class position is not *wholly* specific. By this I mean that its significance does not only lie in its being associated with women, that it is not necessarily unique to women, and that women's class interests are not entirely different from those of any other group.

If we are to understand the place of women in the class structure, a conceptual separation must be made between its component 'aspects'. Although in effect the class position of women may refer to both an available place in the division of labour and to the actual place(s) occupied by women, it is crucial to distinguish these analytically. Unless this is appreciated the question of whether women occupy a distinctive place in the class structure is ruled out of court, and so also the possible contribution of sexual divisions to this place is precluded. Only with the rejection of the notion of derived class can we have a better understanding not only of the class structure and of the class structure as it applies to women, but also of the role of sexual divisions within that structure.

With regard to women, as to men, we should be interested in the significance of class positions in relation to others in the class structure, as well as in the ways in which and the degree to which women's occupancy of those positions is significant. The difficulties are further compounded in as much as, to repeat, arguments ostensibly concerned with women as a class are in fact just as much about both women's actual class position and whether sexual inequalities have anything at all to do with this (Parkin, 1971, pp. 13—18). The notion that women are a class may be justifiably rejected on the grounds of the shared class position of most men and women. But this does not dispose of the question of the possibly distinctive place of women within classes. Classes are extremely broad and complex groupings. They are not homogeneous entities, they are divided by age, skill, sex and ethnicity (Glaberman, 1975; Phizacklea and Miles, 1976). Most men and women may, for instance, be working class, but this should not be a reason for ignoring important distinctions where they exist. On the subject of sexual divisions, conventional arguments have tended to introduce obscurity rather than clarity. For example, while sexual inequalities clearly cannot determine class positions as such,[3] this does not make them irrelevant to the allocation of agents to particular positions. In Parkin's analysis, for instance, there is, with regard to women, a certain confusion between positions in the class system and recruitment — despite his general attempt to separate them — in so far as the family is seen to play a determining role with regard to both processes, and in that he moves from one to the other within the context of the same argument. Further, conflating the issue of women as a class (or sexes as classes) with that of women's class position obscures the wider relationship of sexual and class divisions, for it means ignoring the relationship of sexual divisions and inequalities both to the specificity of a group's position within the class structure and also in terms of class relations.

One of the reasons for a failure in sociological analysis to consider women's occupations seems to be a belief that by so doing one is forced, unrealistically, to acknowledge a middle-class majority in western society or that family members occupy different class positions; given, that is, the increased employment of women, especially married women, in white-collar jobs (Hamilton, 1972, pp. 153–6; Perrow, 1972, p. 206; Szymanski, 1976, pp. 106–12). But to deal with these problems by assimilating women into the family is to use a double standard in class analysis. Serious analysis of female employment is avoided by retreating into conventional platitudes on the family unit and the significance of male jobs. Of course, the problems of including women would not arise if most women's occupations were taken for what they really are — as fundamentally or at least increasingly proletarian. Although the proletarianisation of white-collar work is far from an undisputed reality, analysis of it is hindered, not helped, by a refusal to consider it just because women happen to be the occupants of the jobs in question.

II

I have so far drawn attention to the ways in which, aside from theoretically inadequate conceptualisations, women's place in the class structure is actually ignored, to the way in which issues of concern to this place have been regarded instead as problematic for the class position of men, and also to the way that such tendencies rule out of court consideration of the interrelationship between class and sexual divisions, of questions such as the part the latter play in the class structure. I have also noted the problem of the specificity of women's class position. This requires brief reiteration before proceeding to an examination of some contributions which attempt to bridge these lacunae.

Women have a specific place in the class structure chiefly because of their actual or potential 'dual role'. This is true whether one is merely concerned with the way women's participation in production and the labour market is affected by their position in the family, or with the way in which the material relationships of domestic labour imply that women have specific class interests (Gardiner *et al.*, 1975). Sexual divisions generally also influence the available places in the division of labour outside the home to which women, rather than men, are drawn. But to phrase the issue in this way is already to presuppose that we know what these 'available places' in fact are. We may have relatively few problems if most women can be identified as part of the working class by virtue of their place in the division of labour, and more particularly the labour they perform in production. But can they be? Sociologists and marxists are by no means agreed on this and essentially the problem revolves around the place of white-collar labour, how one analyses it, what has been happening to it, in particular whether or not it has been proletarianised. We also know that women are concentrated in certain types of paid labour: does this, for instance, indicate a specific position as a distinct stratum, a 'subclass' even, of the proletariat, if not of the middle class? Such a question can obviously be answered only by reference to class structuration as a whole. In other words, we cannot grasp the specificity of women's class position unless we also have an understanding of what women's place in the class structure actually is. I do not stress these points merely in order to be pedantic, but because the fact that these are often overlooked can, as I hope to show, permit a misinterpretation not only of women's class position but of the class structure as a whole. This is (especially) true of one of the few contributions to take seriously female paid labour, that of Giddens (1973). Unfortunately two others, Braverman and Poulantzas, while importantly avoiding these traps, tend to concentrate on class places to such an extent that they virtually exclude sexual divisions. However, the work of all three will be examined in detail in an effort to explore the adequacy and limitations of their attempts to understand women's place in the class structure and the functions of female labour, specifically 'white-collar labour', within it.

Giddens has argued that since women

> still have to await their liberation from the family, it
> remains the case in the capitalist societies that female
> workers are largely peripheral to the class system; or,
> expressed differently, women are in a sense the 'underclass'
> of the white collar sector (1973, p. 288).

Women constitute such an underclass because they are sexually disqualified from 'primary' jobs in the labour market as a result of prejudice and interruptions in labour availability due to marriage and childbirth. They thus tend to monopolise 'secondary' jobs, those which have a low economic return, and limited security, lack other economic benefits and chances of promotion. Although his perspective completely misses the sense in which the performance of semi-skilled irregular labour (quite apart from domestic labour) is integral to the entire economic system, this thesis deserves some attention, particularly because of his suggestion that the feminisation of white-collar occupations is one factor, among others, that accounts for the lack of merging between working and middle classes.

Giddens argues in general for the validity of the division between manual working class and white-collar middle class, and against what he calls the 'enormous mythology' that the overlap at the margins of these groups implies an overall merging of the two groupings. He is concerned at several points with the relationship of feminisation to the bases of working- and middle-class structuration, namely differing market capacity, 'paratechnical' and authority relations, neighbourhood segregation, class awareness and unionisation.

Overlap between the two groupings, or classes, in economic terms is confined to segments of skilled manual occupations and sales and clerical occupations. 'But', Giddens points out, 'the major characteristic of these latter occupations is that they are everywhere increasingly monopolised by women.' This is highly significant 'in considering the nature of the boundary between the working and middle classes'. This relates to his discussion of the 'buffer zone' and concerns mobility and conditions of labour. He points out that actual mobility between the two groupings is short range, in and out of a 'buffer zone' which lies across the manual/non-manual division, and argues that this 'acts to cushion any tendency towards the collapse of mobility differentials separating the two' (pp. 180–1). Giddens seems to dismiss the significance of any economic merging between the two groupings on the grounds that it is a merging between male skilled manual and female non-manual occupations, and also rather neglects the fact that much of the short-range mobility is actually between female non-manual occupations on the one hand and female semi- and unskilled manual occupations on the other. That the two classes do not merge via mobility or anything else is not the same thing as the collapse of differentials between segments of both — a point worth making since women's own class membership is also at issue here.

Feminisation also has something of a special place in connection with the way differences in paratechnical relations, independently of similarities in market capacity, serve to distinguish or divide the working from the middle classes. Such relations have to do with size of enterprise, homogeneity and mechanisation, for example. Of the latter Giddens suggests that its use in the office is quite different from its application to factory labour, but in addition it is again women who 'largely monopolise those occupations which are wholly routinised (e.g. typist, stenographer)'. What the significance of this might be is not here made clear. In an earlier passage Giddens notes: 'The very appropriateness of the designation "clerical" becomes questionable in the light of the introduction of mechanical means of carrying out tasks previously involving the "pen pushing" of the clerk.' However, he goes on, the influence of both this and weakened economic differentials 'upon pre-existing class relationships has frequently been exaggerated, not only in terms of their statistical significance, but *also because of the effects of the "feminisation" of clerical labour*' (p. 191; my emphasis). Although he qualifies this statement with the proviso that the changes are none the less real and bear on unionism, the drift of the analysis suggests that women's occupancy of positions in the labour market affects their class character. Against the view that a new process of polarisation is occurring through a massive *déclassement* of routinised white-collar labour, Giddens argues that:

> The fact that most of the occupations in question have become dominated by women workers probably acts to *solidify* as much as to dissolve the 'buffer zone' between the working and middle classes, and *certainly must lead us to reject any of the more sweeping assertions about the 'proletarianisation' of the lower levels of the white collar sector* (p. 288; my emphases).

This in itself, incidentally, suggests that female labour is less marginal than Giddens claims, for how can women workers be 'peripheral' if the 'underclass' they so neatly occupy is part of the 'buffer zone' which helps to prevent polarisation of the two major classes? But aside from this inconsistency there are more important issues.

First, there is the suggestion of a middle-class majority in contemporary capitalism, even if we allow for the possibility that women workers may strictly speaking be part of the 'buffer zone' between the two classes. For if at the same time women are seen, as a result of their increasing dominance of the white-collar sector, as an underclass of such, and if the white-collar sector, whatever its variations, remains fairly sharply distinguished from the working class, and if the 'feminine' nature of these occupations is seen as part of the argument against proletarianisation, then the middle class must be the 'major' class of contemporary capitalist society given the occupational distribution of the adult population and associated socio-economic and technical factors. Leaving aside here the possible political implications, this poses a subsidiary problem. Namely, if married women's white-collar employment denotes a non-proletarian position, the units of the class system, families, will mostly contain adult members who occupy different positions in that system. This might not present any difficulty were it not for the fact that these units are usually held to be indivisible as far as class interests and the like are concerned — why else refer to them as units? The problems presented by Giddens's analysis stem basically from a tacit assumption that women's place in the division of labour can be understood only in relation to women's domestic role. Giddens is not wrong to relate women's occupancy of an 'underclass' to domestic factors, but is incorrect in interpreting the significance of this place and the class membership that goes with it solely in these terms.

Giddens states that women's dominance of the routinised, lowest-level, white-collar occupations must lead us to reject sweeping assertions about proletarianisation. Feminisation is seen as qualifying the objective changes in white-collar work, or at least as altering their significance. His remarks imply that, whatever the systematic discrimination against women in the labour market, the character of certain jobs in that market depends on who occupies them. Indeed it may depend on the meaning of such jobs for their occupants, particularly in that they mean something very different for men and women. His comments on women's monopoly of routinised jobs which economically overlap with skilled manual work seem to be based on some unstated assumption that the

changes matter less for women, that one cannot compare
women's work with men's work, perhaps because women are
not full time breadwinners and are partially insulated from
the world of work. There are reminders of Crozier's suggestion
that 'the proletarianisation of white collar employees does
not have the same meaning at all if it is women, and not
heads of family, who comprise the majority of the group'.
Crozier's use of subjectivist 'explanations' in arriving at this
assessment is explicit: the 'deadening and alienating . . .
assembly line work [of the office] . . . may constitute a promotion' for women who thirty years before 'were' mere
'labourers, seamstresses or maids'. However uninteresting or
badly paid, white-collar work is also now carried out by
women (rather than men), moreover 'by women with
reduced aspirations' (Crozier, 1971, pp. 13–19).

Although Giddens does not make his assumptions explicit,
his analysis does suggest that we cannot read off the signals
we might regarding proletarianization because it is women
who are involved. Thus not only do sexual divisions explain
why women, as agents, occupy a particular place (an 'underclass'), but the agents themselves appear to affect, if not
alter, the very nature of the position occupied. Although
there is obviously some truth in this, the point I wish to
stress here is that positions are certainly not created and
reproduced entirely by those who occupy them. There is no
necessary sense in which an analysis of the changes in relations governing white-collar labour must be confounded by
the phenomenon of feminisation. Although the family and
corresponding sexual divisions influence how women and
to where women are drawn into the labour market, what I am
concerned with here is the problem of determining the class
place that such a position in the labour market implies. Only
when we have adequately established this can we understand
the nature of the distinctive place in the class structure
occupied by women, and indeed why it is women rather than
others who are found there.

If there is ambiguity to women's class membership it stems
much less from their 'dual role' than the complexity and contradictory location of their position in the general division of
labour, specifically their place in production; that is, their
place in economic, 'paratechnical' and authority relations. It

is not coincidental that women occupy the most disputed terrain of the class structure — both in the sense that women's presence there has itself led to confusion and mystification, and, more importantly, in the sense that it is a terrain whose changing features (about which there is such disagreement) have themselves drawn in female rather than male workers. But there are some questions about the place and functions of female labour in production which can only be answered by putting to one side the question of the family and of sexual divisions, and indeed of women as women. That is, we should in the first instance examine not agents in the division of labour but the objective positions to which they are recruited. It is of course marxism that has this emphasis at its core. Class here has to do with position in relation to the means of production but this does not simply mean ownership or non-ownership of such. The types and functions of ownership, and also of possession of control, are differentiated, but so also are their 'opposites'. All workers who sell their labour power perform surplus labour and some are specifically exploited through the production and appropriation of surplus value. The class structure is not a simple division between capital and labour, although its form is precisely given by the contradiction between them. Nor are the relations of production simply economic in the narrow sense but also involve, as will be seen, political and ideological components.

The marxist analysis of classes in capitalism has certain grey areas, precisely those which centre on the critical significance of 'white-collar' labour, and specifically whether it is now part of an expanded proletariat or is the new element of a distinct class, the *petite bourgeoisie*. There is considerable agreement, however, that the white-collar sector is undergoing transformations, that much of it is thus increasingly close to, if not part of, the working class, and that women predominate in the most transformed of the new wage-earning groups. For some, at least, the transformations it has undergone in recent decades are of greater importance than the fact that white-collar, service and sales labour is unproductive. What categories are used to designate and theorise about the new occupations are of more than mere academic interest: they have considerable political implications in that classes are real social forces. If the new groups are, in the final analysis, *petit bourgeois*, then although they may be useful in the struggle of the working class, alliances with them are potentially problematic and such groups may be unreliable class allies. But since it is women who inhabit the grey areas that constitute the disputed boundaries with the working class, the issue I wish to deal with here is whether most female white-collar workers remain outside of rather than being part of the proletariat.

First, let us turn to the transformations. These are to a large extent interlinked. They can be seen at their most extreme in both manual and white-collar service and retail sales labour. The great majority of low-level workers in services — such as restaurant and catering but also in health — and in the commercial sector have found their labour considerably rationalised, their tasks disassembled, their skills thus destroyed and training reduced to a minimum. The changes are manifested in increasing hours of labour time, earnings within a compressed range and linked to output, restricted career opportunities, generally unstable employment and marginality to a bureaucratic hierarchy, if 'workers' are part of it at all.[4] Recent research leaves little doubt as to the general process of deskilling and the way it affects mental labour in the office, particularly that of the clerical worker. Mechanisation is seen not to cause but to hasten the degradation of such work in that, whether automated or not, office machinery reduces mental involvement by controlling information, standardising and simplifying tasks. The product of such labour may be symbolic but it is increasingly produced by manual operations. The classic case of repetitive labour is the typing pool, but many other workers in banking, insurance, administration and related office work are far from immune. The changes affecting office labour are manifested in increased and monitored output and efficiency, and considerable advances in the technical division of labour which split up component tasks and assign them to different 'operatives' (Braverman, 1974, ch. 15; Hamilton, 1972, pp. 349—51; Mumford and Banks, 1967, pp. 27—30 and 183—94).

There is little doubt either that the fragmentation and routinisation of tasks is itself part of a change in the relations governing office labour. But what change exactly? And with what implications for place in the division of labour and thus the class structure? The extent to which the personal operating functions of the capitalist have now become, to a large extent, labour processes in their 'own right' is due both to the increasing importance and complexity of extracting surplus value and struggles over its ownership and distribution, and to the general separation of conception and execution; that is, between administration and planning on the one hand and physical production on the other. The deskilling of mental labour is part of the process of centralisation and the institution of new forms of authority in the modern enterprise, and the way in which the very division between decision (or conception) and execution has become more rigorous in the effort to control and co-ordinate production.

Braverman sees the transformation of clerical labour as due in particular to the application of scientific management to the office from the early decades of the twentieth century which has brought in its wake increasing control, discipline and reorganisation of labour. As with factory labour, wresting control from workers has necessitated the removal of dependence on craft knowledge and experience. But his analysis throws up two related problems. First, there is his questionable conclusion that the office is now entirely analogous to the 'continuous flow' production of the factory and that the processes of rationalisation have replaced the all-round clerical worker by the subdivided detail worker who has merely a 'white collar' to distinguish her from her sister in the factory. Second, his analysis leads to an oversimplistic conception of the working class and admits of barely no differentiation at all (apart from sex), let along cleavages. While he is undoubtedly correct to observe that the sex ratio is virtually reversed in clerical work compared with that of operatives, that changes in sex composition and pay emphasise the discontinuity with clerical work of an earlier period, and that the sex barrier itself has permitted the decline in wages and earnings, this does not necessarily mean that the 'chief remaining distinction' within the working class 'seems to be a division along the lines of sex'. This position stems from his contention that unproductive labour is not only mass labour and waged labour but in terms of its organisation, forms and conditions it is no longer in 'striking contrast' to productive labour but part of 'a continuous mass of employment . . . which has everything in common' (1974, p. 423). Athough Braverman does not completely reject the distinction between productive and unproductive labour, and argues that it enables us to understand the movements of capital and its effects (particularly in that the growth of unproductive labour is contingent on the expansion of surplus value, while productive labour has correspondingly decreased), he is too hasty in suggesting that unproductive labour remains distinct only in that it produces no surplus value, which he uses to argue for a virtually homogeneous mass. It may no longer be in *striking* contrast to the productive, but is this more true of its organisation than of the relations of which it is a part and of its functions (economic or otherwise)? And if so does this mean exclusion from the proletariat?

Such questions bring us specifically to the work of Poulantzas, who, more than any other, has forcefully argued that the new wage-earning groups constitute a distinct class, the new *petite bourgeoisie*. Poulantzas' objections to 'proletar-ianisation' hinge on his analysis of the way in which un-productive mental labour reproduces essentially bourgeois political and ideological relations. The mental–manual labour distinction has thus to do with a highly specific place in social relations, not a mere difference between clean and dirty, brain or hand work. His analysis — of which more below — is undoubtedly useful in countering the crudities of much contemporary marxism, mainly American, which sees almost everyone, from the shop floor and assembly line to the door of the director's office, as part of the working class (Anderson, 1974, ch. 5; Szymanski, 1976; Hacker, 1976). However, the new *petite bourgeoisie* is also seen as inherently fractionalised by cleavages drawn within it, and the transfor-mations affecting unproductive mental labour are seen to 'reinforce still more the polarisation of certain . . . fractions' in the direction of the working class' by being massively focused upon them' (Poulantzas, 1975, pp. 302–3). More-over, the statistically predominant fractions are precisely those which do have a proletarian polarisation, and it is these also which are heavily feminised. The three major fractions are, first, that of low-level sales and service workers; second, that of bureaucratised workers in banking, administration, the civil service, education and so on; and third, that of low-level technicians and engineers.

Now while for Braverman, for instance, an inevitable concomitant of the general expansion of office labour (in the effort to control production) has been its own subjection to control and co-ordination, Poulantzas is more sceptical. He sees the new forms of the division of labour also resulting in the reproduction of the division between mental and manual labour and within mental labour itself, along with the bureaucratisation of enterprises. But far from creating a new proletariat of office and other workers, this merely facilitates their proletarian polarisation. Bureaucratised labour supposedly remains, as will be seen, new *petit bourgeois*. And although low-level commercial and service workers not only comprise the most polarised fraction but also make up a stratum that 'increasingly form[s] *part* of the working class' (p. 321; my emphasis), his criterion here is that much sales work, by involving distribution, has now become productive labour. The work of handling, packing and storage by sales workers in the most concentrated stores, shops and self-service supermarkets is now more akin to transport than to the 'art of selling'.

The question is, therefore, whether in fact the transformations are only such as to intensify polarisation. On what basis are the fractions *petit bourgeois* at all, especially if they are new and polarised towards the working class?

The changes creating the first fraction (of mainly low-level sales and service workers) are most marked with respect to women. For example, their lower educational attainments, compared with men, reflect the degree to which their tasks are the most fragmented and deskilled. It is women's earnings that depress the level of such in this fraction. It is men who practically monopolise commercial managerial positions. And if women virtually dominate the first they are even more significant in the second fraction, that is of 'subaltern' bureaucratised workers for whom fragmentation of tasks, etc., has occurred in the context of increasingly 'authoritarian and hierarchical relations'. It is this fraction that 'has in the last few years experienced the most pronounced and accelerated tendency towards feminisation' resulting in the phenomenon of 'a considerable intensification of the hierarchical cleavages between the massively feminised subaltern levels and their management' (p. 323). Although feminisation is indeed complex, and women may be found among both the most and the least advanced *petit bourgeois* fractions, many female unproductive workers — such as those in retail services — have suffered a relative decline in wage levels compared with skilled female manual workers and there is in fact little evidence that they earn more than the latter (which might otherwise affect their consciousness); there is also much mobility between the two. Leaving aside here considerations of marriage (Poulantzas' discussion of such issues is both brief and ambiguous, but in any case I have already argued that they are here irrelevant) and accepting that a large proportion of commercial workers are in small enterprises where politico-ideological factors such as 'personalised clientism' may operate against working-class polarisation, it is the case that women comprise that stratum of sales workers in the most concentrated stores whose labour, now productive, is in fact proletarianising them. But to reiterate, the question is whether it is only such women workers who are now to be considered working class, and only on such criteria. This question can only be answered by looking briefly at what Poulantzas means by the political and ideological relations inscribing unproductive mental labour.

Mental labour, first, is labour that is distinguished from the 'simple' manual labour of the working class by various 'ideological symbols' (rituals, know-how, secret knowledge — 'general culture' as opposed to 'technical skills') such that it is perceived as intellectually superior, privileged and respectable. Mental labour is also bureaucratised, a process that 'materialises' mental labour as 'separate' from manual labour and reproduces the whole relationship of domination and subordination within itself. It thus reproduces bourgeois political relations and embodies and reproduces class powers as such, by virtue of the fact that its agents are both subordinated themselves and subordinate others. That such workers do not exercise direct political domination over the working class is largely irrelevant to their class position (chs 4 and 5). My argument is not with this general analysis, but with Poulantzas' discussion of how these very same processes of bureaucratisation and the reproduction of the mental–manual division create fractions. This, I believe, is more problematic, as is its application to particular cases. It is questionable how far, for instance, the specific form taken by these processes locate those affected by them as definitively and objectively *petit bourgeois*.

Let us take first the reproduction of bourgeois political relations. I have indicated that unproductive mental labour does this essentially because the relations defining its place are hierarchical rather than relations of domination, but the assumption that such relations are peculiar to the new *petite bourgeoisie* and are correspondingly alien to the working class is at the very least questionable, and indeed this is partly recognised by Poulantzas.[5] More important, bourgeois political relations are said to be reproduced in the 'double-sided process of subordination' in which lies 'the very meaning of the hierarchy' (p. 275). However, if we confine our attention to low-level office and clerical workers, predominantly women – that is, those who are not only a major focus of this paper but are also seen by Poulantzas as of critical significance – the picture looks rather different. For the majority of these workers the possibility of subordinating others does not exist, nor are there opportunities via mobility and promotion for the exercise of such in the future. It is simply not true that 'everyone is at the same time "superior" and "inferior" to everyone else'. Some are merely inferior. Poulantzas begs the empirical question by calling all these workers 'subaltern' in the first place. It is also worth noting that while the notion of cleavages is central to the concept of fractions, cleavages within the bureaucratised ranks are held to be 'hierarchical rather than cleavages of domination'. But can cleavages be hierarchical? Is this not a contradiction in terms, especially if the relations between the lowest and higher ranks are increasingly 'authoritarian'?

It might be objected that the workers in question do none the less perform the functions of capital rather than labour, although this is not really dealt with by Poulantzas and is even rejected as irrelevant. He states quite categorically that the bureaucratised agents are part of an 'intermediate class' not because they are a link or transmission belt in the bourgeoisie's domination over the working class, 'not because it is directly the effective intermediary . . .' but because of the relations the hierarchy expresses. Even so, it might, in principle, be worth asking whether, even if many or most unproductive workers do not directly dominate the working class, they are none the less agents of those who do; that is, whether or not they are part of the whole complex apparatus of control, domination and surveillance. It has been suggested that the labour of employees (clerical, commercial and so on) increasingly has to do with the functions of co-ordination and unity of the labour process, and that such workers are thus no longer petty functionaries ('subaltern') of capital but agents of labour (Carchedi, 1975, pp. 365–90; Crompton, 1976). True, co-ordination itself does not have a purely 'technical' meaning in capitalist relations of production, but the most telling point is, surely, that if being part of the apparatus of control has no empirical effects what meaning can it have? If workers do not in fact have authority, if they do not control, if they do not subordinate others, then what does it mean to be part of 'the work of control'?

However, there remains, Poulantzas reminds us, the question of ideological practices inscribed in mental labour. How do the workers in question fare here? Of secretaries he has no doubt. In referring to the lack of discrepancy between training and jobs he suggests that:

> these subordinate places themselves are thus invested with a 'mental labour' quotient which distances them even more, in a certain way from the working class. If a secretary/ typist with a baccalauréat feels frustrated in her ambitions it is not clear why she should automatically thereby become aligned with the working class. It is just as possible that her 'proximity' to the working class, combined with her educational qualification, reinforces in her those practices that distinguish her from the working class (p. 269).

But this is said of those with an educational qualification of the type which though it may be characteristic of office staff is certainly not of clerical workers. Of course it may be the case that bureaucratised 'subaltern' agents feel they have more in common with those above to whose positions they aspire but this is not a question of their objective class place but a reference to consciousness. If the mental labour quotient of secretarial work compensates for a low-level position, still marking it as separate from working-class labour, can the same be said of typists and clerical workers in general? This quotient refers to commercial and service workers as well as those in offices. Poulantzas' empirical example of how far ideological practices are inscribed here is merely a reference to 'the traditional esteem given to "paper work" and "clerical workers" in general' (p. 258). He cites only one authority to the effect that the training given to female commercial workers is not technical so much as cultural, in that it teaches not skills and rules to be strictly applied but taste, sensitivity, fashion and decorative arts. There is a further problem. Even if all this were true, the point about mental labour is that 'if [its] ideological symbols have little in common with any real differentiation in the order of elements of science they nevertheless legitimise this distinction *as if it had such a basis*' (p. 258; my emphasis). The lack of any real differentiation from productive manual labour in the material labour process is, of course, precisely what Braverman is concerned to emphasise. Poulantzas has claimed that he is demonstrating how mental labour remains separate from manual labour but he is only showing how despite real similarities in many cases it is 'marked' as if it were separate.

In many cases the real collapse of differentiations seems the more interesting phenomenon. Poulantzas remarks in connection with isolating distinctions in the commercial sector that 'those selling "luxury" goods play the part of "mental workers" ' (p. 317). By implication the rest are essentially 'manual workers'. Those commercial and service workers who are increasingly part of the working class lack the ideological symbols ('the art of selling', for instance) of mental labour although it must be stressed that they are proletarianised because their labour has actually become productive. This said, however, it is worth noting that what has replaced the art of selling is 'the distribution of a given mass of goods in a minimum time' (p. 321). This is a reference, in other words, not only to productive labour but also to the significance of the labour process itself, its organisation and subjection to control. Now if this process has changed because such labour is now productive, has, however, the deskilling and fragmentation of tasks of other sales girls and cashiers occurred for the same reason? Are the sales people who are now 'mere demonstrators', the girls on the cash registers — the 'spearhead of struggle in this sector' — equally productive workers, or part of the collective productive worker? Or is it the organisation of their labour that heralds their entry into the working class?

If the fact of becoming productive has transformed some labour in circulation into manual labour, it is also true that much clerical labour, which is clearly neither productive in the strict sense nor part of the material labour process, is also increasingly subject to time control, output quotas, etc. Like Braverman, in fact, Poulantzas is forced to take account of the increasing 'fragmentation and standardisation of tasks of the great mass of subaltern agents' (p. 322), also subject to obscured knowledge. Although bureaucratised workers are seen on average as having better career opportunities than sales and service workers and there is more emphasis on mental labour, these 'privileges' would appear to be due to the fact that the group he is here considering includes civil servants, research workers, teachers and possibly also specialised and highly skilled office 'technicians'. Apart from the typing pool, Poulantzas observes that

> In banking and insurance, for example, to say nothing of the giro sector . . . the handling of records by subaltern agents consists more and more in simply filling in stereotyped boxes with a cross, and here we see clearly the indirect effects of computer 'techniques'; it is not without reason that these agents have been described as semi-skilled red-tape workers (p. 323).

With promotion effectively blocked as well, these workers too, therefore, have ceased to perform mental labour in the sense in which Poulantzas uses the term: and this in spite of the strictly economic functions of such labour. Is such clerical labour really esteemed in the way it once was? And if such non-productive labour has lost its 'ideological symbols', if manual labour has been reproduced 'on the mental side' of the division, all that can distinguish it from the 'simple manual labour' of the working class is its reproduction of political relations. This, I have suggested, does not essentially describe the functions of a substantial sector of unproductive labour.

My argument here – apart from an interpretation of the actual political and ideological relations involved – is essentially that changes in the labour process and its organisation cannot be theorised away in understanding the class structure. What we can call the 'conditions' of labour are particularly important if the overall place in the division of labour has no empirical effects. And ultimately, of course, 'conditions' may be precisely the mediating links between class place and class consciousness.[6] In addition, by redrawing boundaries we do not have to imply their total collapse. Indeed the same changes leading to deskilling also create, however temporarily, new skills 'higher up'; they too stratify the grouping of employees. To be concerned with the lowest levels of the non-productive sales, service and clerical workers is not to merge the whole sector into the working class (Carchedi, 1975, pp. 392 and 398–401; Braverman, 1974, ch. 18; Crompton, 1976, p. 420). Poulantzas seems to equate any view of proletarianisation with a dualist image of society. His fractions, particularly of bureaucratised workers, are very large, and like many of the sociologists he criticises, he wants to see their 'top' and 'bottom' extremes as part of a continuum. In a sense, he does not even reject the category of labour implied in the term 'white collar': he only rejects the supposed reasons for its growth and suggests alternative theoretical bases for its constituting a class. For these reasons and also because he is concerned primarily with the bourgeoisie and its 'offshoots', while Braverman deals with the working class as a whole, he is unable to agree that 'the problem of the so called employee or white collar worker . . . has been unambiguously clarified by the polarisation of office employment and the growth *at one pole* of an immense mass of wage workers' (Braverman, 1974, p. 355; my emphasis).

None of this is to argue either for an undifferentiated working class or for the irrelevance of ideological relations, perhaps especially to consciousness: as Carchedi says of the employee: 'his condition approaches more and more the proletarian one while he is asked to stick to an ideology and political practice which is based on a lost position of privilege' and which denies the unfolding reality (1975, pp. 395 and

397), a point also echoed by Glaberman (1975). Even a certain community of interests at certain times between workers and the proletarianised strata does not necessarily mean proletarian class consciousness among the latter. As far as differentiation is concerned we should be equally wary of assuming that a similarity in condition or situation is all that needs to be noted. Differences between girls punching cards and workers on a conveyor belt may have ceased to be decisive for class membership but not, as Carchedi suggests, simply because the former works on a 'paper conveyor belt'. The organisation of their labour process may be equivalent, but a paper conveyor belt is a paper conveyor belt — part of that labour process which has to do with unity and co-ordination and which may not necessarily involve the direct production of value. The functions (economic and 'political') are not by any means identical, and above all these should sensitise us to differences between productive and unproductive — especially commercial — labour as well as contradictory consequences of the expansion and significance of the latter. Finally there are, for instance, offices and offices. The fact that some are located in a factory and others are total organisations must be expected to produce different effects.

What finally, of sexual divisions, which the preceding discussion has tended to overlook? That these have been overlooked is not surprising, for the logic of the above approaches is to suggest that sexual divisions play only a contributory part in the class structure, by reinforcing the impact of transformations or in terms of the consequential differentiations or cleavages that exist, while the logic of much sociology, usually despite stated intentions, is to elevate marriage and family relations, if not sexual divisions as such, to the place of virtually sole determinants.

   Here I wish to comment briefly on what I see as one particularly crucial question, namely how sexual divisions affect the class structure by accounting for (as well as being descriptive of) women's monopoly of certain positions. Marxists stress that the distribution of labour and the form it takes are largely a 'function' of or response to the movements of capital. But the agents who fill positions which are becoming increasingly deskilled, whether productive or unproductive, are mainly and increasingly women. Why is this? Why are women concentrated in this sector? Clearly deskilling of labour is a major reason why agents drawn in can be those with a lower value to their labour power, such as women or migrants. Barron and Norris (1976) have shown also that the 'fit' between the characteristics of secondary jobs and those employed in them lies in such factors as dispensability, visible social differentiation from primary workers and so on. But sex and women's place in the family are seen as factors used to justify, not determine, the allocation of women to the secondary sector of the labour market. For instance, Barron and Norris argue that many if not most of the attributes of female employees themselves are in fact characteristics of the jobs they do, even though they see a relationship between attributes required by the job (by employers) and those determined independently of the market. They stress that high turnover rates are characteristics of jobs, not women (or men); that apart from higher redundancy, women may want to leave jobs more often than men, but such voluntary turnover can also reflect job properties such as insecurity and low pay. Low organisation is seen to reflect such conditions too, in particular low pay, scattered work places and high incidence of temporary jobs. Dispensability is seen to derive largely from employers' need to maintain a depressed and unstable secondary sector and thus 'manipulate' employment levels in relation to product demand, retention of key (core, primary) workers and so on. They suggest, however, that attributes are a product of the relation between employer and employees. Those attributes that women bring to the labour market by virtue of family obligations and socialisation are used by employers to select them for the secondary sector.

However, such observations do not go far enough. Conditions in the labour market, deskilling and other such factors do not explain why women are drawn in rather than migrants, or school leavers, or indeed men displaced from other sectors of the economy. We want to know, for instance, why it is precisely women's labour that can be hired more cheaply. The answers may seem obvious but, perhaps surprisingly, they are often not sought. Poulantzas and Braverman, for example, both put much store by women's large numbers.

for Braverman, in fact, this largely explains why women are such an ideal reserve of labour for the new mass occupations and help keep wages in them low. This is related to what he sees as the two apparently opposing forms taken by the increased relative surplus population created by monopoly capital. The attraction of women into industry and trade is only 'the other side of the coin' of the repulsion of men. As men are displaced, increasing the stagnant part of the reserve army, women's employment grows, but in a way that increases the floating and stagnant parts in that women are drawn into jobs characterised by high turnover and mobility or into part time or casual employment. Women do not have to vanish from the labour market in periods of high general unemployment to constitute a part of the reserve army — as long as we also recognise that much actual female unemployment is hidden. However, if the reserve army is understood in this way then women have always been a substantial part of it. What has largely happened is that there has been a relative shift of female labour from casual or part time employment in and on the fringes of industry (including, for example, outwork) — much of it uncounted or hidden in official returns (Land, 1975; Scott and Tilly, 1975). Of course, not all 'new' female employment represents such a shift,[7] but women's large numbers are by no means simply guaranteed by a 'lower economic participation' in the early period of monopoly capital. There is also some displacement of women from traditional sectors, a movement of female labour from manufacturing into services.

Moreover, women's large numbers, whatever their source, are far from the only reason, and certainly not the most significant, for helping to maintain low wage levels. Women's cheap, flexible and disposable labour power, their situation both when employed and unemployed, stems fundamentally from their actual and assumed role in the family. Beechey rightly emphasises in her contribution to this volume that 'a crucial determinant of the specificity of the position of female wage labour' is the sexual division of labour which assigns women to the family and the dominant patriarchal ideology relating to this. The historical basis of low-paid female employment and the related exclusion of women from certain sectors of the labour market (their exclusion,

for instance, from skilled work towards the end of the nineteenth century and the relationship of this to the growth of
the ideology of the dependent housewife, gaining ground
particularly among skilled working-class men) has to be
understood in this context. Numerous assumptions and
practices — the social security and taxation systems, trade
union policies, and so on — reinforce the notion that women
are or should be economically dependent on men, and among
these is, of course, the reproduction of the deskilled, low-
wage sector itself. The family alone does not account for the
position of women in the class structure. The sexual division
of labour locates women to a particular place within the
structure of labour, that place being itself determined by the
forces of capitalist production.

Nevertheless, the consequences of sustaining the ideology
of the male breadwinner, as Land argues, not only assist the
economic exploitation of women but help to maintain the
belief 'that women's wages [are] either for their sole support
or to supplement a man's wage' and 'by allowing women . . .
to supplement rather than substitute for a man's wage, low
wages for men are perpetuated and men's work incentive
preserved' (1975, p. 73). Female wage labour, combined with
domestic labour, thus has highly complex consequences for
the class structure and class consciousness. Ultimately, of
course, an integrated analysis of both domestic and paid
labour is necessary, as is consideration of the ways in which
sexual divisions have their effect and take their form in relation to class practices such as trade unionism, sectionalism
and the conjuncturally specific nature of demands. We should
also consider the relationship and possible contradictions
between consciousness and the processes of proletarianisation:
how far does the presence of women help these objective
processes and yet perhaps exist in contradiction with the way
they are perceived by the agents involved, or hinder certain
forms of group identification or solidarity?

This paper has looked at one part of the whole, one hitherto
neglected or ignored; the question, first, of how one concep-
tualises women's position in the class structure and, second,
how concretely we should assess the class position of most
female white-collar workers. I have emphasised that we must
concern ourselves with women as workers. For it is through

labour, in particular paid labour, that women (just like men, of course) engage in the relations of production that are the pivot of the class structure. If relations of the labour process have been particularly stressed this is only because they are in a sense the immediate form of and 'key' to more fundamental production relations and are those through which the latter are experienced. 'Condition' is not equivalent to place in the social division of labour and may, theoretically, exist in contradiction with it, but nor is it chance that the condition of so much unproductive 'white-collar' labour increasingly approximates that of productive manual workers — perhaps indeed because the relations defining its overall place have themselves changed. If there is no doubt that women manual workers are part of the working class in their own right by virtue of the labour they perform, there is today much less doubt that most women non-manual workers also are — objectively speaking — part of the proletariat. This said, such women workers may still, as Poulantzas maintains, have to be won for the working class in terms of class struggle, but this is due not only to the complexities of their own class position but also to the fundamental problems of sexism within the working class which is itself fostered by the way sexual divisions and intraclass divisions interrelate.

Notes

1 In Britain in 1971, 42.7 per cent of all women aged fifteen and over were 'economically active' (*Women and Work*, Manpower Paper no. 9, HMSO, London, 1974, Table 1, p. 44). In 1974 this figure was 42.4 per cent of all unmarried females (including divorced, etc.), and 49 per cent of all married females (*Social Trends*, no. 7, 1976, Table 4.6, p. 97). On part time work, estimates vary — in 1972 from 32.1 per cent to 45.5 per cent of female employees; the proportion in manufacturing is lower (about one in five). See 'Part-time women workers 1950—1972', *Department of Employment Gazette*, November 1973. In 1966, 46 per cent of part time women workers were married (*Women and Work*, op. cit., p. 13).

2 Interestingly in a passage on the problems of delineating the lower and upper middle class in terms of the arbitrary criterion of family income, Hamilton (1972, pp. 339—41) points to the significant minority of American 'upper' middle class families who are only there by virtue of being two-income households and are only there for a time. Further down the economic hierarchy the greater, on the whole, the proportion of working wives and their lifelong employ-

ment participation (see, for instance, A. Hunt, *A Survey of Women's Employment*, Government Social Survey, HMSO, London, 1968).

3 Although the logic of the conventional argument is that they do. This assumes that sexual divisions are inconsequential since men are the main breadwinners. In fact the opposite is the case. In so far as men are the chief breadwinners it is because of the interrelationship between higher male earnings and female dependency. This surely is a situation of sexual inequality, and to imply that it is irrelevant to the class position of women or to the family's existence as a unit is absurd. This is simply to recognise that when the 'family' is invoked as a reason for the supposedly derived class position of women, or for the statement that sexual inequalities are not an important component of stratification, what is being thoroughly obscured behind the language of harmony (the family, the unit) is the way in which internal divisions, inequalities within the family are closely related to sexual inequalities in society as a whole.

4 Poulantzas remarks that these workers are 'least affected by the tendency towards bureaucratisation . . . because they are nearest the barrier of manual labour' (1975, p. 317). Braverman's suggestion that the distinctions between manufacturing and service labour are now 'meaningless, even ridiculous' is essentially based on the way that the labour of restaurant workers, chambermaids, etc., involves assembly-type operations and the production of tangible, vendible commodities (1974, ch. 16 and 19). Although he confused the question of productive/unproductive labour by drawing something of an analogy with material production, the real issue is whether such labour is subject to the same or similar relations of control and organisation of labour.

5 Poulantzas recognises that the mental–manual division has been reproduced in manual work but claims that the working-class strata of skilled, semi-skilled and unskilled with all their gradations do not exercise over those below them authority relations and a monopoly of knowledge, at least 'certainly not in the same way' nor assuming the same forms as characterise mental labour. However, hierarchies of promotion are being reproduced in substantial sections of manual labour, and control of some workers by others may well involve authority if not actual secrecy of knowledge. Indeed Poulantzas seems aware of these changes and refers to capital's attempt to introduce the same relations in the working class, which has to proceed via the labour aristocracy and 'class collaborationist trade unions' (1975, p. 276). He suggests that this attempt has been constantly undermined by working-class work relations and solidarity, but, even were he to offer proof of this, the very mention of the labour aristocracy in this context invites scepticism of his claim that bourgeois political relations are reproduced only in unproductive labour.

6 My thanks to Theo Nichols for his point. See his article on class (1978) which also goes beyond the discussion in Wright (1976).

7 The increase in female participation is frequently attributed to the

entry of married women in particular, but it should be noted that
this concerns (a) largely older married women — see *Women and
Work* (op. cit., pp. 7—8 and Table 2, p. 44), and (b) an increase in
'economic activity' among certain types of married women, such as
those married to 'middle-class' men or to skilled workers — substantial numbers of working-class women have always worked outside
the home: see Land (1975); Scott and Tilly (1975); M. Anderson,
The Family in Nineteenth Century Lancashire, Cambridge University
Press, 1971; and J. Gardiner, 'Women's work in the Industrial
Revolution' in S. Allen, L. Sanders and J. Wallis, *Conditions of
Illusion*, Feminist Books, Leeds, 1974.

References

Acker, J. (1973), 'Women and social stratification: a case of intellectual
    sexism', *American Journal of Sociology*, vol. 78, pp. 936—45.
Anderson, C. H. (1974), *The Political Economy of Social Class*,
    Prentice-Hall, New Jersey.
Barron, R. D., and Norris, G. M. (1976), 'Sexual divisions and the dual
    labour market' in D. L. Barker and S. Allen, *Dependence and Exploi-
    tation in Work and Marriage*, Longman, London.
Bell, C., and Newby, H. (1976), 'Husbands and wives: the dynamic of
    the deferential dialectic' in D. Barker and S. Allen, *Dependence and
    Exploitation in Work and Marriage*, Longman, London.
Braverman, H. (1974), *Labor and Monopoly Capital*, Monthly Review
    Press, New York.
Carchedi, G. (1975), 'Reproduction of social classes at the level of
    production relations', *Economy and Society*, vol. 4, pp. 361—417.
Coulson, M., Magaš, B., and Wainwright, H. (1975), ' "The housewife
    and her labour under capitalism" — a critique', *New Left Review*, no.
    89, pp. 59—71.
Crompton, R. (1976), 'Approaches to the study of white collar union-
    ism', *Sociology*, vol. 10, pp. 407—26.
Crozier, M. (1971), *The World of the Office Worker*, University of
    Chicago Press.
Gardiner, J. (1975), 'Women's domestic labour', *New Left Review*, no.
    89, pp. 47—58.
Gardiner, J., Himmelweit, S., and Mackintosh, M. (1975), 'Women's
    domestic labour', *Bulletin of the Conference of Socialist Econom-
    ists*, vol. 4, part 2, pp. 1—11.
Giddens, A. (1973), *The Class Structure of the Advanced Societies*,
    Hutchinson, London.
Gillespie, D. (1972), 'Who has the power? The marital struggle' in
    H. P. Dreitzel, *Family, Marriage and the Struggle of the Sexes*,
    Macmillan, New York.
Glaberman, M. (1975), *The Working Class and Social Change*, New
    Hogtown Press, Toronto.
Hacker, A. (1976), 'Cutting classes', *New York Review of Books* vol.
    23, 4 March, pp. 15—18.

Hamilton, R. (1972), *Class and Politics in the United States*, Wiley, New York.

Hutton, C. (1974), *Secondhand Status: Stratification Terms and the Sociological Subordination of Women*, paper presented at BSA Annual Conference.

Land, H. (1975), 'The myth of the male breadwinner', *New Society*, 9 October, pp. 71–3.

Land, H. (1976), 'Women: supporters or supported?' in D. L. Barker and S. Allen, *Sexual Divisions and Society: Process and Change*, Tavistock, London.

MacRae, D. G. (1972), 'Classlessness?', *New Society*, 26 October, pp. 208–10.

Marceau, J. (1976), 'Marriage, role division and social cohesion: the case of some French upper class families' in D. Barker and S. Allen, *Dependence and Exploitation in Work and Marriage*, Longman, London.

Middleton, C. (1974), 'Sexual inequality and stratification theory' in F. Parkin, *The Social Analysis of Class Structure*, Tavistock, London.

Mumford, E., and Banks, O. (1967), *The Computer and the Clerk*, Routledge & Kegan Paul, London.

Nichols, T. (1978), 'Social class: official, sociological and marxist' in J. Evans, J. Irvine and I. Miles, *Demystifying Social Statistics*, Pluto Press, London.

Oakley, A. (1974), *The Sociology of Housework*, Martin Robertson, London.

Parkin, F. (1971), *Class Inequality and Political Order*, MacGibbon & Kee, London.

Perrow, C. (1972), *The Radical Attack on Business*, Harcourt Brace, New York.

Phizacklea, A., and Miles, R. (1976), *Class, Ethnicity and Political Action*, SSRC Research Unit on Ethnic Relations, Bristol.

Poulantzas, N. (1975), *Classes in Contemporary Capitalism*, New Left Books, London.

Scott, J., and Tilly, L. (1975), 'Women's work and the family in nineteenth century Europe', *Comparative Studies in Society and History*, vol. 17, pp. 36–64.

Seccombe, W. (1974), 'The housewife and her labour under capitalism', *New Left Review*, no. 83, pp. 3–24.

Szymanski, A. (1976), 'Trends in the American class structure', *Socialist Revolution*, no. 10, pp. 101–22.

Whitehead, A. (1976), 'Sexual antagonism in Herefordshire' in D. Barker and S. Allen, *Dependence and Exploitation in Work and Marriage*, Longman, London.

Wright, E. O. (1976), 'Class boundaries in advanced capitalist societies', *New Left Review*, no. 98, pp. 3–43.

10 The state and the oppression of women

Mary McIntosh

It is quite clear, as the papers in this book indicate, that women's oppression and subordination to men are to be located within the operation of the family and the labour process. But it is the way in which the state sustains these relations of oppression and subordination that Mary McIntosh's paper discusses. The state steps in to maintain the social conditions of reproduction. The way in which state intervention occurs is analysed in relation to crucial aspects of women's position: that is, their relation to the family and to wage labour. In justification of the position put forward here, it is argued that the 'key problem is the relative inflexibility of the family as a social institution structured by ideologies of human nature, tradition, religion, and so on, as well as by state policy', a point which is pursued in the conclusion that the 'state simply steps in to maintain the social conditions of reproduction'. The effectiveness of the operation of the state on the maintenance of the conditions of reproduction constitutes the topic of analysis, the starting-point being a consideration of the way in which the state exercises specific forms of social control over women, mainly in relation to the family; but this is addressed by moving beyond the concept of patriarchy to that of the relationship that exists between the state and the capitalist mode of production, in which the state plays a part in the production and reproduction of conditions of reproduction. Here there is a need to examine the relationships between the state, the labour process, and the family institution, and it is such an examination which constitutes the main project of this paper. The prime concern is to analyse state intervention in the maintenance of the family household. The actual reproduction of labour power instances the way in which the state intervenes in such questions as the rate of fertility (an aspect of family life which is at certain conjunctures closely connected to mode of production, as Kate Young's contribution indicates) and the subsequent care of children. Through the allocation of certain welfare benefits the concrete form of state intervention is demonstrated, and serves 'to bolster the family household system by dealing with the instances where the needs of the reproduction of the working class are not met by the system'. The crucial issue of the relation of the state to women as paid workers is also addressed, and it is here that an argument found in the contributions by both Veronica Beechey and Jackie West is reiterated: that the value of women's labour power is below that required for the reproduction of the worker. Using this argument an explanation is offered of the nature of the intervention of the state through such means as the creation of crêches, maternity benefits, and so on, which relate not only to changes in household management but also to the labour requirements of the economy.

Women have been subordinated to men and oppressed by them in many different sorts of society.[1] In the most general terms, the oppression of women is not unique to capitalism. But the relations between the sexes nevertheless take different forms in different social formations and even at different periods of development in capitalist societies. One of the features of capitalist societies, especially in the more advanced stages of capitalism, is the important part played by the state in the economy and in the society at large. It is not surprising, therefore, to find that the state plays a part in the oppression of women.

In this paper it will be argued that the state does this not directly but through its support for a specific form of household: the family household dependent largely upon a male wage and upon female domestic servicing. This household system is in turn related to capitalist production in that it serves (though inadequately) for the reproduction of the working class and for the maintenance of women as a reserve army of labour, low-paid when they are in jobs and often unemployed. This two-pronged relationship involves contradictions and, furthermore, the family household system has its own history and roots in pre-capitalist society, so that state effort cannot achieve a perfect fit between the household and the various needs of capitalism. State policy is thus constantly juggling to keep several balls in the air at once.

I

The way in which the state is commonly understood is in terms of the relations between the 'state' and the 'citizen'. The state is seen as an alien body interfering in private lives. Radicals of both right and left deplore state intervention as limiting the spontaneity and freedom of individuals. People could run their businesses and bring up their children (according to the right) or run their local communities, solve their personal problems and educate themselves (according to the left) much better without central government meddling in their affairs.

This kind of perspective has informed some strands of thought in the women's liberation movement. The state is seen as denying us freedom to choose abortion, say, or to decide whether to do wage work or housework; as a purveyor of oppressively sexist ideologies in education, social services and medicine; as practising economic and legal discrimination against women in relation to Supplementary Benefit, social security and taxation, and in relation to rape, domestic violence and prostitution. All of this is true of course, and such analyses are indeed immediately useful given the exigencies of day-to-day struggles for improvements and resistance to threats to worsen our already bad situation.

It is none the less surprising that women have borrowed the idea of the state as a directly repressive mechanism from the libertarian and radical left. For, if intervention is conceived as a relationship between the citizen and agents of the state, one of the striking features of the situation is that the state 'intervenes' less conspicuously in the lives of women than of men, and when it does so it appears to be done more benevolently. It is not mere casuistry to point out that the notorious 'cohabitation rule', and the equally iniquitous rule from which it derives whereby a married woman, or a cohabiting one, cannot claim Supplementary Benefit for herself or her children, are rules *preventing* the government department's officers from intervening in a woman's life. They enter, albeit in the most intrusive manner, only if she attempts to claim the benefit. What this indicates is that we cannot expect to understand the impact of the state on the position of women in this sphere if we see the conflict between claimant and government officer as the observable form of that impact. Much more important is the non-claimant status of so many women. We must look at the whole structure of benefits, the part they play in the economy as a whole and the patterns of social relations that they establish and sustain.

The relation of women to state agents is much more often indirect than that of men. The state frequently defines a space, the family, in which its agents will not interfere but in which control is left to the man. In relation to the control of children, this is obvious and explicit. Fathers are held responsible for sending their children to school and providing minimum support and care. But how they do this, short of cruelty or neglect, is left largely to them and social workers are extremely reluctant to intervene by removing children from the parental home. Women are now full citizens in most purely legal respects; they have the right to vote, to own and dispose of property, to make contracts, to go to law, to hold passports. In many ways, however, the state relates to married women through their husbands, especially in income tax and the social security system, which will be examined more fully later.

The general pattern of non-interference and relative benevolence comes out most clearly in the exercise of the criminal law. Most laws apply to men and women alike and those that do not (like 'living on immoral earnings' and the 'age of consent') are designed to protect women against predatory man. Yet far more men are convicted of crimes than women, and far more men are sent to prison and other forms of harsh institution, and for far longer terms. The analysis of criminal statistics is a complex matter, but the differences are so gross that there can be no doubt that the main reason is that there are more laws against the kinds of thing that men and boys do than against the kind of thing that women and girls do. Either women do not 'deviate' (whatever that may mean) so much, or their deviations are not counted as criminal but are subject to other forms of control. Furthermore, though this is less easy to demonstrate, it seems that even when women do commit crimes that are detected by the police they are more likely to be treated leniently by police and by courts; and the regime in prison, if they ever get that far, is more comfortable and less authoritarian. The prevailing ideology that women are not voluntarily criminal, that they must have been led astray, unbalanced by emotional or hormonal disturbances or else mentally sick, seems to inform the treatment of women criminals at every stage. They are let off with a caution, given a conditional discharge, or put on probation much more readily. Except for a tiny handful, the 'worst' prison cases are sent to the new Holloway prison which is vaunted as a place of treatment rather than of punishment.

Feminist criminologists are hard put to it to find a point of attack. Commonly they turn instead upon the invidious nature of the kind of explanations that are offered for female criminality and the kinds of stereotypical motivations that are attributed to women by agents of social control and by criminologists. Recently, however, the apparently benevolent non-interference of the state towards women has been examined more critically and it has been seen that the social controls outside the criminal law — the family, social work and ultimately psychiatry — are every bit as coercive and even more intrusive (Smart, 1976; Snäre and Steng-Dahl, 1978; Fox, 1977).

The situations in which the state's non-interference with women is most obviously less benevolent are those in which women are denied the adequate protection of the law: in rape and in domestic violence. Here the assumption that women's contexts are too private and personal to be subject to criminal sanction leaves women exposed to violence and abuse. In both cases the behaviour is seen as an extension of normal male–female relations, the boundary is too obscure for a jury to decide reliably and the whole issue is cast in an ambiguous light by the attribution of ambivalent motivations to the women victims. It is said that women often say 'no' to sex when they don't really mean it; or wives continue to live with husbands who beat them and though they may complain to the police at night, they refuse to press charges in the morning. The supposed irrationality of women places these in the category of 'victim-precipitated crimes' which cannot be solved satisfactorily by the supposed rationality of the law.

The study of such specific injustices is important for immediate political campaigns. But it can tell us little about the part played by the state in the oppression of women. Here the overall pattern of non-interference, of the family and personal relationships as mediators of social control, of the siting of women in the private rather than the public sphere are of much greater importance.

The level of analysis that is needed is one on which we ask not simply 'How does the state oppress women?', but 'What part does the state play in establishing and sustaining systems in which women are oppressed and subordinated to men?'

At this stage it can be stated simply that in capitalism the two systems in question are the family household and wage labour.[2] In the first, women and men are defined *with respect to each other* and located in asymmetrical relations of production, distribution and authority. In the second, women occupy relatively disadvantaged positions as compared to male wage workers, and usually also submit to supervisors who are men. The two systems are both closely interdependent and contradictory; some of the links will be discussed in a later section. As Margaret Coulson put it: 'The position of women is structured by the *contradictory* tendencies which derive from the relationship between the private sphere of the family and the public sphere of general production' (1974, p. 2). But although these are systems in which women are oppressed by men, this oppression, as such, is neither their defining characteristic nor their *raison d'être*.

The part played by the state in these institutions is a complex one; and the state, like society, cannot be analysed simply in terms of 'patriarchy'. Capitalist society is one in which men as men dominate women; yet it is not this but class domination that is fundamental to the society. It is a society in which the dominant class is composed mainly of men; yet it is not as men but as capitalists that they are dominant.

Some writers, notably Christine Delphy (1970), have conceptualized a relation between capitalism and patriarchy in terms of a 'family mode of production', with its own patriarchal relations of appropriation, existing within the same social formation as the capitalist mode of production. This may well be a useful approach, but to conclude, as Delphy does, that this patriarchal system of production can be overthrown by 'seizing the political power over ourselves at present held by others', if this means 'over women by men', is mistaken. The state must be seen as a capitalist one, or at least as one that is to be understood primarily in relation to the capitalist mode of production.

Furthermore, the state cannot be conceived as external to the dominant mode of production, as is sometimes implied by a mechanical separation of the economic, the political and the ideological in which the state is located in the political sphere. The idea of contrasting an interventionist with a non-interventionist state — *laissez-faire* versus state control — is a mistaken one, since even *laissez-faire* capitalism depends, for the conditions of its existence, upon the bourgeois state. Capital itself, with its mode of extracting surplus value, is a specific form of property established by a complex set of laws administered (with an ultimate sanction of coercion) through specific institutions. The 'free exchange' of commodities requires quite different laws from those of, say, feudal production as well as new forms of regulated money and credit. Thus although we may speak of state monopoly capitalism as a relatively late stage in the development of the capitalist mode of production in order to indicate the increasing scale of the state institutions and their direct involvement in capitalist enterprise, we must not suppose that the part played by the state was any less essential in the earlier 'competitive' stage.

This paper will adopt the idea of 'capitalist reproduction' to conceptualize this relation: the capitalist state plays a part in producing and reproducing the conditions for capital accumulation at any given stage. It must be frankly admitted, however, that this formulation leads to an analysis that is functionalist in character. Some ways of mitigating this are suggested at the end of the paper, but they do not alter the fundamental functionalism of the approach.

II

In general terms, no mode of production can persist over

time unless its conditions of existence are continually reproduced. If the labour process is analysed in terms of two distinct levels, the relations of production and the forces of production, then each of these must be reproduced. In capitalism, both are reproduced first and foremost within production itself. Some production is of commodities like machinery, raw materials and so forth, which are purchased and transformed into constant capital for the production of articles of consumption. In the production of commodities workers are paid a wage that is sufficient to reproduce their labour power, so that they can arrive at work each day in the same condition as the day before and provide for their children who will grow up to replace them;[3] capital, however (since commodity production is also production of surplus value), is each day expanded by the process of production. Marx explains how the wage relation reproduces both itself as a relation of production and labour power as a productive force:

> The money which the labourer receives is spent by him in order to preserve his labour-power, or — viewing the capitalist class and the working-class in their totality — in order to preserve for the capitalist the instrument by means of which alone he can remain a capitalist. Thus the continuous purchase and sale of labour-power perpetuates on the one hand labour-power as an element of capital, by virtue of which the latter appears as the creator of commodities, articles of use having value, by virtue of which, furthermore, that portion of capital which buys labour-power is continually restored by labour-power's own production, and consequently the labourer himself constantly creates the fund of capital out of which he himself is paid. On the other hand, the constant sale of labour-power becomes the source, ever renewing itself, of the maintenance of the labourer and hence his labour-power appears as that faculty through which he secures the revenue by which he lives (Marx, 1972, p. 385).

In this conception, then, consumption appears as a phase in the great 'circuit of capital' and as necessary to the self-expansion of capital. The usual 'social welfare' approach, which sees the central problem of consumption as one of unequal distribution, is thus displaced by one that focuses instead on the part played by consumption in the expanded reproduction of capital.

Although capitalist reproduction takes place first and foremost within production, politics and ideology have also played an essential part. The state has undertaken important tasks of reproduction. Even the reproduction of machines and raw materials, for instance, cannot always be undertaken by capital itself. Certainly a single firm cannot be self-sustaining, but even a multiplicity of firms cannot always provide all the raw materials and essential services that they need. Some items such as fuels, communications and transport systems require large capital investment, but 'without any immediate prospect of profit' (Engels, 1975, p. 147) and tend to be either established as legal monopolies or state enterprises, held on behalf, as it were, of all the individual capitals.

Similarly the reproduction of labour power takes place outside capitalist production itself. A central argument of this paper will relate to the part played by the state in this process. For the wage serves with certainty for the reproduction only of the workers themselves and although to a large extent the mediation of the wage for the reproduction of the class as a whole is provided through the institution of the family, this institution has required state support and, even when supported, has not been adequate to the task.[4]

In the nineteenth century it was a matter of great concern to the bourgeoisie that industry was working its labourers so hard and paying them so little that it exhausted them before the next generation was produced. No individual firm would benefit from stopping this; but the state, under pressure from the 'Ten Hours' movement, as well as from elements of the bourgeoisie, was able to restrict hours of work, especially for women and children, and to insist on somewhat improved conditions. In the twentieth century, the state has become massively involved in the education, housing, health and income maintenance of working people.

As far as the relations of production are concerned, Marx tended to concentrate on questions such as the property relation, the wage relation; so much so that in *Capital*, ideology appears in the rarified form of 'commodity fetishism'. Recent writers have looked at a wide range of aspects

of ideological reproduction in a reaction against the 'economism' of the previous period of marxist thought. They have
pointed to the fact that although state coercion is sometimes
used to establish capitalist relations, for the most part these
are assured by ideological reproduction. Althusser (1971)
has even gone so far as to identify a series of institutions
(religious, educational, family, legal, political, trade union,
communications and cultural) as ideological state apparatuses,
since these perform what for him and for Poulantzas were
state functions — the state being the 'cement' in the social
formation and the 'factor of social cohesion'. The impact of
Althusser's idea has been immense. It has enabled sociologists
studying education, politics, medicine, socialization, culture
and the media, industrial relations, social policy — indeed
almost all the traditional fields of sociology — to relate their
work to marxism, since they are able to show how the institutions they are concerned with function as ideological state
apparatuses. The danger is that their work may still be fundamentally sociological rather than marxist in the problems it
poses.[5]

There has been a tendency, however, to concentrate on
ideological reproduction and to ignore the ways in which
other aspects of the capital–labour relation are reproduced.
Thus, matters such as the developing nature of labour law,
company law and the determinations of the value of labour
power have not been analysed sufficiently. The state has
played a considerable part in the establishment of labour
power as a commodity, that is, in the creation of a proletariat
forced to sell its labour power in order to subsist. Historically
in Britain this meant the virtual abolition of self-subsistence
through such measures as the Enclosures, and the shrinking
of the lumpenproletariat of the casual poor. By now (unless
they have wealth, or engage in crime or prostitution, or join
the for-ever-swallowed-and-recreated *petite bourgeoisie* of
small business people) there are only four ways in which
most of the population subsist: wage labour, dependence on
state support, dependence on relatives, private pensions and
savings. Given the relative inflexibility of the last two, the
state is able, through the social security system, to define the
size and structure of the workforce to a considerable extent
(as well as to push down the price of labour power by keeping

the state subsistence minimum as low as possible (Ginsburg, 1977)). In the case of women, the social security system has worked in a curious way, on the one hand to establish married women as dependent upon their husbands (and therefore as not entirely reliant upon wage labour) but on the other hand by restricting their direct eligibility for social security benefits, to make them more vulnerable to use as cheap labour power when they do have to engage in wage labour.

The notion of capitalist reproduction thus enables us to identify two distinct functions of the state, relating to the two major systems in which women are oppressed. On the one hand, for the reproduction of labour power the state sustains a family household system in which a number of people are dependent for financial support on the wages of a few adult members, primarily of a male breadwinner, and in which they are all dependent for cleaning, food preparation and so forth on the unpaid work done chiefly by a woman. At the same time, the state itself carries out some of these functions of financial support and of servicing; yet it usually does so under such ideological conditions that it is seen as 'taking over' functions properly belonging to the family or as 'substituting' for work that 'should' be done by a housewife.

On the other hand, for the reproduction of relations of production (specifically the nature of labour power as a commodity), the state has played an important part in establishing married women as a latent reserve army of labour, again by sustaining the family household system and particularly by assuring the financial dependence of unemployed wives on their husbands so that married women are not fully proletarianized even during a period when they are increasingly drawn into wage labour.

Marx wrote: 'The maintenance and reproduction of the working-class is, and must even be, a necessary condition to the reproduction of capital. But the capitalist may safely leave its fulfilment to the labourer's instincts of self-preservation and of propagation' (Marx, 1970, p. 572). Unfortunately, matters are not quite as simple as Marx suggests. If the maintenance and reproduction of the working class is seen as involving at least the housing, feeding and clothing of all the members of the class, then it includes provision for children, the sick and disabled, the retired, the unemployed and those who do the domestic work, as well as provision for today's workers themselves. To a large extent, as stated earlier, this is provided from the worker's wage through the institution of the family. Yet it will be argued, first, that the specific form that the family takes is not simply an effect of 'the labourer's instinct of self-preservation and of propagation' but is a result in part of state policies, and, second, that the family is not adequate on its own to distribute support and maintenance through the class.

It may well be the case that the (male) labourer's 'instinct for self-preservation' would lead him to form a relationship something like that of marriage. For he might well wish to arrange a situation in which, in exchange for financial support, he would gain the domestic, sexual and emotional services of a woman on a long-term basis. Marriage is indeed such a relationship. But it is more than that, for marriage has never been a completely private affair, nor even a contract between the two parties. It has always involved the state or the church or some form of public regulation. One of the reasons that the state or, earlier, the church have sought to control weddings and provide for the formal solemnizing and recording of marriages has been that they could not conduct their jurisdiction over property and inheritance unless they could establish who was and who was not married.

Some writers, following Christine Delphy's interpretation of marriage as a unique form of labour contract (Delphy, 1970 and 1976), argue that the basis of the state's involvement is to guarantee, on behalf of men in general, a relationship in which men exploit women. Diana Leonard Barker writes:

> The usual reasons advanced to justify legal regulation of, support for, and intervention into marriage and the family, are: the protection of women and children (assuring support obligation and assigning responsibility for child care), ensuring family stability (for the psychic good of all its members, and hence the stability and well-being of the polity), and the promotion of public morality. I suggest that a more important reason for the regulation of marriage — indeed *the* most important reason — is that in supporting marriage the (male) state supports a particular,

exploitative relationship between men and women; whereby
the wife provides unpaid domestic and sexual services,
childbearing and rearing, and wage-earning and contribution to household income when convenient (i.e. her labour
for life — with limited rights to quit, and herself as an
instrument of production) in exchange for protection,
assured upkeep and some rights to children (Barker, 1978,
p. 239 — italics and parentheses in original).

This position is a great advance upon much of what is written
on family policy in that it recognizes the family as the prime
location of the oppression of women, as the place where the
relations of men and women *vis-à-vis* one another are defined.
'Family policy' purports to bolster the family in the interests
of women. It is indeed true that marriage can provide certain
protective rights for women; but these are best seen as secondary gains in a situation where women are at an overall dis-
advantage. Thus while in the short run desertion by a husband
or widowhood may be a catastrophe, in the long run women
as a whole would be better off without the institution of
marriage as it stands.

The weakness of this position, however, is that it sees
domestic production in marriage relations as a separate form;
it does not enable us to raise questions about historical
variations in this form as the dominant mode of production
changes. The state is seen as a 'male' state, rather than as also,
at one time, a feudal state and, at another, a capitalist state;
its intervention is therefore in the (presumably unchanging)
interests of men.

Nevertheless, writers in this vein have been right to emphasize the important part played by the state in sustaining
the family. Hilary Land has done an immense amount of
valuable work in exploring both the assumptions behind
British family policy and the consequences of it (Land, 1976;
Land, 1977; Land and Parker, 1978). She has also argued
that the income maintenance system, in particular, assumes
that married women will be financially dependent on their
husbands. In fact, in 1974, there were in Britain over half a
million married couples where the wife was the sole or
primary earner, and out of eleven million couples with the
husband under sixty-five, there were seven million working
wives contributing an average of 25 per cent of the family

budget (Hamill, 1976). Yet the massive weight of the official assumption of the economic dependence of wives and co-habiting women must surely play a part in keeping these numbers down: the ineligibility of the wife for many benefits makes it unwise for a couple to rely too heavily on her income (Lister and Wilson, 1976) and makes her more likely to take low-paid work; such provisions as the widow's pension (under both social security and occupational schemes) make it less necessary for a wife to be able to support herself alone.

It is clear, then, that the family household as we know it is not merely the social expression of an instinct but is importantly structured and constrained by state policies. The question is, what function does the state serve in its family policies? Barker, in the passage quoted earlier, says that 'the state supports a particular, exploitative relationship between men and women'. Land and Parker have pointed out that in studying the 'hidden dimensions' of family policies it is

> important to examine and understand the needs and obligations which are presumed to arise from marriage quite separately from those which are presumed to arise from parenthood. If not, the nature of marriage will too often be equated with that of parenthood (1978, pp. 3–4).

They offer evidence that there are many presumptions that support a specific dependent–breadwinner form of marriage, regardless of whether there are any dependent children or not. A glaring instance is the 'married man's tax allowance', which he receives regardless of whether his wife works or not and regardless of whether there are children or other people in need of care in the household. Unlike Barker, though, they emphasize that:

> At the same time as preserving an unequal marriage relationship social policies which impinge on the family have not been allowed to interfere with work incentives for men. Indeed, we would argue that by assuming an unequal economic relationship between men and women, the man's duty to participate in the labour market is reinforced and although the wife may take paid employment too, her first duty is in caring for her husband, children and sick or elderly relatives (p. 17).

They thus see a link between the family household and men's wage work in social production and see state policies as being concerned with establishing the link as well as with confirming men's dominant position in the family.

The family household of contemporary capitalist society is very different from that of, say, peasant society, where the family depends for its subsistence directly upon the productive work of its members, rather than upon a wage or wages to purchase needed commodities. The history of the Poor Laws and other 'income maintenance' policies, and the history of the protective legislation (see, for instance, Smelser, 1959) which limited the hours and conditions of women's and children's work in factories during the nineteenth century, are witness to the impact of the wage system, especially in its industrial form, upon the family. They represent the establishment of definitions of mutual financial dependence and of a social separation of 'work' from 'home' which are needed only under a wage system. Though such policies have often been seen by their proponents as attempts to support and defend a timeless family form, rooted in human nature and morality, in fact the end result has been a family form that is specific to capitalism and that changes, too, as capitalism develops.

One important feature of this family household, and the concomitant of the woman's dependence within it, is the woman's work as housewife. Housework, as the production, from commodities purchased with the wages, of use values for private consumption within the household, develops as the almost exclusive province of the wife and as the only productive activity within the household. It becomes rationalized and involves an increasing proportion of commodities (Davidoff, 1976; Ehrenreich and English, 1975). There has been a considerable debate about the analysis of the part played by this domestic labour in the daily reproduction of the husband's labour power (see the paper by Paul Smith, chapter 8 in this volume). Much of this has revolved around the question of whether domestic labour is productive or unproductive for capital and the implications for the class location of housewives. Undoubtedly the existence of this domestic labour reduces the amount of commodities needed to reproduce the husband's labour power. At any given time, therefore, it reduces the value of these commodities. For instance, men whose jobs take them away from home are usually paid a great deal extra in wages or expenses. Domestic labour therefore helps to keep down the value of labour power, and so keep down wages. But the daily reproduction of the husband's labour power is only one aspect of the relation of the family household to capitalism.

It is, however, striking that, from the point of view of the reproduction of the working class as a whole in capitalism, the family household system is an extremely inadequate one; it may be this that explains both state efforts to force the family into a particular mould and the fact that the state itself undertakes some of these tasks of reproduction.

Even the biological reproduction of future members of the class cannot always be safely left to individuals. In Britain, where very little in the way of explicit population policy has been needed by the state, we are inclined to forget that in many countries the problem of 'underpopulation' or 'overpopulation' has been experienced as acute. Here pronatalist propaganda has been thought sufficient, despite the recommendation of the Royal Commission on Population (1949) that nurseries and maternity leave and benefits would make motherhood more attractive. Yet, writing in France, where policies to combat underpopulation have been given priority, Patrice Grevet (1976, pp. 430 ff.) has argued that there is a law of population specific to the capitalist wage system which tends to produce difficulties in the renewal of generations. The reason, he says, is that the material needs of the child (even for the average family size for renewal) are not recognized in the wage.[6] In certain circumstances, especially as needs and the awareness of needs develop in the monopoly stage of capitalism, this non-recognition results in a low birth rate. Grevet sees this problem of the renewal of generations as an important factor in the interwar crisis of the maintenance system in France, whose solution was to be the beginnings of a comprehensive social security system. Grevet's 'law of population' has, of course, to be seen as a countertendency to the one that Marx wrote of in *Capital*, vol. I, when he pointed out that the working population make some of their own number redundant by producing so much that future production involves more machines and fewer workers:

The labouring population therefore produces, along with the accumulation of capital produced by it, the means by which itself is made relatively superfluous, is turned into a relative surplus-population; and it does this to an always increasing extent. This is a law of population peculiar to the capitalist mode of production; and in fact every special historic mode of production has its own special laws of population, historically valid within its limits alone (Marx, 1970, pp. 631–2).

Immigration, too, may help to solve the problem of the non-renewal of generations. Yet neither the growth of a relative surplus-population (which is in any case valuable to capital in keeping wages down), nor immigration, can explain why Britain has not had the absolute decline in birth rate that France experienced. The state support for an ideology of family and parenthood, especially motherhood, of which Elizabeth Wilson (1977) has written, may well have played a part in making a more explicit population policy and financial subsidies for parenthood unnecessary.

Grevet's idea of the non-recognition of certain needs in the capitalist wage system draws our attention to other ways in which the family is inadequate to the task of making the wage pay for the reproduction of the working class. It would be possible to imagine this task of reproduction being carried out in a world where every member of the class (children, trainees, the sick and disabled, the retired and people engaged in caring for all of these) lived in a household where there was at least one breadwinner permanently in work and where every household had the same ratio of earners to dependants so that a uniform wage could be fixed at such a level as to provide adequate maintenance for all. In practice, however, since not all wage earners have dependents, unless the working class resists, wages can be pushed down to such a level that they will not support them, the wage being just enough to maintain the workers themselves.

Furthermore, there are many would-be breadwinners who are out of work at any given time. These are the 'relative surplus population' of which Marx wrote (1970, p. 640 ff.). Some (the 'floating') may be able to survive because they are unemployed only briefly; others (the 'latent') because they have some source of support, say in agriculture, to which they can return; but others (the 'stagnant') 'dwell in the sphere of pauperism', that is to say they depend upon state support through the provisions of the nineteenth-century Poor Laws or parts of the twentieth-century social security.

Finally, and most imporantly, in practice the *family* system of forming households results in a much less tidy pattern than can easily be supported through a wage system. Variations in numbers of children, and the chances of disablement, sickness, longevity and death produce households with very varying needs, in no way related to variations in the wages coming in to them. To a large extent the effects of these variations are simply absorbed by the families concerned. Households with many wage earners and few dependents live fairly well and households with large numbers of children are known to be in the greatest povery (Child Poverty Action Group, 1976). Within these poor households it is women in particular who suffer since they normally sacrifice more than their share of consumption and have to work harder in order to convert a smaller amount of commodities into as high a standard of living as possible; in addition, they usually have to go out to work, or take in 'out work', in order to raise the household income. There are some social security provisions that serve to iron out some of the differences between family households, though they do not do so very effectively. Among these are child benefits, family income supplements (which, however, only apply where the male in the household is the full-time wage earner), disablement benefits, invalid care allowances, temporary sickness and unemployment benefits. In so far as these are effective at all on a wide scale, they serve to bolster the family household system by dealing with the instances where the needs of the reproduction of the working class are not met by the wage system. In doing so, as has been said earlier, they bolster a specific family household system in which the wife is assumed to be dependent and in which she is assumed to provide household services for all the other members.

The current concern about the 'one-parent family' has focused attention on many of the problems that arise from the attempt to rely on the 'normal' family. The solutions proposed all involve helping this odd family to approximate to the normal one in its effectiveness — to assist the one parent to play the part of two — without making the breaking-up of two-parent families or unmarried motherhood too attractive. The concern is in part a very old one, which flourished in the nineteenth century, about how to provide adequately for all children without encouraging immorality. To say that the emphasis on morality helped to establish a form of household that was as convenient to the capitalist wage system as any family-based household could be is not to deny the morality of female chastity its own dynamic, which could at times go far beyond the call of its duty to capitalism. Similarly today many of the anxieties about provisions for single parents are rooted only in morality; but many, like Sir Keith Joseph's (1972), are genuinely related to the needs of capital. The fear that unmarried women and women who have many children will bring them up less well-suited to modern wage labour is probably well-founded. They become involved in what Joseph called a 'cycle of deprivation'. On the whole, then, the policy will tend to be one of seeking a way to give support to the one-parent family that did not choose it or the 'genuine case of involuntary role-reversal'.[7] It will give minimal support to any who may have chosen to reject the normal pattern. But, above all, it will not encourage alternatives such as public responsibility for children or the disabled.

The extension and intensification of children's dependence upon their parents is a marked feature of the past hundred years. Universal elementary, and later primary and secondary education, made it impossible for children to earn wages or work in any way to support themselves. As long as they continue their education (up to the age of twenty-five or marriage) they are counted as dependents. The means test in grants for students in higher education, for instance, is applied to the parents' income, and unemployed school leavers living with their parents get smaller supplementary benefits than those living away. Children cannot easily be sent to live in another household. They are not company or help to the elderly, they do not care for younger children, they do not work in the home or in anything productive, they cannot be apprenticed until they are sixteen, nor can they be servants. The most usual ways for them to live apart from at least one parent are formalized fostering and adoption, where they are assimilated completely as children of the household. In 1851, in contrast, a large proportion of households contained children who were living with relatives other than their own parents. This pattern was a common one, probably in situations where the mother was unmarried, or had remarried, or where she was dead (Anderson, 1971, p. 84 ff.). A major reason why single motherhood is such a burden is the total dependence of children in the present period. The non-recognition of their needs by the state is premised on an assumption that in 'normal' cases there will be two parents to shoulder this dependence – the one financially, the other practically – and that this is viable.

Old age and the disablement of men are the two situations where the state has to some extent recognized needs unmet by the wage system and allowed the principle of individual dependence on the state regardless of household circumstances. In the case of old age, this has in part been made necessary by the fact that the practice of supporting old parents, of sharing a household with them if they had nothing to contribute, has never been a universal one in Britain (Anderson, 1971). Nevertheless the state pensions for the retired and disabled have always been barely adequate for financial support. In practice, an enormous amount of care and domestic servicing is provided for the old and disabled by the women in their families, especially their daughters and their daughters-in-law (Land and Parker, 1978; Cartwright et al., 1973; Moroney, 1976). About a quarter of old people are now in the same household as their children (Central Statistical Office, 1975, p. 78). The state provision for these needs takes the form only of institutions which appear to be planned as places of last resort.

Unemployment benefits and supplementary benefits represent, among other things, a partial state recognition of the needs, unrecognized in the wage system, arising from Marx's 'floating' and 'stagnant' reserve army of labour. But these benefits are not merely substitute wages for those who cannot find work. Women living with their husbands or lovers and school leavers living with their parents do not have the same benefit rights as men. A woman in such a situation cannot claim supplementary benefit at all; she can only claim unemployment benefit if she has paid full contributions rather than taken the 'married women's option' (now being phased out, but formerly very common) to pay a tiny amount, and her benefit even then covers only herself and not her husband or her children. The benefits are thus largely geared to the needs of the *male* members of the industrial reserve army and their dependents, rather than to the needs of any workers who are not employed.

In various and piecemeal ways, then, state policy has sought, sometimes unsuccessfully, to remedy the fact that the family household system is inadequate for mediating the wage and the reproduction of the working class. It has always done so in such a way as to sustain that family system of a male breadwinner, dependent children and a dependent wife responsible for domestic and childrearing work. Where this would be seriously threatened, the needs have remained unmet.

Grevet does not introduce the notion of needs unrecognized by the wage system in order to examine family policy. He himself is concerned with a much wider problem: that of the growing need for collective forms of consumption, as, with the development of technology and the division of labour, people's needs become more diversified, more subject to risk and longer in phase, so that things like education, housing, health protection and transportation of people cannot be provided through a wage system in which labour power is purchased for only a brief period (Grevet, 1976, p. 120). He argues that in the stage of state monopoly capitalism, not only has state financing of the military and of research grown, along with state financing of production:

> But another public financing of consumption has played a growing role, under pressure from the people. This is the public financing of personal consumption: *education, health, housing, social security*, etc. This financing temporarily resolves the contradiction between the character of labour power as a commodity and the growth of needs that take more and more socialized forms. It intervenes directly in establishing new conditions of the productivity, the demand and the maintenance of labour power (p. 524, my translation).

What Grevet refers to as 'collective consumption' has also had a very particular relation to the family. Its introduction is frequently accomplished with an ideology that retains a definition of the need as one that, in some sense, *should* be served by the family – and especially by the wife-mother. This idea that the family is the proper location of these needs can often be found in linguistic usage. One has only to think, in the commercial sphere, of the name 'Mother's Pride' for white, sliced, factory-baked bread or, in the sphere of the state, of the French *école maternelle* for a nursery school. Functionalist sociology reflects this ideology with its picture of a pre-industrial family of a multi-functional type and a complex internal structure transformed in the course of industrialization into a simpler structure with an irreducible minimum of functions: 'stable satisfaction of sex need, production and rearing of children, and provision of a home', according to MacIver and Page (1950, p. 264). In this picture, the functions remain the same – they are the requisites of all societies – but, with the advent of industrialization and the general evolutionary tendency towards the increasing complexity of overall structure and the increasing structural simplicity and functional specificity of parts, they are 'taken over' from the family by various specialized institutions, frequently ones that are related in the state. (For a full critique of these theories, see Morgan (1975).) The image of functions that once belonged to the family being taken over by the state is a very powerful one. The different functions vary in the degree to which their removal from the family is seen as being legitimate. Land and Parker (1978) have pointed out that the removal of education of small children is legitimate, whereas the removal of care is not, so that the state provision for the under-fives is largely in the form of nursery *schools*, whereas other forms of day care (nurseries and child minders) are largely private.

Child care (both preschool and during times when the schools are closed or the child is unwell) is indeed an example of the nature of state involvement with the family. In the period since the Second World War there has been a reaction against the policy of placing children from broken or incompetent homes in institutions, and immense efforts have been made by the new breed of social workers, caseworkers, using watered-down psychoanalytic theory, to enable these children to live in their mothers' homes and to persuade mothers to take responsibility for them in the officially approved manner (Wilson, 1977, p. 84 ff.). 'Shared care' — the care of children and other dependents shared between social agencies and the family — is a concept that has been discussed in social policy circles recently but that has little relation to practice. '. . . the state (both centrally and locally) has hitherto tended *either* to assume responsibility for child care *or* to leave the family to cope as best it can until crisis or tragedy occur' (Land and Parker, 1977; italics in original).

The health services, on the other hand, represent a more thoroughgoing 'takeover' by state institutions. Tasks that were carried out at home by women have been replaced by professional activities in clinics and hospitals. Most babies are born in hospital; the home confinement attended by a midwife is a declining practice. Ante-natal and post-natal care, and regular check-ups in schools, have made health a matter of professional expertise from an early stage. Many senile people are looked after in hospitals, subject to geriatric care for a medical or psychiatric condition rather than in suitably organized old people's homes. Yet even this extensive change still wears the ideological garb of a 'takeover'. The recent cutbacks in public spending have revealed that when the money is not available for state provision, the responsibility for many fringe forms of care 'reverts' to women relatives (Counter Information Services, 1976, p. 27; Moroney, 1976). When homes for the old or the handicapped are not provided, or when schools work half days because they do not have enough teachers, these people who need supervision and care are sent 'home' and women have to give up wage work or work odd hours in order to be with them. The policy of 'community care' for the mentally ill, as embodied in the Mental Health Act of 1959, was a longer-term policy that reduced state expenditure (as well as the evil effects of institutionalization) by keeping hospital stays as short as possible and getting relatives — again mainly women — to provide care, with social work support, during periods when the patient's symptoms were controlled by drugs.

Thus, given the ideology that these forms of care belong in the family, the ultimate possibility of these aspects of reproduction being organized through the family household

remains. The family is ever ready to provide care for dependents: the men to spread their wage a little further (though
pensions often help to make this less necessary), the women
to take on an extra burden of emotional and practical
servicing.[8]

III

It is not necessary to argue here that women's — and above
all married women's — place in wage labour is that of a
reserve army. Veronica Beechey presents this position in
detail in chapter 7 of this volume (see also Gardiner, 1975).
As far as the state is concerned, there are two aspects of this
analysis that need to be developed: state participation in
determining the conditions of employment and state participation in maintaining a situation in which married women are
only semi-proletarianized.

The question of the conditions of employment raises a
number of analytical problems that are not yet resolved. On
the one hand the Sex Discrimination Act (1975), in breaking
down occupational segregation, appears to make women
more readily substitutable for men and therefore to enhance
their usefulness as a reserve army, by locating throughout the
occupational structure those workers who can both help in
keeping the general level of wages down and be more easily
laid off. Some problems of occupational segregation and the
reserve army have been discussed by Milkman (1976). On the
other hand we know that an Act geared to equality of
opportunity for individuals and with almost no enforcement
procedure other than an inadequate one of individual com-
plaints is likely to have very little effect on occupational
segregation. Or again, on the one hand the Employment
Protection Act (1976), under which the jobs of some women
have to be kept open for them when they have babies,
appears to make women less easily disposed of by employers.
On the other hand, the provisions only apply where the
worker has been employed for two years or more, a condition
that probably one half of women workers can satisfy, precisely
because of their 'reserve army' character. These contradictory
implications of recent state policies affecting women wage
workers suggest that the state does not play a significant role

in establishing the conditions of employment that permit or inhibit the use of married women as a reserve army of labour. Much more important are the various endeavours of trade unions and employers and the changes in the labour process discussed by Beechey (this volume and 1977).

The other aspect of women's position in the labour market relates again to the family household system examined in the last section. For as well as being a system through which women's work contributes to the reproduction of the working class as a whole, it is also one of mutual financial dependence, which means that married women are not dependent on their own wages for the costs of the reproduction of their labour power. This enables them to be paid wages that are below the value of their labour power (Beechey, 1977) and it also enables them to 'disappear almost without trace back into the family' (Beechey, this volume) when they are redundant to waged employed.

In this last respect they provide an interesting parallel and contrast with Marx's example (an agricultural labouring population) of his concept of 'a constant latent surplus-population' (Marx, 1970, p. 642). For Marx saw these wage labourers as no longer needed with the increasing mechanization of agriculture and 'therefore constantly on the point of passing over into an urban or manufacturing proletariat'. The extent of the surplus population, he said, 'becomes evident only when its channels of outlet open to exceptional width'. So, too, do many married women remain only latent proletarians, not entering the statistics of the 'economically active' until there are job openings available to them. But in Marx's example, the process of primitive accumulation in agriculture as well as of the self-reproduction of capital in manufacturing play a part in the constitution of this element of the surplus population. The first provides a source that is 'constantly flowing'; the second results in both attraction and repulsion as effects of the expansion of capital and of its rising organic composition. In the case of married women, the attraction and repulsion of workers by modern capitalism (and, by repercussion, non-capitalist employment) is still relevant. The attraction–repulsion produces varied needs for labour power at different times and places and this is one of the reasons why a reserve army of labour is needed, as well as how it is produced. However, married women are not a source that is constantly flowing or awaiting transformation from a latent situation to a proletarian one. Rather they are constantly flowing to and fro, sometimes latently at home or semi-employed, sometimes fully employed, but never fully proletarian in the sense of being entirely dependent on wage labour for their livelihood. For, unlike agricultural labourers in Marx's day, they are not less and less needed in their sphere of latency, for there are no overall changes in the family household system but those originating in the capitalist sphere or indirectly in response to changes there.

The question of the role of the state is thus a particularly significant one, because the state can initiate or guide changes in the family household system in relation to capital's need for the labour power of married women as well as in relation to the reproduction of the class in general.[9] The immensely expanded welfare services during the Second World War are an example of this (Titmuss, 1950; Wilson, 1977, ch. 7). In part, improved provisions for diet, health, mother-and-baby clinics and so forth were a response to a new recognition of the unfitness of many working-class people revealed by military service and evacuation; in part provisions like residential nurseries were an attempt to deal with the problems of family break-up which evacuation and military service brought about; but to a large extent, day nurseries, canteens and better maternity services were the price that had to be paid to draw married women into war work. The state provided these alternatives and aids to women's work in the household, not just because of changed needs in the reproduction of the working class, but also because these women were needed for waged labour. There is dispute as to the extent to which the social policy introduced in wartime initiated permanent changes in welfare provisions. It is certain, though, that the taking over of practical servicing was largely reversed in the postwar period. While the financial support provided by the social security system may have been consolidated as a result of wartime experience, women's household work was re-established in the late 1940s and 1950s, often with considerable effort by state agencies as well as by ideologues like John Bowlby.

Women's dependence on their husbands makes them very

suitable as a latent reserve of labour. But apart from such massive upheavals as those of wartime, this dependence is not open to short-term manipulation by the state. On its own it would sustain a latent reserve that could respond simply to openings in the labour market. However, it has been shown earlier that in practice many women do not have husbands who can be depended on. For these women, as for any people who have no one to depend on, the state provides if they are not employed. For these women the conditions of state provision establish their relation to the labour market: a generous and unconditioned provision could keep them out of employment altogether; a meagre provision could force them to seek employment at whatever wages; a provision conditional on, say, having household responsibility could force some to look for work and enable others to stay at home. This area of welfare policy is therefore potentially a fairly flexible instrument keeping women more or less in reserve for wage labour.

Norman Ginsburg (1977) sees one of the main functions of poor relief and social insurance expenditures and administrations as being 'reconstructing labour and reproducing the front-line of the industrial reserve army of labour'. The Poor Law Amendment Act of 1834 played an important part in the creation of a proletariat dependent on wages for its livelihood, for it sought to eliminate any poor relief at levels higher than local wages or under conditions as attractive as those of the free wage labourer. At various periods women have been differentiated into categories and differentiated from men. Those defined as 'undeserving' or those for whom it was thought a 'liable relative' should be responsible could be subjected either to the 'workhouse test' or to the test of their willingness to seek work (Thane, 1977). Such people would presumably constitute the front line of the reserve army, or what Marx called the 'floating' element. Others, like the widowed mothers of young children, have nearly always qualified for outdoor (unconditional) relief, and only the inadequacy of the payments would make them want to take paid work at all. A more detailed historical analysis, relating changes in the organization of welfare payments to women to changes in the labour requirements of capital, needs to be done; the materials are there (see for instance Webb and

Webb, 1910; Finer and McGregor, 1974; Thane, 1977) but they have not yet been analysed in this way.

It is possible to summarize the present situation as one in which:

(1) Women living with husbands or male sexual partners are assumed by the state to be dependent upon them (and so either *are* dependent on them or are forced to work at, possibly, very disadvantageous rates of pay).
(2) Women living with their children and without a man, and some other older widows, are supposed to be allowed to depend on state payments without being expected to seek work. In practice, however, they are often under pressure to accept jobs (Marsden, 1973).
(3) Most other women are required to seek work or prove disablement, as (almost) all men are, before they can get either contributory or supplementary benefits.

When unemployed, the first two categories may be said to constitute a 'latent' reserve army and the third a 'floating' one.

IV

Up till now in this paper, the different ways in which the state contributes to sustaining systems of family household and wage labour in which women are oppressed have been described as functional for capital — as providing part of the social conditions for the accumulation of capital. There are certain dangers in this kind of 'marxist functionalism', as indeed in any form of functionalism, and so it is necessary to point out how the analysis here avoids these dangers. The great weakness of functionalism is that it presents a picture of society as an integrated whole in which any disturbances are met by equilibrating and adaptive mechanisms, so that the general tendency is towards equilibrium rather than disequilibrium. By contrast, in marxist theory, the social formation (particularly in its capitalist form), whilst conceived as an integrated whole, none the less contains internal contradictions of ever-increasing severity. These ultimately result in the destruction of the formation and its transformation into something new.

However, since the fundamental contradictions in society are found in the mode of production and since the tenets of materialism require that analysis ultimately relates all elements of the social formation to the economic level (even if the relation is conceived as one of relative autonomy), marxist statements on particular social developments often run the risk of taking a non-dialectical form, explaining them simply as serving certain 'needs of capital'. Paul Corrigan has pointed out that such forms of marxist functionalism in the study of the 'welfare state' have curious political implications:

> if we accept that welfare is controlled by capital and acts against the welfare of working people, then why should we fight the cuts? We should welcome them . . . as a direct cut in the power of the ruling class over the working class (Corrigan, 1977, p. 88).

The corresponding political positions are 'always negative and utopian' since, under capitalism, welfare can only serve the needs of the ruling class.

There are two common ways of introducing a dialectical element into the analysis. One is to reassert the fundamental contradictions of the mode of production — to point out, for instance, that the accumulation of capital intensifies the contradiction between the social character of production and the private character of appropriation. But this does not really help in making a more politically useful analysis, since it still provides no space for welfare politics, or education politics, or women's politics within capitalism. The other common way is to counterpose working-class struggle to ruling-class efforts to satisfy the 'needs of capital' and to see social policies as ways of guaranteeing the social conditions for the reproduction of capital whose specific forms are the outcome of class struggle. To some extent working-class struggle is the other side of the medal of functionalism. For if school dinners or a national health service help keep the working class healthy, they fulfil aspirations of the class as well as merely help to reproduce it; or, if welfare payments are used to damp down the fires of working-class protests, they can be seen as an achievement of that protest. The value of introducing the idea of class struggle can only be seen in concrete analyses of specific situations. Corrigan argues that

Marx's discussion of the Factory Acts in *Capital*, vol. I, is a detailed analysis that unravels the various results (in the *form* that the legislation took) of a complex class struggle at a specific stage in the development of capitalist production.

Another problem that needs to be approached in this way is that of the historical determination of the value of labour power. Indeed, one of the questions that is central to the theme of this paper but has not yet been adequately analysed is whether the value of labour power includes the cost of reproducing the worker alone or the entire family of the worker. This is not a theoretical question but an historical one, since the value of labour power is socially determined by the class struggle and is different at different times. Jane Humphries (1977, pp. 247 ff.) argues that the 'family wage' for the married man, and his wife and children staying at home, was a goal and to some extent an achievement of working-class struggle during the nineteenth century.

The analysis in this paper points to further contradictions of a different sort: those between the sphere of the family and the sphere of capitalist production. Thus, it has been argued here that a specific form of family household (in which there is joint consumption based on the income from a limited number of wage earners and the domestic labour of a wife and in which the wife is, or can be, a dependent) functions broadly both with respect to the reproduction of the working class and with respect to maintaining married women as a latent reserve army of labour. It has been further argued that the state plays a vital part in sustaining this form of family household or in providing substitute support that approximates to it in its effects. Yet at any given conjuncture there may well be contradiction between the state policies needed for the reproduction of the class and those needed for reproducing the relation of women as a reserve army.

For example, pro-natalist policies, or policies geared to combating child poverty may suggest child benefits and large-family benefits at such a level that mothers — and sometimes even fathers — of large families do not find it worthwhile to go out to work at the available low wages. Another example: when the expansion of production calls for an increase in the size of the labour force, wages may increase; but this means that in each family the man's wages have gone up and it may be less necessary for the woman to go out to work; in this case the reserve army, instead of advancing to the front, goes into retreat.

The key problem is the relative inflexibility of the family, as a social institution structured by ideologies of human nature, tradition, religion and so on, as well as by state policy. A pure functionalist analysis might lead to the conclusion that 'if the basis for the present family household form had not existed when capitalism emerged, it would have had to be invented'. The implication of the argument presented here, on the other hand, is that it would be possible to imagine systems for the reproduction of the working class and systems for sustaining reserve armies of labour that would function more effectively for capitalism. This is not to suggest, however, that there is any tendency to move from the present position towards any such imaginable systems.

A problem that has preoccupied feminist thought is whether there is any tendency within capitalism towards the socialization of domestic labour. The question may be interpreted in a number of different ways and the analysis presented here should help to clarify some of the issues. In one interpretation the question is a spurious one: in so far as this labour is domestic it is private and cannot be social.[10] In another, it is a belated one: the increasing use of commodities, both as raw materials and as instruments of production, in the home testifies to the increasing component of 'dead' social labour in domestic production. Yet, as the demands made on them rise, women continue to spend long hours in domestic labour. In a third interpretation, the 'taking over' of certain functions by the state from the family constitutes a form of socialization. Yet this 'taking over' is either provisional in nature or else involves newly developed kinds of activity like specialized education or advanced medical care in hospitals.

At some periods, such as wartime, the state may take over more activities from women in the household, in order to free them for wage labour. At other periods there may be a shortage of labour in social production and if women's wages are sufficiently high, they may be able to afford more 'convenience goods' and 'labour saving devices' produced as commodities by capitalist enterprise (often, indeed, by the wage labour of the same women). In general, however, unpaid domestic labour reduces the value of labour power, so that maintaining the system in which it is performed benefits capital.

As well as the various contradictory tendencies found in the two systems that relate to the oppression of women, there are other more general contradictions such as those relating to the 'welfare state' in general, which affect these two systems. In this paper it has been assumed that the state simply steps in to maintain the social conditions of reproduction. Yet in doing so it is undertaking expenditure and thus performing an economic function.[11] From a feminist point of view, it is not merely the size but also the consequences of such state expenditure for sexual divisions that become objects of struggle.

If this paper can contribute anything towards guiding such struggle, it is in showing the ambiguities involved in the state support of a system of family households which can be dependent on a male wage and in which women carry out domestic production and servicing. This household system mediates the individual worker's wage for the reproduction of the working class as a whole; as such it is supported by the state. Yet since, for historical and ideological reasons, it is formed on a kinship basis, it is always inadequate to performing this function fully; the state then provides substitutes for the wage where this is missing. At the same time, the fact that married women can often fall back on dependency on a man's wage keeps them semi-proletarianized, enabling them to serve as a very flexible latent reserve army of wage labour. Yet the varying need for women in wage labour is unlikely to coincide with the rather less varying need for them in the domestic labour of reproducing the working class. Such contradictions mean that there are always a number of conflicting principles articulated in state policy, so that there is always room for change.

Notes

1 My thanks to the following friends who have kindly given me comments on an earlier version of this paper: Michèle Barrett, Veronica Beechey, Helen Crowley, Norman Ginsburg, Annette Kuhn, Maxine

Molyneux, Kerry Schott, Harold Wolpe. They are not, however, to be held responsible for the outcome.

2 It is common to make the central question of women's oppression, 'How do women become different from and subordinated to men?' The position taken here is that these processes of socialization, and the institutions such as education (see Wolpe, this volume) in which they take place, can only be understood in relation to these two key systems. Ideology, sexuality, personality are all important elements in women's oppression, but they remain without an historical dynamic unless we relate them, through these two systems, to the capitalist mode of production.

3 The question of the size of the wage, which in marxist theory tends to be equivalent to the value of labour power, is a complex one. The aspect that has been most discussed recently is the effect that women's domestic labour has on the value of their husbands' labour power. Less discussed has been the question of whether the reproduction of the housewife and of the next generation is included in the value of the wage earner's labour power. Himmelweit and Mohun (1977) suggest that

> The value of labour power should be seen as the mediating link with which to analyze changes in women's role in production. It is determined partly by the extent of domestic labour and, relatedly, by the number of wage-labourers in the family. In turn, the value of labour power determines the extent to which women must work, both in wage-labour and at home, in order to provide an acceptable standard of living for their families.

It is important to note that not only are the amount and combination of housework and commodities required to reproduce and socialize an individual historically determined by class struggle (rather than being biologically fixed), but also the number of people dependent on each wage for their reproduction is an historical and not a theoretical question (see, for instance, Humphries (1977)). This paper will bypass these issues by taking up, in the next section, the more general question of the reproduction of the working class as a *whole*, which is obviously less amenable to quantitative analysis in terms of the value of labour power.

4 To write of the 'adequacy' or 'inadequacy' of the family as an institution for serving certain 'needs of capital' highlights some of the problems inherent in the functionalist approach. It can, however, be understood as a necessary preliminary to an analysis of class struggle. Thus, to specify the requirements for the reproduction of capital is to specify the material basis on which ruling-class policies will be formed; though it may tell us little about the particular shape that these will take in the political class struggle.

5 For a full critique of the idea of ideological reproduction, see Hirst (1976).

6 There is not space here to elaborate Grevet's concept of 'needs'. It is not a biological one, but involves both an objective and a subjective

moment, the former resulting from external exigencies connected with the forces of production and social relations, the latter being the conscious reflection of the objective moment. In capitalist society, 'even the limited covering of needs comes through the struggle for wages and other forms of resources for the people, a struggle which itself presupposes a consciousness of the needs to be satisfied' (Grevet, 1976, p. 65).

7 This phrase is used in a letter from Brian O'Malley, Minister of State at the Department of Health and Social Security, to the Woman's Liberation Campaign for Legal and Financial Independence, 14 May 1975.

8 David (1978) has a much more sophisticated discussion of the complexities of the relation of family to education system.

9 A comparable analysis of the reserve army of African labour in South Africa has been made by Legassick and Wolpe (1977). They see the state policy of creating Bantustans in much the same way as the state policy of supporting families is described here.

10 This seems to be the position of Adamson *et al.* (1976) who offer a very interesting discussion of the debate on domestic labour and women's oppression, but ultimately simply *assert* that domestic labour cannot be socialized under capitalism.

11 There is, at present, dispute between neo-Richardians (Gough, 1977) and marxists (e.g. Fine and Harris, 1977) about the analysis of the 'social wage'. Gough sees this as similar to the ordinary wage and equally an object of class struggle. Fine and Harris argue a similar position to that of this paper: that the 'social wage' is not a wage at all, in the sense of being an exchange for equivalent labour power, but, unlike the wage, is primarily the outcome of political struggle.

References

Adamson, O., Brown, C., Harrison, J., and Price, J. (1976), 'Women's oppression under capitalism', *Revolutionary Communist*, no. 5, pp. 2–48.

Althusser, L. (1971), 'Ideology and ideological state apparatuses' in *Lenin and Philosophy and Other Essays*, New Left Books, London.

Anderson, M. (1971), 'Family, housework and the industrial revolution' in *Sociology of the Family*, Penguin, Harmondsworth.

Anderson, M. (1972), *Family Structure in Nineteenth Century England*, Cambridge University Press.

Barker, D. L. (1978), 'The regulation of marriage: repressive benevolence' in Littlejohn *et al.* (1978).

Beechey, V. (1977), 'Female wage labour in capitalist production', *Capital and Class*, no. 3, pp. 45–66.

Cartwright, A., Hockey, L., and Anderson, J. L. (1973), *Life Before Death*, Routledge & Kegan Paul, London.

Central Statistical Office (1975), *Social Trends*, no. 6, HMSO, London.

Child Poverty Action Group (1976), *Child Benefit Now*, CPAG, London.

Corrigan, P. (1977), 'The welfare state as an arena of class struggle', *Marxism Today*, vol. 21, pp. 87–93.

Coulson, Margaret (1974), 'The family and the sexual division of labour in capitalism', paper presented at the British Sociological Association annual conference.

Counter Information Services (1976), *Crisis: Women Under Attack*, CIS, London.

David, M. E. (1978), 'The state, education and the family' in Littlejohn *et al.* (1978).

Davidoff, L. (1976), 'The rationalisation of housework' in D. L. Barker and S. Allen, *Dependence and exploitation in Work and Marriage*, Longman, London.

Delphy, C. (1970), 'L'ennemi principal', *Partisans*, no. 54–5; translated as 'The main enemy' in *The Main Enemy: a Materialist Analysis of Women's Oppression*, Women's Research and Resources Centre, London, 1977.

Delphy, C. (1976), 'Continuities and discontinuities in marriage and divorce' in D. L. Barket and S. Allen, *Sexual Divisions and Society*, Tavistock, London.

Ehrenreich, B., and English, D. (1975), 'The manufacture of housework', *Socialist Revolution*, no. 26, pp. 5–40.

Engels, F. (1975), *Selected Works of Marx and Engels*, Progress Publishers, Moscow.

Fine, B., and Harris, L. (1977), 'State expenditure in advanced capitalism: a critique' *New Left Review*, no. 98, pp. 97–112.

Finer, M., and McGregor, O. R. (1974), 'The history of the obligation to maintain' in *Report of the Committee on One-parent Families*, vol. 2, HMSO, London.

Fox, G. (1977), 'Nice girl: social control of women through a value construct', *Signs: Journal of Women in Culture and Society*, vol. 2, pp. 805–17.

Gardiner, J. (1975) 'Women and unemployment', *Red Rag*, no. 10, pp. 12–15.

Ginsburg, N. (1977), 'Poor relief: the development of state policy in the context of class struggle and struggle for accumulation', paper presented at the Conference of Socialist Economists, July.

Gough, I. (1976), 'State expenditure in advanced capitalism', *New Left Review*, no. 92, pp. 53–92.

Grevet, P. (1976), *Besoins populaires et financement publique*, Éditions Sociales, Paris.

Hamill, L. (1976), 'Wives as sole and joint breadwinners', paper presented at the SSRC Social Security Research Workshop.

Himmelweit, S., and Mohun, S. (1977), 'Domestic labour and capital', *Cambridge Journal of Economics*, vol. 1, pp. 15–31.

Hirst, P. Q., (1976), 'Althusser's theory of ideology', *Economy and Society*, vol. 5, pp. 385–412.

Humphries, J. (1977), 'Class struggle and the persistence of the working-class family', *Cambridge Journal of Economics*, vol. 1, pp. 241—58.

Joseph, Sir K. (1972), speech to the Pre-school Playgroups Association, 29 June.

Land, H. (1976), 'Women: supporters or supported?' in D. L. Barker and S. Allen, *Sexual Divisions and Society: Process and Change*, Tavistock, London.

Land, H. (1977), 'Social Security and the division of unpaid work in the home and paid employment in the labour market' in Department of Health and Social Security, *Social Security Research Seminar*, HMSO, London.

Land, H., and Parker, R. (1978), 'Family policies in Britain: the hidden dimension' in J. Kahn and S. B. Kammerman, *Family Policy*, Columbia University Press, New York.

Legassick, M., and Wolpe, H. (1977), 'The Bantustans and capital accumulation in South Africa', *Review of African Political Economy*, no. 7, pp. 87—107.

Lister, R., and Wilson, L. (1976), *The Unequal Breadwinner*, National Council for Civil Liberties, London.

Littlejohn, G., Wakeford, J., Smart, B., and Yuval-Davis, N. (1978), *Power and the State*, Croom Helm, London.

MacIver, R. M., and Page, C. H. (1950), *Society: an Introductory Analysis*, Macmillan, London.

Marsden, D. (1973), *Mothers Alone*, Penguin, Harmondsworth.

Marx, K. (1970), *Capital*, vol. I, Lawrence & Wishart, London.

Marx, K. (1972), *Capital*, vol. II, Lawrence & Wishart, London.

Milkman, R. (1976), 'Women's work and the economic crisis: some lessons of the great depression', *Review of Radical Political Economy*, vol. 8, pp. 73—97.

Morgan, D. H. J. (1975), *Social Theory and the Family*, Routledge & Kegan Paul, London.

Moroney, R. M. (1976), *The Family and the State: Considerations for Social Policy*, Longman, London.

Royal Commission on Population (1949), *Report*, HMSO, London.

Smart, C. (1976), *Women, Crime and Criminology*, Routledge & Kegan Paul, London.

Smelser, N. J. (1959), *Social Change in the Industrial Revolution*, Routledge & Kegan Paul, London.

Snäre, A., and Steng-Dahl, T. (1978), 'The coercion of privacy' in C. Smart and B. Smart, *Women, Sex and Social Control*, Routledge & Kegan Paul, London.

Thane, P. (1977), 'Women and state "welfare" in Victorian and Edwardian England', paper presented at the SSRC Social Security Research Workshop.

Titmuss, R. M. (1975), *Problems of Social Policy*, U.K. History of the Second World War, HMSO, London.

Webb, B., and Webb, S. (1910), *English Poor Law Policy*, Longman, London.

Wilson, E. (1977), *Women and the Welfare State*, Tavistock, London.

11 Education and the sexual division of labour

AnnMarie Wolpe

Much sociological work on the position of women in the educational system has been taken up with the problem of accounting for the difference in levels of attainment between boys and girls within educational institutions. To this end, a number of accounts have been given of the causes of this differences. Direct action has followed as a consequence, mainly in the USA where publishers, for example, with the possibility of being sued under Title Nine, are making efforts to expunge any form of sexism from textbooks. While such actions are commendable, clearly these steps will not in themselves effect a change in women's position *vis-à-vis* the educational system. Sexism in education is not simply derived from the way in which culture is transmitted, but is a far more complex process. In this paper AnnMarie Wolpe examines some of the conventional approaches which 'explain' differential achievement between the sexes, and suggests that such approaches are derived from a 'subjectivist' position and hence can do no more than describe the processes at work within the educational system. To propose an alternative materialist problematic within which to think the terms of the relationship between women and the educational system is immediately to encounter difficulties arising from the underdeveloped character of work in this area. A necessary prerequisite of a feminist and materialist approach to education must be a full consideration of the implications of the sexual division of labour and the uneven and contradictory nature of the reproduction of capital. Only then is it possible to understand either the ways in which the educational system relates to transformations of the division of labour or the mechanisms by which subjects are reproduced and allocated in that division of labour. And it is only then that the question of the specificity of the position of women with regard to the educational system can be raised. Because the initial groundwork for such a project yet remains to be undertaken, the parameters within which the precise question of women may be considered can at present only be drawn in outline.

Apart from the 'new sociology of education', which has been largely concerned with what constitutes 'knowledge', the field of the sociology of education has been dominated by the 'inequalities' debate — the role that the educational system plays in the production of the disparities which exist within society. In the main this work has been firmly located within one or another version of stratification theory. Initially, in the analyses made from this standpoint, no attention was paid to gender differentiation within the educational or stratification systems and it was simply assumed that the position of women was determined by the position of men. Recently, a body of literature has begun to appear which, while remaining within the framework of stratification analysis, has attempted to account for the inequalities between boys and girls in education and in the stratification system. The literature has primarily chronicled the inequalities within the school itself, and has then set out to account for the divergencies in the levels of educational attainment of girls as compared to boys and, thereby, to explain their inescapable failure to achieve equality with boys in the higher levels of the occupational system. This paper has a twofold aim. In the first instance, its purpose is to point to certain fundamental limitations of stratification theory and to demonstrate the effect of these on women-centred studies. The second aim is to pose the question of the position of women in a different way and to indicate tentatively the concepts which may be necessary for the development of an alternative analysis.

I

Central to stratification theory is the interrelationship between occupation, income and status (Jackson, 1968;

Parkin, 1971). According to this theory, occupation is the fundamental determinant of an individual's class position. As Parkin expressed it, 'the backbone of the class structure is the occupational order'. Income and status attach to occupations and hence the hierarchy of the income and status orders are correlated with, correspond to, the hierarchy of the occupational order. This correlation is in turn a function of the expertise, the skill, entailed in different occupations. It was, of course, Weber who introduced these concepts. In a well-known passage Weber defined class in terms of the situation of individuals who share a

> typical chance for a supply of goods, external living conditions, and personal life experiences, insofar as this chance is determined by the amount and kind of power, or lack of such, to dispose of such goods or skills for the sake of income in a given economic order (Gerth and Mills, 1964, p. 181).

Parkin echoes this when he states: 'marketable expertise is the most important single determinant of occupational rewards, and therefore one of the key elements in the system of class inequality' (1971, p. 21). It follows from this that the entry of an individual into the occupational order and hence into class and status positions must be seen as a function of the acquisition of skills and expertise which are disposable on the market. The crucial question which now arises is: How are these marketable skills obtained?

In the literature on social stratification, the educational system is accorded a special role: it is conceived of as the agency or mechanism whereby pupils attain differential marketable skills — skills which in turn open up the way to positions in the occupational structure. The next problem that should be posed is what determines the education an individual will receive? Here one of the main underlying assumptions is that access to education and its advantages is largely equal, so that the way is open to all to compete on an equal footing to acquire qualifications and to again compete for jobs in the hierarchical occupational structure. As Bowles and Gintis put in their comments on the sociology of education, in this type of approach the availability of equal opportunity in education is thought to provide an open, objective and ostensibly meritocratic mechanism for assigning individuals to unequal economic positions. The educational system fosters and reinforces the belief that economic success depends essentially on the possession of technical and cognitive skills — skills which it is organized to provide in an efficient, equitable, and unbiased manner on the basis of meritocratic principle (1976, p. 103).

The educational system appears therefore to operate in a purely functional manner, that is to say in a manner which ensures the rational allocation of individuals into jobs appropriate to their levels of attainment.

The inequality evident in the occupational structure is therefore seen as directly linked to the educational system itself. The difference between individuals in the levels of skills and expertise reached suggests that there is an unequal use of equal educational facilities. This unequal use is often accounted for on the basis of certain qualities individuals possess, qualities which are internal to the individuals themselves, and it is this which accounts for their different levels of attainment. These explications differ in emphasis; an examination of the literature produces examples of some of the reasons which are given for these differences, such as lack of 'clarity' amongst pupils themselves who 'follow the course of least resistance into whatever slots the economy makes available' (Jencks, 1973), or resignation and acceptance (Runciman, 1966), or the pupils' own motivation (Turner, 1964b), or their innate ability (Jensen, 1969).

Other writers have attributed these differences to phenomena which are related to the stratified society and which operate at the level of educational institution. The type of explanation offered here may rest, for example, on a notion of cultural deprivation, derived from the individual's class position and resulting in the individual being unable to benefit fully from the educational facilities available. The extensive literature on the relationship between education and the occupational structure focuses almost exclusively on males. There appears to be no necessary theoretical reason for this within the framework of stratification theory. The failure to deal with the differential position of men and women in the stratification system must be attributed to the effect, in these studies of the operation of preconceptions concerning the marginality of women – conceptions which themselves constitute elements of the ideological structures of the societies under investigation. Briefly, we may note how this effect is produced.

First, in the analysis of the occupational structure it is assumed that gender differentiation is irrelevant (by contrast, for example, with racial or ethnic distinctions) and, as a consequence, the specific and unequal situation of women becomes totally obscured. The fact that women do comprise a significant proportion of the labour force (over 40 per cent) and also their disproportionate clustering at the lowest levels of the occupational hierarchy, in terms of both pay and skills, do not appear (Department of Employment Report, 1975; Barron and Norris, 1976). Second, only those occupations which relate specifically to economic activity are regarded as relevant in stratification analysis. Therefore housewives who are defined as 'economically inactive' are excluded from stratification analyses. According to the last census (1971), almost 58 per cent of all women were married, classified as housewives and 'economically inactive', and this not inconsiderable group of women is totally overlooked in stratification terms.

Third, and following from the above, the position of women in the status hierarchy is generally treated as deriving unproblematically from the position of men. Status, as was pointed out above, is seen to be determined by occupation – incumbency of an occupational role carries with it a certain estimation of prestige both within the job situation and in the broader social world (Jackson, 1968). There is, as Parkin has put it, a 'congruence in the two dimensions of inequality based on the division of labour'. Since the position of women in the occupational structure is treated as peripheral, the allocation of their status is derived from that of men. When status is actually measured, it is derived only in terms of the position of the *male* head of the household. This situation is justified on the grounds that the family comprises the basic unit for analysis in stratification terms, and that the man's role in the occupational structure is the major one for the maintenance of the household. Parkin puts this position quite succinctly:

Now female status certainly carries many disadvantages
compared with that of males in various areas of social life
including employment opportunities, property ownership,
income and so on. However, these inequalities associated
with sex differences are not usefully thought of as components of stratification. This is because for the great majority
of women the allocation of social and economic rewards
is determined primarily by the position of their families —
and, in particular, that of the male head. Although women
today have certain status attributes in common, simply by
virtue of their sex, their claims over resources are not
primarily determined by their occupation but, more commonly, by that of their fathers or husbands (1971, pp.
14—15).

Recently, there have been several attempts to come to
terms with these inadequacies, which are due to the exclusive
concentration on men, by explicitly utilising stratification
theory to account for the differential position of men and
women in the stratification system. It will be shown in what
follows that it is possible, in a variety of ways, to extend
stratification theory, without at all tampering with its basic
postulates, to include an analysis of the differential position
of men and women in the stratification hierarchies. It is
precisely because the literature I am about to outline does this
that it is unable to transcend the limitations of stratification
theory and becomes subject to all the inadequacies of that
theory. Acker (1973) poses the problem of the way in which
sexual inequalities can be dealt with using a stratification
model. She suggests that the 'classic definitions of class',
with the family as the basic unit, is being replaced by a consideration of the individual. This, she says, could 'cut across
class lines' and enable analyses to be carried out of 'interrelated hierarchies of positions or persons', as well as provide
a 'basis of evaluation which affects the placement of individuals in particular hierarchies'. She poses in addition the
problem of assigning a status to women not engaged in paid
work and suggests: 'the position of the non-employed wife
may be determined by a combination of the ranking of
housewife, conferred status, and pre-marriage deference
entitlements belonging to the woman herself' (1973, p. 942).
    Graham and Llewellyn have, on the other hand, argued for

a reconsideration of the relationship that women have to the occupational structure.

> It would appear that because *occupation per se* is used as a determinant of class position in mobility research, and broader economic and social relational considerations are omitted, attempts to redress the balance by analyses of female occupational intergenerational mobility, or marital mobility, do not add significantly to an understanding of the class position of women. This is because such studies are still based on the same assumptions as male mobility studies, and a quite different relationship that women have to the occupational structure is never explained (1976, p. 5).

Their solution to the problem of explaining the 'quite different relationship that women have to the occupational structure' is to examine the actors' perceptions of the employment situation (that is, the way women regard their work) and how factors relating to mobility within an occupational group affect women.

While Acker and Graham and Llewellyn consider the way in which gender based stratification could be inserted into the general study of stratification systems, another trend (emanating largely, but not exclusively, from feminist writers) has been concerned specifically with the relationship between gender variables, equal opportunity, education and occupation. Turner (1964a and 1964b), whose work is firmly located within a stratification model, regards society as divided into strata which are ranked in accordance with status 'and the possession of goods and power'. He says: 'In any open class society — one which allows vertical mobility — ambition is likely to find expression in the pursuit of upward mobility. Ambition then becomes a desire to abandon one social position and attain another' (1964b, p. 2). Education, and appropriate qualifications, constitute the instrument realising ambition; education being seen in purely pragmatic terms. Because of his concern that most of the studies dealing with the nature of ambition have concentrated on males and male values in relation to the higher social strata, Turner sets out to examine specifically the content of women's ambition. He does so through a survey of a large number of eighteen-year-old women. He says that 'a man works toward some goal that the sociologist can locate on the stratification grid'. This is not so, he argues, with women, except for those who 'acquire in certain respects a less feminine constellation of values than other girls'. In other words, girls who display ambition congruent with that of men appear 'deviant', and non-feminine. He finds that amongst the vast majority of women, the nature of ambition and the form it takes differ considerably from those of men. Woman's ambition is tied to her role in marriage and to the goals directly related to marriage, whereas man's ambition is linked to his occupation and as such is of a material nature.

> The fundamental differentiation of women's ambition, related to direct and indirect pursuit of goals imposed by the married woman's role, appears to be the key to the data at hand . . . the educational and occupational ambitions are substantially related to material ambitions for men, but women's own educational and career aspirations bear little relationship to their material existence (Turner, 1964b, p. 271).

In order to give some political credence to this analysis, Turner tentatively suggests that it may be useful to distinguish two basic types of rewards, 'intrinsic' and 'extrinsic', the characteristics of the former being related to a 'striving for exellence within' an occupation, and 'extrinsic' reward being directly linked to material aspects. He argues that women are concerned with intrinsic rewards, with a 'striving for excellence' because of their traditional roles as housewives. Men, on the other hand, because of their role in work, are concerned with extrinsic, material rewards. He draws a number of conclusions (which he offers as 'plausible inferences') to account for the 'fact' that women, if they do choose a career, are none the less more concerned with intrinsic rewards in their occupational roles rather than with material, extrinsic rewards. Thus, in Turner's analysis, it is the orientation of women towards ambition which determines their actions. The reason for the failure of women to compete on an equal footing with men is that their ambition, and hence their orientation towards success in work, is not related to work; the form of their ambition characteristically varies from that of men. So differences between men and women are accounted for by gender specific orientations. It would seem then that differences are explained in terms of the 'traditional' roles that men and women perform — men at work and women in the home. Women do not work, nor do they want to 'succeed' at work because they are concerned with their familial roles, and this in turn is seen to determine the nature of women's ambition. The nature of this ambition itself has an effect on the way in which girls will utilise the equal educational facilities which are available to them. The circle is complete.

King (1971), like Turner, is concerned with the absence of 'sex variables in the discussion on inequality of opportunity' but he proposes a different approach. His aim is to devise a model which includes both sex and 'class' variables. He accepts both that there is 'equality of opportunity' in education and that 'the class gap has closed to some extent in the last forty years', although he does recognise that it 'has closed least at the university level'. None the less, he notes that 'equality has not emerged, in spite of the educational system', and proceeds to examine the four main models which are usually utilised to explain this fact. As none of these explanations, he maintains, can account at all for girls in the educational system, he formulates a model which will in fact include women, whilst at the same time retaining the analytical categories of class and status; he believes that this model will be able to account for the different educational experiences of four basic pupil types, middle-class boys, middle-class girls, working-class boys and working-class girls. This distinction is necessary because he observes that:

> At each level of education the sex-gap is bigger for the working class than the middle class, and the class-gap is bigger for girls than for boys. As the level of education rises the sex-gap widens for both classes, but widens more for the working class. The class-gap also widens for both sexes, but more for girls than for boys (p. 171).

He draws a distinction between 'symbolic' and 'functional' values of education. The former he defines as the 'indicator of social status', and the latter as the 'means to the desired occupation' (although he does not define what he means by either 'social status' or 'desired occupation'). According to him the lower down the social scale one goes the less likely is education to have a great deal of 'symbolic' significance. The 'symbolic' function is more relevant to middle-class girls who might wish to gain access to certain occupations, but it is less important for them than for middle-class boys who are likely to utilise education as a means of acquiring not only a desired occupation, but also a particular status; working-class boys use education merely 'functionally':

Middle class boys show a high evaluation of education for both symbolic and functional purposes; they have to maintain status and gain entry to occupations through certification. Working class boys do not have status that is confirmed by the receipt of education but may gain access to desired occupations through education; hence their low symbolic evaluation and possibly high functional evaluation. Middle class girls have a high symbolic evaluation (status confirming), but a lower functional one related to their stronger orientation to marriage. Working class girls show a low evaluation of both the symbolic and the functional; their orientation is towards early marriage, they have no status to confirm. This model could be elaborated by the inclusion of ability and adaptation variables (King, 1971, p. 173).

Thus, King, like Turner, ultimately explains the situation of women through their orientations which are themselves derived from their position in the occupational/class structure. The assumption is that the educational system offers equal opportunities alike to all boys and all girls. The unequal use of equal opportunities results from the different orientations of different actors. It is the actors themselves who are responsible for perpetuating their own inequality.

A more recent example of failure to account for the position of women is evident in a much acclaimed book by Bowles and Gintis (1976), which purports to offer an analysis which will overcome the problems of conventional approaches in the sociology of education. They relate the educational system to a broad societal base utilising, they claim, a materialist analysis. Their concern is with the passage of the individual through the educational system into a society dominated by a 'corporate form of capitalism'. They maintain that it is necessary for individuals to be 'integrated' into the various sectors of the capitalist society. While it is beyond the scope of this paper to appraise this work comprehensively, one general point can be made. The concern here, as with King and Turner, is with the individual as a knowing subject whose personal development is related to and even determined by the educational system. They say:

> It is a mistake to think of the educational system in rela-
> tion to the economy simply in 'technical' terms of the
> skills it supplies students and for this employers pay in the
> labour market. To capture the economic impact of
> education we must relate its social structure to the forms
> of consciousness, interpersonal behaviour, and personality
> it fosters in the student (Bowles and Gintis, 1976, p. 9).

They are correct in viewing the educational system as producing more than just 'technical skills'; but to concentrate, as they do, on the individual actor in this way is to be concerned essentially with a subjectivist approach — for them the way in which the actor perceives and reacts becomes important. They thereby overlook the structural determinants of the situation. More specifically, perhaps, their regard for the individual leads them into an analysis in which it is the 'inequalities' in society which demarcate one individual from another; but it is these 'inequalities' which themselves need to be explained. They say that the 'dynamics of economic life' are based on differences in levels of income and so they are forced to 'explain' how these disparities come about. Such an analysis cannot be said to be a marxist one in spite of assertions as to the importance of the class structure. It is perhaps an indication of the pluralism of Bowles' and Gintis' approach that they attribute an important role to specific elements such as ethnicity and sex. The maintenance of income differentials, they say, derives

> largely from the class structure and the structure of racial
> and sexual privilege. In a more proximate sense, differences
> in wages or salaries are associated with differing personal
> characteristics of workers, and differences in geographical
> and sectional situations facing them (Bowles and Gintis,
> 1976, p. 91).

To introduce, as they do, income differentials, status and occupation is to commit the common error of confusing class position with occupational structure. Their failure to provide a coherent account of the position of women is quite clear. In the final analysis all they do is ascribe to women a particular position which is determined by their sex.

It may now be asked what the contribution of feminist writers has been to the analysis of the position of women in education and society. An examination of the work of several of these writers reveals that they are in fact operating within the same conceptual terrain as Turner and King. What unites the work of the feminist writers, despite differences of emphasis and some theoretical variation, is a common concern with a political problem — how to obtain parity for women with men in society. In this literature, education is considered to be directly linked with the occupation structure and is thus seen as the *major* means to a successful economic career. Achievement is defined in terms of entry into highly prestigious and rewarding jobs. The acquisition of qualifications in the educational system, either directly, or through opening up the way for further training, is seen as providing the key to success. Thus, if girls are to achieve as well as boys, it is argued that they need to acquire the skills which will enable them to compete with boys for the high-status or well rewarded jobs. The question which presents itself to the feminist writers is: How is the relative lack of attainment by girls, their failure to acquire parity within academic terms as measured by success in public examinations with boys — despite earlier cognitive advantages — to be explained? (Boocock, 1975; Maccoby, 1966; Shaw, 1976; Wolpe, 1977).

Certain variants of this approach may be located within a social psychological framework, in which case there is a tendency to reject the results of psychological tests which have been utilised to measure the differences between men and women on the basis of performance in experimental situations. The argument mobilised is that such tests are culturally specific and therefore not a valid means for explaining gender differentials (Hartnett, 1976). As Boocock points out:

> Studies comparing sex differences in intelligence tend to show negligible overall differences but substantial differences in specific ability areas. The findings are generally

consistent with popular stereotypes; males out-perform females on mathematical reasoning, judgement and manipulation of spatial relations, while females excel at vocabulary and verbal fluency and tasks involving straight memory. Test scores also indicate, however, that superior or highly developed ability is more or less equally distributed among boys and girls; and on all measures there is considerable overlap between and distribution of scores for the two sexes (1975, p. 81).

In adopting the notion of cultural specificity, an attempt is made to establish categories of social forms of behaviour patterns which can be attributed to males and females and to define a related list of gender specific personality traits (Maccoby, 1966). According to this approach, the internalisation of values which define adult male and female behaviour patterns is seen to occur as an integral part of normal childhood development; and it is the internalisation of 'female' values which, it is argued, affects women's occupational attainment in adulthood (Rendel, 1975). An example of this can be seen in the way in which aggression is conceptualised as a determinant of women's use of education. Boocock, who accepts the premise that there are specific personality traits congruent with achievement, cites aggression as one of these. Aggression is defined as a 'masculine trait' and since girls are socialised not to display such masculine traits, they are, it is suggested, bound to underachieve.

Aggression, however, is not the only trait which comes under scrutiny. Anxiety is another element routinely used to account for gender differences. Byrne reported:

An important discovery of the National Child Development Study . . . however was that while more boys than girls showed anxiety for acceptance by their peer groups, many more girls than boys showed anxiety for *adult* acceptance. And proportionately far more girls than boys from the manual social classes III (b), and IV and V showed this anxiety. Thus girls are far more likely than boys to conform to an adult-set stereotype of expected behaviour pattern, educational aim or social behaviour (1975, p. 189).

Such approaches as these concentrate on specific variables selected from a large range of possible variables; specific elements in social behaviour. They do not resort to attributing gender differences to inherent qualities in men and women; rather they are concerned to show that these behaviour patterns are derived from society, that they are socially constructed. The difficulty, however, is that the conditions under which the behaviour patterns in question come into existence and are transformed are not discussed in this work. The result is that we are left with given behaviour patterns which are acquired through socialisation and are functional to individual achievement on an already given stratification system. As with Turner and King, the analysis is located within a stratification model and as such is subject to the same criticisms.

A more 'structural' type of analysis is exemplified in the work of Cynthia Fuchs Epstein who is concerned to explain why women who indeed have managed to become highly qualified, nevertheless fail to 'achieve'. As she put it, 'our best women — those in whom society has invested most heavily — underperform, underachieve and underproduce. We waste them and they waste themselves' (1973, p. 4). Whilst she is basically concerned with an elite group, many of the points she makes are general in their application. The concept of status is central to her explanation. For women, she sees sex status as crucial (although she does not in fact explain why this should be so):

> Certain ascribed statuses — sex status and racial status for example — are central in controlling the choices of most individuals. The status of 'women' is one such dominant and often salient status. For a woman, sex status is primary and privotal and it inevitably determines much of the course of her life, especially because of rigid cultural definitions which limit the range of other statuses she may acquire (Epstein, 1973, p. 92).

The fact that individuals occupy a number of status positions opens up the possibility of 'role conflict' because a multiplicity of statuses is conducive to 'social structural ambiguity'. While her notion of structural ambiguity is by no means clear, she illustrates how it works by means of an example:

> The young girl is asked to be studious and learn but she

increasingly becomes aware that she may not be asked to demonstrate her knowledge. She is asked to be good-looking, and charming and deferential to men, yet she must go to school and compete with young men at all levels of educational training. The syndrome has a variety of labels, like cultural discontinuity and identity stress. Here is where social structural ambiguity or sociological ambivalence come in (p. 61).

Social ambivalence is derived from calling on the girl, particularly the middle-class girl, to achieve and do well at school, while at the same time she is subjected to those pressures where 'all arrows direct the girl to marriage' (Epstein, 1973). Empirical evidence is cited by Epstein in support of the claim that college girls who are potentially bright turn their sights away from commitment to intellectual, professional or other career pursuits because of marriage or the prospect of marriage. Epstein suggests that it would greatly assist individual girls if they had 'role models' in which these conflicts had been resolved, and with whom young girls could identify. She concludes that the only way in which women may achieve any equality is through opening up more jobs to women, and then ensuring that they are sufficiently motivated to take up these opportunities. In this way Epstein is able to ignore what she earlier indicated as an inevitable contradiction — 'social structural ambiguity' — in adult female roles and statuses, and instead to visualise change being brought about through a change on an individual level only. She does not preclude other alterations occurring but reduces these to an undifferentiated notion of 'wider societal changes' which, she cautiously says, 'may contribute to the greater participation of women and heightens the burdens assumed by today's professional women' (p. 199).

Although Epstein apparently starts out from a structural frame of reference, her position is, in the final analysis, no different from the others, whose work has been considered above. She overwhelmingly concentrates on the actions and orientations of the individual actor. Provided that all occupations are open to women, she implies change will come about if and when women's attitudes towards these opportunities undergo a marked modification. From this viewpoint, the rational use of womanpower resides in the hands of the women themselves; women will cease to underachieve when they discard their attitudes. At this point a major difficulty arises in Epstein's analysis. On the one hand, she argues that the female status, like all statuses, is 'ascribed' and consequently outside the control of the actor. On the other hand, she also asserts that it is open to women to alter their status through a change in their orientations or attitudes. This contradiction remains unresolved in Epstein's work because she offers no propositions concerning the relationship between ascribed roles and actors' orientations, nor does she suggest the causes or mechanisms which may effect a transformation in either.

From a brief account of the work of both feminist and non-feminist writers it emerges quite clearly that, differences notwithstanding, all this work operates within a common problematic, the parameters of which are set by the concepts of stratification theory and the notion of the orientations of the individual actor. In summary form this common problematic may be characterised as follows:

(1) The social system is conceived in terms of an hierarchised system of social stratification. The key elements in this system are occupational roles which are differentially rewarded both in respect of material rewards (particularly income) and in degree of prestige. The hierarchical order of the occupational structure corresponds to the hierarchical order of material rewards and prestige attached to the occupational roles.

(2) The determinant of the level of income and prestige which is accorded to occupational roles is the extent of expertise or skill required to fulfil that role. That skill can be acquired by means of the educational system. The opportunity to utilise the educational system to gain the skills required to enter into the occupational structure is, more or less, equally available to all actors in the social system.

(3) However, although the facilities of the educational system and opportunities for education and training are generally available, the use to which those facilities are put varies considerably as between individual actors. The reason for this unequal usage of equal facilities is to be found in the different individual qualities of each actor.

These individual qualities relate either to innate skills or to the orientations of the actors.

(4) In the case of gender differences in the stratification system, the position of women is to be explained by the fact that women do not have sufficient aggression, or have too much anxiety, or are otherwise incumbents of inappropriate personality traits; or, again, by the fact that their orientations are towards 'intrinsic' or 'symbolic' or other rewards which are not functional to an 'adequate' utilisation of the educational system.

This type of approach is open to a number of objections on both empirical and theoretical grounds. While it is not possible to discuss these in detail in the present context, it is necessary to state the grounds upon which stratification analysis is argued to be inadequate in order to lead into a discussion of what might constitute an alternative approach.

Empirically, the accounts discussed above are unsatisfactory because they ignore important conditions which, when taken into account, cast considerable doubt on the explanations offered for the unequal position of men and women. Thus, on the one hand, the assumption that equal educational opportunities are available simply ignores the entire body of work in the sociology of education which analyses the differential availability of and access to educational facilities for different classes, races, religious groups and so on. These studies discuss the economic and other pressures which lead to early school leaving, lack of resources, of adequately trained teachers, of teaching material, of subject options, of libraries, of adequate buildings, and so on, which characterise the educational conditions of many, but not of all, groups. Other studies have shown that certain of these disadvantages apply also to girls at school. In addition, the studies surveyed, in discussing women's orientation, tend to make the simplistic assumption that essentially all women are engaged exclusively in the family as mothers and wives. This is to ignore the fact that an ever-growing proportion of households, both in Britain and America, are solely supported by women who are employed also in the economy (Land, 1975; Acker, 1973). Furthermore, it is to ignore that 40 per cent of the British workforce is composed of women (a figure which would be much higher if part-time workers for whom no returns are made were included), and that women work in all types of roles in the occupational structure.

More important, however, are the theoretical limitations which emerge from the work under consideration. Two major points may be made here. First, if we accept the existence of a stratified occupational structure, the question which presents itself is: How is the emergence of the particular occupational structure and its order of hierarchy to be explained? Stratification analysis in general and the work on women in particular have nothing to offer in answer to this question. The theory can merely give a description of an unequal system of material and status rewards which is said to attach to occupations, but it does not in any way tell us how that system of inequality is itself produced. Indeed, in the work dealing with women, the concentration on the subordinate position they occupy in the stratification system relative to men has the paradoxical effect that it leads either to a narrow focus on the small minority of women who, given equal opportunities, could achieve educational and occupational parity with men at the higher levels, or upon the possibility of the *pro rata* redistribution of men and women through all levels of an hierarchical and therefore unequal system of stratification. That is to say, since it does not deal with the conditions of existence of the inequality, it can only concern itself with a redistribution of actors while retaining the unequal system.

Second, and relatedly, while the mechanism of redistribution is said to reside in the transformation of the orientations of women actors, nothing is said about the conditions which will produce or make possible such transformations. Instead, we are presented with a circular argument which attributes women's orientations to their role in the social structure while at the same time explaining their allocation to particular roles in terms of their orientations. With this is coupled the suggestion, as I pointed out above, that women's roles will change with changing orientations.

Now it is clear that what is absent from these analyses is any conception of the relationship between the occupational structure — or rather the division of labour — and the conditions which produce changes in it, the social relations and conflicts which determine the different conditions within the division of labour. Nor are any conceptualisations offered for an analysis of the complex relationships operating between changes in the division of labour and in other structures, such as the family, and other discourses, such as the ideological, within society.

II

The analysis of the specific position of women in the educational system and in the division of labour depends in the first place on adequate conceptualisation of the complex relationship between capitalist production, the division of labour, the family and the educational system. In the previous section attention was drawn to the absence of discussion of these relations, except in an extremely partial and simplistic way, in the literature on stratification. On the other hand, while within marxism a number of recent contributions have made important points (Poulantzas, 1975; Bowles and Gintis, 1976; Hussain, 1976), there is as yet no systematic analysis of these relationships. What does emerge from this work is that in some sense the necessary organising concept for the analysis of the educational system relates to the process of the reproduction of agents — as economic, ideological, political and social agents, that is — and their allocation into 'places' in the system of social relations. An attempt will be made to elaborate and extend the insights contained in the above-mentioned work.

The point of departure must be certain general characteristics of the capitalist mode of production. In the production phase of the circuit of extended accumulation, capital undergoes a continuous process of restructuring in both its constant and variable forms. In general it can be said that this process of restructuring is an effect of the struggle to counter the tendency of the rate of profit to decline. The restructuring in turn has effects on the mode of extraction of surplus value. Marx draws a distinction between absolute and relative surplus value:

> The surplus value produced by the prolongation of the working day [or by the intensification of labour], I call *absolute surplus-value*. On the other hand, the surplus-value arising from the curtailment of the necessary labour-

time, and from the corresponding alteration in the respective lengths of the two components of the working-day, I
call *relative surplus-value* (1970, p. 315).

Relative surplus value is the result of an increase in the
productivity of labour which is brought about through the
revolutionisation of the means of production and consequent
changes in the labour process:

By increase in the productiveness of labour, we mean,
generally, an alteration in the labour process, of such a
kind as to shorten the labour-time socially necessary for
the production of a commodity, and to endow a given
quantity of labour with the power of producing a greater
quantity of use-value (1970, p. 314).

It is clear that the extraction of absolute and relative surplus
value implies not only different labour processes but also, as
a necessary concomitant of this, different divisions of labour,
and furthermore the transformation of the labour process
with the tendency towards relative surplus value implying a
continuous transformation of the division of labour. It is
important to note, however, that the tendency towards the
development of the mode of relative surplus value extraction
and its dominance does not imply the elimination of the
extraction of absolute surplus value. Absolute and relative
surplus value coexist within the capitalist mode of production, but in unequal degrees and in an asymmetrical and
contradictory relationship. As Marx insisted, capital accumulation is both an uneven and contradictory process:

Considering the social capital in its totality, the movement
of its accumulation now causes periodical changes, affecting it more or less as a whole, now distributes its various
phases simultaneously over the different spheres of production. In some spheres a change in the composition of
capital without increase of its absolute magnitude, as a consequence of simple centralization; in others the absolute
growth of capital is connected with absolute diminution of
its variable constituent, or of the labour-power absorbed
by it; in others, again, capital continues growing for a time
on its given technical basis, and attracts additional labour-
power in proportion to its increase, while at other times it

undergoes organic change, and lessens its variable constituent; in all spheres, the increase of the variable part of
capital, and therefore the number of labourers employed
by it, is always connected with violent fluctuations and
transitory production of surplus-population, whether this
takes the more striking form of repulsion of labourers
already employed, or the less evident but not less real form
of the more difficult absorption of the additional labouring population through the usual channels. With the magnitude of the social capital already functioning, and the
degree of its increase, with the extension of the scale of
production, and the mass of labourers set in motion, with
the development of the productiveness of their labour, . . .
there is an extension of the scale on which greater attraction of labourers by capital is accompanied by their greater
repulsion; the rapidity of the change in the organic composition of capital, and in its technical form increases, and
an increasing number of spheres of production becomes
involved in this change, now simultaneously, now alter-
nately (1970, pp. 630–1).

The implications of this passage are of considerable importance in a number of respects, but here I want to focus upon
its relevance to changes in the labour process and division of
labour. The transformations in the division of labour occur
unequally both in the different departments of production
and within different sectors and, indeed, enterprises within
departments. However, not only does the degree of transformation vary in this way but the tempo of change is also
uneven and erratic. The effect of this is that varied, contradictory and opposing demands are set up for quantities
of labour power possessing differing skills and qualities.
The complex nature of these demands can be indicated
briefly by reference to some of the detailed processes which
occur. Changes in the labour process render certain types of
skills redundant (or at least diminish the demand for them),
increase the demand for others, introduce new, increasingly
complex skill requirements and at the same time produce a
process of deskilling.

It is important to note here that what has been said in
regard to industrial production applies also to a considerable
extent to the sphere of 'unproductive' labour — that is to say,

to the labour processes in the non-productive spheres of the extended reproduction of capital. The transformation of the labour process in the spheres of the circulation of commodities, financial and banking institutions, bureaucratic organisations and so on has become a prominent feature of advanced capitalism.

The continuously present and yet changing multiplicity of requirements for varying quantities and differing types of labour power is expressed in contradictory demands on all types of labour producing institutions and organisations — schools, colleges of further education, universities, polytechnics, and so on. The attempt to mould educational and training policies to suit particular types of demands thus becomes the site of political and ideological struggles which have consequences for the system of education. In this regard it may be noted that the demand on the educational system for labour with specific skills is coupled with the further demand, related precisely to the rapid changes in the division of labour, for labour power which is generally trained and, in any event, highly adaptable. Before dealing with this, however, it is necessary to draw attention to a sphere which is of considerable importance in relation to education, but in which the division of labour, by contrast with the sectors of the economy referred to above, has remained relatively static over the period of capitalist development. Despite the availability of domestic 'labour saving' devices, processed foods, consumer durables and the like, the division of labour between men and women in the household has tended to remain remarkably static in capitalist society. It is still the woman's role generally to manage the household, to conduct or supervise 'domestic labour', while the man's activities in the household tend to be restricted to periodic tasks of 'maintenance' of property and to the management of 'external' monetary matters. The point is that from the perspective of domestic labour a range of relatively unchanging skills seems to be called for.

I referred above to the variant and contradictory demands which are made on the educational/training system in response to the transformation of the division of labour in the different circuits of the capitalist production process. It was not intended to suggest by this that the requirements for labour power of particular qualities and quantities which arise in production are automatically and directly translated into effective demands of the educational system: far from it. In the first instance, at any given moment, for whatever reasons, a particular fraction of capital may be dominant in the social formation and may be able to assert its demands more strongly and effectively than other classes or fractions of classes. This may be of particular pertinence in the period of advanced monopoly capital when the state intervenes directly and on a large scale in the economy and, in particular, in the process of the reproduction of labour power. In short, policies on training and education are themselves the outcome of struggle between the dominant classes. In the second instance, however, the struggle between the dominant classes takes place within the context of the capital–labour contradiction. Thus, working-class organisations not only resist certain changes in the division of labour (illustrated, for example, in trade union resistance to job dilution, deskilling and job redefinition) but also attempt to influence education and training policies.

In the discussion so far I have focused exclusively, in an extremely general and schematic way, on the processes which tend to generate labour power requirements while at the same time pointing to the fact that the translation of requirements into policy demands is overdetermined by the operation of class struggle. It does not follow, however, that education policies advanced by even the hegemonic fraction of the dominant classes will actually be carried into effect within the system of education. The reason for this is that the educational system does not immediately and directly reflect the 'necessities' of the economy. That is to say, the educational system is not functional for production in the sense that the 'functional' requirements of production can be met through the operation of educational institutions. The point is that the educational sector is itself the site of struggles not only within the structure of the educational system but also in so far as, for example, 'interests' within the system resist or support 'external' demands made on it from different sectors of the economy. These struggles are fought out in terms of educational ideologies and within structures — forms of administration, class-room, curricula and so on — which define the specificity of the educational system. Despite its ambiguity, it can be said that these 'factors' place the educational system in a position of relative autonomy with regard to the economy: that is, the struggles which occur both within and outside educational institutions tend to result in 'compromises' in the operation of the system, and these 'compromises' constitute the form and content of the struggle which is itself in part structured by the ideological and organisational conditions of education. As Bourdieu and Boltanski have put it: 'The educational system has a strong relative autonomy with respect to the economy and hence a structural duration particularly out of phase with that of the economy' (1977, p. 4). Concretely, this relative autonomy is reflected in debates about the 'purposes' of education, such as whether it should aim to be vocational or non-vocational, the validation of 'qualifications' and the setting of 'standards', decisions over the content of curricula and so forth.

III

A conceptualisation, such as that advanced here, of the educational system as a structure, which has a relative autonomy *vis-à-vis* the capitalist mode of production and which is the site of the operation of the contradictions and uneven development of that mode, is crucial to an understanding of the operation of the educational system in its historical specificity. In this section I want to consider the educational system, first, as a mechanism of *reproduction* of 'agents' in the sense that it operates, more or less successfully, to qualify them both 'technically' and ideologically; and second, as a mediating agency in the *allocation* of agents into the division of labour. Poulantzas argues that:

> The reproduction of agents, in particular the notorious 'training' of the agents of actual production, is no simple technical division of labour (technical education) but also a real training and subjection which extends into political and ideological relations (1975, p. 33).

While Poulantzas justifiably draws attention to the political and ideological relationships, that which constitutes 'training' is itself highly problematic and needs careful consideration. It is necessary to consider what constitutes skill, and to examine the claim that the educational system produces agents each with a particular level of skill.

It has been pointed out that the process of capital accumulation entails a rapid transformation and expansion of the skills required in the labour process; it is necessary to reiterate that this applies not only to industrial production but throughout all the sectors of the economy. Precisely because of the struggles in relation to the educational system which were referred to previously, there is at any one moment a necessary disjunction between the 'requirements' of the economy and the range of skills the educational system can produce. The way in which the demand for skills becomes translated in the educational system is to an overwhelming extent at the level of the school in the form of a more or less general training which is itself ideologically overdetermined. The notion of 'skills', for example, turns out to be ill-defined and extremely unclear and the actual relationship between 'skills' acquired at school, and likewise the notion of the demands of the labour market remains extremely problematic.

This is to some extent indicated by the relatively small numbers of school leavers who are seen to have definite or specific skills which correspond to the 'needs' of the labour market. Nor does the use of the term 'skill' enable one to incorporate the wide variations in the levels of attainment of school leavers. For example, just over half of all British girl school leavers in 1974 had no 'graded result' in public examinations, or had one or more grades which were below the ordinary or advanced certificates of education. This group probably comprises part of the 78 per cent of school leavers who went directly into employment on leaving school. The chances of this group possessing specific vocational skills are small, as the work of the Manpower Services Commission is constantly emphasising. Indeed, it was estimated (Department of Employment, 1977) that 45 per cent were likely to attain qualifications during the course of their employment, with 26.5 per cent apprenticed, 17 per cent likely to obtain 'planned training' while at work, and 1.5 per cent in jobs which could lead them to professional status (p. 233). So for this 45 per cent, qualifications (at whatever

level) would be obtained contemporaneously with employment and not necessarily within the boundaries of a formal
educational system. The chances of the other 55 per cent of
new labour recruits receiving formal, recognised training are
extremely slight. As for full-time education, there were
approximately 9 per cent who continued formal education
either at degree level or in teacher training colleges. For the
rest who continued in full-time education (13 per cent), more
than a third — mostly women — enrolled in catering, nursing,
or secretarial courses, embarked on the General Certificate of
Education (GCE) ordinary ('O') or advanced ('A') level
courses.

Perhaps it may be suggested that the struggle which results
in the educational system operating in this way is structured
by two contradictory processes, both of which are related
to the rate and nature of transformation in the division of
labour. On the one hand, the outcome of conflicts over
education is the establishment of structures and organisations which, because of vested interests, both 'internal' and
'external', display a relative inertia in the face of rapid change
in the economy — there is thus a 'lag' in the rate at which
the education can meet the demand for new skills. On the
other hand, the counterpart of the demand for new skills is
a process of deskilling which in relation to the educational
system manifests itself in the declining demand for skills
which were earlier required. But these factors are not necessarily taken into account in the course of the internal
organisation of various educational institutions. It may be
that resources, teaching skills, expertise and so on which
were once in effective use in the educational system tend
to become redundant.

It is precisely tendencies of this kind which underlie the
Manpower Planning Commissions and reports which regularly
appeared in Britain from the 1940s onwards. Fundamental to
these reports and underpinning their analyses and proposals
is the belief that increased productivity, improvement in the
country's standard of living, and reduction in unemployment,
are directly linked to the level of attainment reached by
school leavers and university graduates. In regard to this
group, Manpower Planning reports up to the late 1960s consistently embody the belief that all these improvements

would result from an increased production of skilled technologists at degree level. With this assumption, attention was
focused on a number of problem areas: the ways in which
applied technology could become as popular with pupils as
pure science and art subjects, the ways in which the total
number of skilled technologists could be increased, the ways
in which to improve the calibre of the type of student
recruited into applied technology — and here they even
considered that women represented a vast potential source
of adequate 'manpower' yet to be tapped, the ways in which
the school curriculum could be adjusted in order to encourage
a greater interest in the sciences, especially applied science.
Nor has this emphasis been greatly altered in recent years. In
the now famous Green Paper dealing with 'Education in the
Schools' and heralding the 'Great Debate' one out of eight
of the stated aims of education is 'to provide a basis of
mathematical, scientific and technical knowledge, enabling
boys and girls to learn the essential skills needed in a fast
changing world of work' (Department of Education and
Science, 1977, p. 7). There is only a token recognition that
the labour process is continually changing; the report is more
concerned with how 'essential skills' are to be 'imparted' to
boys and girls with a great deal of emphasis being placed on
the development of a core corriculum which would ensure
that all pupils do acquire 'basic knowledge'; it is not seen as

> the task of schools to prepare pupils for specific jobs but
> experience has long shown that studies and activities that
> are practical and obviously relevant to working life can be
> valuable as a means of learning, including the learning of
> basic skills (p. 11).

The basic skills go beyond the mastering of reading,
writing and calculating figures. Although not clearly articulated in official statements, even though essential to the aims
of education as set out in the Green Paper, the ideological
and political components of education are inextricably
linked.

Closely linked to the area of skill is the ideological discourse of the educational system, and it is in this field that
analysis is least developed. The way in which knowledge is
produced is highly complex. While this process has been

discussed in broad terms in recent literature, an analysis of its operation in the educational system — the way in which the educational system produces and reproduces knowledge — has yet to be undertaken. While recognising the difficulties, it is nevertheless necessary to draw attention to some of the problems which arise, since this is of particular relevance to the way in which curricula are not only constructed but also provide the main vehicle for the transmission of knowledge. In addition it becomes of special interest when the specific situation of women is considered.

Unfortunately when the educational system is thought of as an ideological discourse it is conceptualized in a monolithic manner, a tendency particularly evident in the work of Bowles and Gintis who talk in terms of the way in which individuals internalise a belief system which 'plays a central role in preparing individuals for work of alienated and stratified work relationships' (1976, p. 124). The way this is achieved is through the 'dual function of education' which imparts 'technical and social skills and appropriate motivations'. They consider that education fulfils an 'integrative' role, a function which ensures that labour is both 'suitably motivated' and 'adequately disciplined'.

> Education plays a dual role in the social process whereby surplus value, i.e. profit is created and expropriated. On the one hand by imparting technical and social skills and appropriate motivations, education increases the productive capacities of workers. On the other hand, education helps defuse and depoliticize the potentially explosive class relations of the production process and thus serves to perpetuate the social, political and economic contributions through which a portion of the product of labour is expropriated in profits (1976, p. 11).

Elsewhere they say:

> schooling was seen [by the elite] as a means of producing the new forms of motivations and discipline required in the emerging corporate order . . . . [Schooling] would discipline a new proletariat, fragment it and eventually stratify it along racial, ethnic and sexual lines (p. 186).

What Bowles and Gintis in effect assert is that embedded in

the educational system is an ideological structure embodying beliefs essential for the maintenance of the corporate system. The 'appropriate' ideology — appropriate, that is, to all elements and strata in society — becomes an integral part of the make-up of emerging members of the labour force.

The starting point for a consideration of the ideological instance in education may be the way in which its effectivity is constituted in the process of the generation and reproduction of ideologies, bearing in mind the relative autonomy of the educational system. Given the relative autonomy, and given the contradictions embodied in it, it would seem likely that an educational system would not constitute a homogeneous ideological discourse. That this is the case for Britain is apparent in the stated aims of the Green Paper (1977):

The majority of people would probably agree with the following attempt to set out these aims, though they may differ in emphasis to be placed on one or the other:
   (i) to help children develop lively enquiring minds;
  (ii) to instil respect for moral values, for other people and for oneself, and tolerance of other races, religions, and ways of life;
 (iii) to help children understand the world in which we live, and the interdependence of nations;
 (iv) to help children to use the language effectively and imaginatively in reading, writing and speaking;
  (v) to help children to appreciate how the nation earns and maintains its standard of living and properly to esteem the essential role of industry and commerce in this process;
 (vi) to provide a basis of mathematical, scientific and technical knowledge, enabling boys and girls to learn the essential skills needed in a fast-changing world of work;
 (vii) to teach children about human achievement and aspirations in the arts and sciences, in religion, and in the search for a more just social order;
(viii) to encourage and foster the development of the children whose social or environmental disadvantages cripple their capacity to learn, if necessary by making

additional resources available to them (DES, 1977, pp. 6—7).

Even a cursory reading of these aims produces a series of contradictions. What is being suggested is that the educational system should at one and the same time develop individual qualities and abilities in pupils, but that it should also promote an attribute combining the necessity for tolerance with an ideal of competition. If children, in fact, learn 'to appreciate how the nation earns and maintains its standard of living' then it is likely to be a difficult task for these same children, the bulk of whom are destined to work in conditions of capitalist production, to be as 'tolerant' and 'compliant' as would appear necessary for the maintenance of such a system.

Counter to the state policy of making all schools comprehensive in terms of a composition of pupils representing the full range of 'ability', is a view expressed in a series of pamphlets published under the title of Black Papers which have had a 'major impact on the debate' in education. An examination of these Black Papers also reveals a series of marked tensions. As Wright (1977, p. 157) has pointed out, 'two distinct strands pervade [their] educational discussion. One is the "instrumental" or "utilitarian" view . . . the other is the idea of a "liberal" or "general" education.' He says many of the writers of the Black Papers are themselves ambivalent and adopt both positions.

The specific series of ideological discourses inscribed in the British educational system are themselves the site of contradiction. All that can be done here, however, is to draw attention to the complexities of the operation and reproduction of ideology in the educational system and the contradictory nature of such an operation. What is indisputable is that the ideologies operate critically at a relatively autonomous level of the educational system which needs to be analysed in its specificity.

In attempting an examination of the allocation of agents to adult social positions it may be — and frequently is — argued that the educational system filters agents into their future occupational roles. Nor is the allocation of agents dependent upon their own choices and aspirations, as Poulantzas (1975) has pointed out in the course of his criticism of the 'equal opportunities' position. It is actually capital which reproduces the places ('roles') and is responsible for the form the division of labour takes, and not the educational system. Class division and class structure, in marxist terms, are precisely characteristic of modes of production and are in no way reproduced except through the reproduction of the mode of production. The educational system is, on one level, and albeit in a contradictory manner concerned with the reproduction of agents to be allocated to the diverse positions in the division of labour. It is useful to avoid the tendency to confuse the reproduction of classes and reproduction of agents who will fit into an occupational structure. The occupational structure is nothing more nor less than the social and detailed division between numerous and diverse jobs in our society, while the mode of production provides the conditions for changes in the nature of occupations, the latter as such are distinct from, and are not to be confused with, the class structure:

> Classes and division of the labour force into functional groups are not the same thing . . . classes do not correspond to the division of the labour force: managerial/non-managerial, manual/non-manual, skilled/unskilled, etc. . . . (Hirst, 1976, p. 391).

It is necessary to maintain this distinction: labour as 'abstract' is independent of the form it takes and has meaning only in so far as it relates to capital, but agents may be classified according to wide differences in terms of the jobs they perform, the status they are accorded, the incomes they earn, their ethnic and sexual membership, although these factors can never, in themselves, be used as explanatory tools.

If this is the case, the relationship between the educational system and the allocation of agents requires some consideration. Hussain (1976) makes the point that qualifications by no means guarantee entry into specific parts of the labour market: they provide no more than access to the *possibility* of getting a particular job. The allocation of agents is not a function of the level of skills and qualifications attained. Even empirical material mobilised within the stratification problematic dispels the presuppositions of the 'equal opportunities' position which suggests that all that is needed are the right qualifications plus the necessary motivation in order to move into those jobs which carry with them prestige, status, and a correspondingly good income.

One major element in the social reproduction of labour which has not yet been discussed is the family unit. It is clear, as other contributions (notably those of Beechey and McIntosh) to this book indicate, that the family structure is highly pertinent in the operation of the dominant mode of production, and that the place of women within that structure may be argued as crucial in a variety of ways. The family provides a structure for the reproduction of the labour force in terms both of reproducing the new generation of workers and of the daily maintenance of the existing labour force. Another aspect of the family structure is that it provides an effective way of apparently reabsorbing unemployed women workers, and also of providing a covert sanctuary for a significant part of the reserve army of labour. The relatively unchanging nature of the sexual division of labour within the family is an important element in the legitimation process for the specific condition of women in the labour force. On the basis that it is seen as the woman's major role to care for and maintain the family, a wide range of 'reasons' can be called upon to justify the low wages women earn, the relatively unskilled nature of their jobs, and the preference given to employing men rather than women in certain areas.

This prejudice is not confined to the capitalist class but is evident within different fractions of the working class. Trade union practices have, up to recent times, effectively excluded women from gaining access to apprenticeships and so to skilled status. Though such practices are no longer legitimate, trade union organisation is still dominated by men and in spite of the rapid increase of women's membership in trade unions, they have still not penetrated these male bastions. These positions which are held are constantly reinforced through the machinations of the network of the media. Content analyses clearly demonstrate the role of the media in upholding the image of women as wives and mothers and the underplaying of the role of women in the labour force.

These observations are relevant to a consideration of the way in which demands for women's labour are generated. I have argued above that it is the mode of production which is responsible for the demand for specific characteristics in the labour force, and that these demands are both uneven and contradictory. There are, however, two outstanding features which can be noted when discussing such demands in relation to women. In the first instance, although technological innovations have generated a whole new range of jobs which do require specific technical skills, women have not benefitted from these new jobs. Second, those areas where women do work and which previously have had a skill component are arguably being deskilled. This is particularly the case in the area of clerical work, which accounts for nearly 30 per cent of employed women in Britain. Braverman (1974) has noted that

> in the clerical routine of offices the use of the brain is never entirely done away with any more than it is entirely done away with in any form of manual work. The mental processes are rendered repetitious and routine or they are reduced to so small a factor in the work process that the speed and dexterity with which the manual portion of the operation can be performed dominates the labour process as a whole (p. 325).

He also refers to the introduction of new machines and equipment which have resulted in the 'need to know the sequence or the alphabet or numerals' becoming superfluous. What is clear and what he states unequivocally is:

> The fact that the introduction of machines and systems is becoming increasingly common in trade and service areas indicates that much automated equipment is so simple to operate that it requires no training whatsoever; it also foreshadows the weakening of the demand for labour in fields of employment that have been expanding rapidly (p. 341).

It is the field in which the influx of women into the labour force has found employment. The relative ease with which deskilling takes place in such areas of work is associated with the less powerful trade union organisation which represents women's interests.

However, the demand for women's labour is closely associated with its compliant nature. Their low level of skill enables their relatively easy redeployment. Moreover, at certain moments they can be brought into and expelled from the labour force with relative ease.

Like the media, the educational system does contribute to the reinforcement of the ideal wife–mother image. But such a process itself obviously works within a series of contradictions not only inherent in the capitalist system but also within the relatively autonomous structure of the educational system. On the one hand it is required to prepare the youth to adapt to a highly technological society which has specific needs for a skilled labour force; on the other hand it is concerned with educational aims which are in direct conflict with such requirements, aims which are related to abstract notions about the self-development which results in a dedication, as far as girls are concerned, to roles which are exclusive of a technological commitment.

IV

It is at this point that the position of women in the educational system may be considered, but it is not possible here to do any more than draw attention to some of the more global problems which include the reproduction of skills and qualifications, the ideological process, and the way in which the educational system mediates in the process of allocation of young women to their adult roles.

In order to discuss in more concrete terms the level of skills attained by girls on leaving school and what happens to them afterwards, an overall view may be useful. Table 1 lists the qualifications girls have on leaving school, their destination, and the main areas in which women's employment occurs.

Without entering into an analysis of the occupational distribution of women, it is clear overall that there are only two categories of employment for women which require some degree of 'skill' – the professional–scientific and clerical groups. While these groups account for 40 per cent of employed women the range of 'skills' varies enormously. Amongst clerical workers the majority, though, do not require post-school training, nor for that matter can it be assumed that all women in the professional–scientific categories have undergone further and higher education. For many of these women what training they have had has been gained during the course of their work (Wolpe, 1978). If a relationship is drawn between the qualifications of school leavers and likely areas of employment, it is quite clear that there is little homology between skills acquired during the course of schooling and actual job specifications. To attempt such a comparison indeed is to invite conclusions about the obvious 'wastage' of girls' potentials.

Table 1

Qualifications of all female school leavers		Destination on leaving school		Areas in which women work	
1974–5	%	1974–5	%	1971	%
1+ 'A' levels	14.5	Degree	4.9	Professional/scientific	11.9
5+ 'O' levels	9.7	Teacher training	3.5	Sales workers	10.7
1–4 'O' levels	26.9	GCE	2.8	Clerical workers	29.1
No qualifications	48.8	Secretarial	5.5	Service industries	23.2
		Others	8.7	All other employed	25.1
		Employment	74.5		

Note: Entrance to institutions of higher education usually requires 'A' level (advanced) examination attainment, while 'O' levels (ordinary) may be required by institutions of further education.

In this context it is clearly relevant to consider the way in which the curriculum in schools is organised: such a discussion would also have to take into account the 'ideological' components of the curriculum, particularly as this provides the basis for the way in which the stock of socially organised knowledge is legitimated through transmission. While there is no standard curriculum for state education in Britain and no uniformity in the courses available for pupils, there is an ever growing tendency to provide a 'core' curriculum in the first three years of comprehensive secondary education. This core curriculum which includes a general science background, pays lip service, to an ever increasing degree, to the notion of not discriminating between boys and girls. It could thus be argued that girls, as well as boys, are given an equal chance after having taken the foundation courses in general science to 'choose' to do physical science at the advanced level. But the numbers taking such a subject to this level are small and insignificant — of those who did obtain 'A' level passes in 1974 only 3 per cent studied science subjects either with or without mathematics. The explanation for this 'failure' of girls to pursue pure science subjects must go beyond discussions which are based on individual motivation and aspiration — as suggested in the Green Paper. It is rather the structural constraints at work in the education specifically relating to girls which need to be taken into account.

Apart from this broad dichotomy between science-technological and non-science subjects, is that broad range of subject specialisms in the social sciences and humanities. These subjects incorporate areas which are regarded as eminently suitable for the more 'academic' type school girls, such as modern languages, English and history. It is here that the structuring of the curriculum and schools' organisation contribute to the preponderance of girls in these areas.

Such a body of knowledge is institutionalised in a number of separate subject or curriculum areas in schools and colleges but it is that area which falls generally under the heading of 'vocational' courses that is particularly relevant to the question of the position of women with regard to the educational system. Even in schools which pride themselves on non-discriminatory practices, the way in which the subjects are presented and their actual content frequently make them gender specific. For example the *raison d'etre* for boys to do home economics is seen, by staff and pupils alike, in terms of boys 'helping out' at some future date when their wives are incapacitated, or prior to marriage during their bachelor days; or for boys, home economics is sometimes linked to cookery which may be seen in terms of future employment in the catering industry. On the other hand, for girls home economics is justified in terms of their future roles as wives and mothers — child care, home care, providing balanced meals for a family, home decoration, and so on. Where girls are allowed, or even encouraged, to do woodwork or metalwork, this is justified again in terms of domestic duties — mending a broken toy or putting up shelves. Such subjects are never offered to girls within the overt context of future jobs (Wolpe, 1977).

The effect of school organisation and curricular structure

cannot therefore be dissociated from the overall division of labour both in regard to paid employment and within the family.

That the ideological discourse of the educational system is a contradictory one has already been argued in the theoretical discussion above. This becomes evident when the aims of education are seen in relation to both the family structure and the labour process. For a prevailing strand of that ideology, the familial position of women assumes an ascendancy over other aspects of their lives. Women do not appear to feature at all in history: they are relegated to the kitchen sink. Teachers who themselves work within and negotiate these ideological structures may be seen as constituted by the process of transmission of knowledge. Even if they are aware of some of the contradictory aspects of the ideological structure, they have to face the consequences of the way in which the pupils are themselves subject to the operation of these structures. By the time teenage girls reach school leaving age they articulate their future in terms of family responsibilities. They reject, often realistically, advice about pursuing school subjects which could open up new avenues; the jobs they anticipate are not only within their scope, but more importantly are easily accessible to them and in conformity with their future familial responsibilities (Wolpe, 1977).

This is closely linked with the way in which the educational system mediates between girls and their allocation to their future roles. Even if girls and young women were able to get the necessary qualifications which would give them access to a wider range of occupations, this would in no way guarantee their entry to those occupations. Factors which relate not only the availability of jobs through employment opportunities but also to the struggle within fractions of the working class need to be considered. Finally the way in which the reserve army of labour operates at any moment, particularly in relation to the family structure, must be borne in mind.

It is not intended to suggest that the analysis outlined in this final section represents a full account of the determinations of the position of women in education. Its purpose has been no more than to indicate the line of concrete analysis which follows from the theoretical arguments in the earlier parts of the paper.

Acknowledgments

I wish to thank most especially Annette Kuhn, Harold Wolpe and Mary McIntosh, who have given me invaluable help and support in working through many of the problems in this paper. During the course of its production, Annette Kuhn has carried the major burden of editorial work on the book as a whole and has given a degree of support which has gone beyond the bounds of partnership in such a venture.

References

Acker, J. (1973), 'Women and social stratification', *American Journal of Sociology*, vol. 78, pp. 936–45.

Barron, R. D., and Norris, G. M. (1976), 'Sexual divisions and the dual labour market' in D. L. Barker and S. Allen (eds), *Dependence and Exploitation in Work and Marriage*, Longman, London.

Boocock, S. (1975), *An Introduction to the Sociology of Learning*, Houghton Mifflin, Boston, Mass.

Bourdieu, P., and Boltanski, L. (1977), 'Qualifications and jobs' in *Two Bourdieu Texts*, stencilled occasional paper, Centre for Contemporary Cultural Studies, Birmingham.

Bowles, S., and Gintis, H. (1976), *Schooling in Capitalist America*, Routledge & Kegan Paul, London.

Braverman, H. (1974), *Labor and Monopoly Capital*, Monthly Review Press, New York.

Byrne, E. M. (1975), 'Inequality in educational — discriminal resource — allocation in school', *Educational Review*, vol. 17, pp. 179–91.

Department of Education and Science (1977), *Education in Schools: a Consultative Document*, Cmnd. 6869, HMSO, London.

Department of Employment (1975), *Women and Work*, Manpower Paper No. 9, HMSO, London.

Department of Employment (1977), *British Labour Statistics, Year Book, 1975*, HMSO, London.

Fuchs Epstein, C. (1973), *Woman's Place*, University of California Press.

Gerth, H. H. and Mills, C. W. (1964) *Essays in Sociology*, Routledge & Kegan Paul, London.

Graham S., and Llewellyn, C. (1976), *Women in the Occupational Structure: A Case Study of Banking*, Mimeographed Paper.

Hartnett, O. (1976), in a discussion paper given to the Sexual Divisions and Society Study Group of the British Sociological Association.

Hirst, P. (1976), 'Althusser and the theory of ideology' in *Economy and Society*, vol. 5, pp. 385–412.

Hussain, A. (1976), 'The economy and the educational system in capitalistic societies', *Economy and Society*, vol. 5, pp. 413–34.

Jackson, J. A. (ed.) (1968), *Social Stratification*, Cambridge University Press.

Jencks, C. (1975), *Inequality*, Penguin, Harmondsworth.

328   AnnMarie Wolpe

Jensen, C. (1969), 'How much can we boost I.Q. and scholastic achievement?' in *Harvard Educational Review*, vol. 39, pp. 1—123.
King, J. (1971), 'Unequal access in education — sex and social class' in *Social and Economic Administration*, vol. 5, pp. 167—75.
Land, H. (1975), *Social Security: A System of Maintaining Women's Dependence on Men*, mimeographed paper given to British Association for The Advancement of Science.
Maccoby, E. E. (ed.), (1966), *The Development of Sex Differences*, Stanford University Press.
Marx, K. (1970), *Capital*, vol. I, Lawrence & Wishart, London.
Parkin, F. (1971), *Class, Inequality and Political Disorder*, Paladin, St Albans.
Poulantzas, N. (1975), *Classes in Contemporary Capitalism*, New Left Book, London.
Rendel, M. (1975), 'Men and women in higher education', *Educational Review*, vol. 17, pp. 192—201.
Runciman, W. G. (1966), *Relative Deprivation and Social Justice*, Routledge & Kegan Paul, London.
Shaw, J. (1976), 'Finishing school: some implications of sex-segregated education' in D. L. Barker and S. Allen, (eds) *Sexual Divisions and Society: Process and Change*, Tavistock, London.
Turner, R. (1964a), 'Some aspects of women's ambition', *American Journal of Sociology*, vol. 70, pp. 271—84.
Turner, R. (1964b), *The Social Context of Ambition*, Chandler Publishing Co., San Francisco.
Wolpe, A. M. (1977), *Some Processes in Sexist Education*, Women's Research and Resources Centre Publication, London.
Wolpe, A. M. (1978), 'Girls and economic survival', *British Journal of Educational Studies*, vol. 26, forthcoming.
Wright, N. (1977), *Progress in Education*, Croom Helm, London.

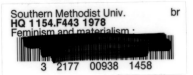